IN SEARCH OF THE LOST

Richard Carter lived and worked with the Melanesian Brotherhood as Tutor, Chaplain and Mission Coordinator between 1990 and 2005, based at Tabalia on the Island of Guadalcanal. He became a member of the Melanesian Brotherhood himself. He is presently Assistant Priest at St Martin-in-the-Fields in London.

Blessed are the peacemakers for they shall be called the children of God.

Matthew 5.9

In Loving memory of

Brother Robin Lindsay
Brother Francis Tofi
Brother Tony Sirihi
Brother Alfred Hill
Brother Patteson Gatu
Brother Ini Paratabatu
Brother Nathaniel Sado

and all those we have loved and who have shown us the way to Christ.

Set me as a seal upon your heart, as a seal upon your arm;
for love is strong as death, passion fierce as the grave.
Its flashes are flashes of fire, a raging flame.
Many waters cannot quench love,
neither can floods drown it.

For Martyrs: Common Worship cf. Song of Solomon 8.6,7

No one could tell me where my soul might be;
I sought for God but God eluded me;
I sought my brother out and found all three
My soul, my God and all humanity.

A prisoner of war

In Search of the Lost

The Death and Life of Seven Peacemakers
of the Melanesian Brotherhood

Richard Anthony Carter

Rachael
As we exchange books!
This also is a story
of struggle but also
of God's blessing
with my prayers
Richard
July 2007

CANTERBURY
PRESS
Norwich

First published in 2006 by the Canterbury Press Norwich
(a publishing imprint of Hymns Ancient & Modern Limited,
a registered charity)
9–17 St Alban's Place, London N1 0NX

www.scm-canterburypress.co.uk

Illustrations are from Rebecca Jewell and Jude Philp: *Pacific Designs*,
British Museum Press, 1998

British Library Cataloguing in Publication data

A catalogue record for this book is available
from the British Library

ISBN 1-85311-780-3/978-1-85311-780-0

Typeset in Bulmer by Regent Typesetting, London
Printed and bound by
William Clowes Ltd, Beccles, Suffolk

Contents

Preface

The history of Christian mission – especially Anglican mission – in the Pacific is a distinctive one. From the beginning, from the days of Selwyn and Patteson, there has been an emphasis on the creative involvement of local people in shaping the life of the Church. In Melanesia, this was not only about ordaining indigenous clergy, though this began very early on. It was about a whole vision of how the faith could become truly local as well as universal. And the development of the Melanesian Brotherhood is the most outstanding example of this – a religious order inspired by classical Christian models yet profoundly rooted in the life and culture of the islands.

Perhaps what anchors such an enterprise most deeply in the life of a community is the knowledge that those involved are ready to take risks for the sake of truth and justice – to be there on behalf of all, whatever the cost. In recent years, this has been demonstrated in one of the major episodes of Christian witness in our age. The members of the Melanesian Brotherhood who sought to mediate in the civil strife that engulfed Solomon Islands in the opening years of the twenty-first century, and who lost their lives in the course of that sacrificially brave attempt, deserve to be commemorated alongside all those who have written the gospel in their blood across the ages.

But there is more than this. When the Brothers – and Sisters – proclaim the gospel now, whether in the Pacific or in their visits to the Western world, this story has become inseparably linked with their identity. The reality of death and resurrection has embedded itself so deeply in the awareness and identity of the Brotherhood that their unforgettable presentation of the Good News in dance and story and drama becomes a living-out of the hope that the story of their martyred friends embodies.

This is the Word truly made flesh in proclamation, and all those who have encountered the Brotherhood will agree that it is a supremely precious gift to us.

Richard Carter has worked with the Brotherhood through these recent times and has become a very effective spokesman for their work. This wonderful book brings to life the vision of the Brotherhood, the struggle to make sense of the sacrifice and trauma of these last years, trauma for the Brothers and for the whole community of the Solomons, the overflowing joy of their witness and their freedom to communicate across cultures with confidence and vigour. It is one of the most truly evangelical books I have read for a long time: Good News for all of us, a testimony to the fidelity of Jesus Christ in his people and to his people, the world over.

+Rowan Cantuar

Prologue

On 8 August 2003 Christians throughout the world were shocked to hear the news that six Melanesian Brothers had been brutally murdered on the Weather Coast of Guadalcanal. This Anglican order of Christian brothers, living a simple and prayerful life of poverty, chastity and obedience, had become well known in the South Pacific and beyond for their work for peace. For three months the Melanesian Brotherhood and other members of the Church had been waiting and hoping and praying that these Brothers who had been taken hostage on 24 April were alive and would return safely. But on 8 August their worst fears were confirmed. The Melanesian Brotherhood was officially told by the Police Commissioner that all six were dead, as was the brother for whom they had gone in search. These seven brothers were brave, talented and greatly loved men and it was hard to come to terms with the enormity of their loss and the tragic ending of such good, young and holy lives. What happened and why did they die? This is the story of the deaths of these seven brothers and the aftermath of those deaths. It is also my story and the story of the Melanesian Brotherhood as we faced both conflict and tragedy and tried to make sense of our faith. Beyond those seven deaths it is also a reflection on trying to live the Christian faith when confronted by fear and great loss. It is in truth the Christian story both of death and resurrection. It is based on a diary and letters that I wrote during the time the events took place.

Acknowledgements

First of all I would like to thank the Melanesian Brotherhood. This Community will always hold my heart. There are too many Brothers to single out any one Brother or Novice for special mention, but I would like to thank the Headbrother Caulton Weris, and former Headbrothers Jude Alfred and Harry Gereniu as a mark of my respect for each Brother and Novice with whom I have shared so much, and of course to acknowledge the seven Brothers who lost their lives for peace and to whom this book is dedicated. I would also like to acknowledge all those Brothers and Novices, past and present, who suffered in the conflict. My thanks go to Archbishop Ellison Pogo, and all members of the Church of Melanesia, a Church I have been fortunate to work for since first arriving in Solomon Islands in 1988.

Many people have supported me in the South Pacific, and I would like to acknowledge Fr Peter Orudiana, his wife Emily and family who have been such loyal friends; also Brother John Blyth; Bishop Terry Brown; Fr Thomas Rowland; Matthew Jones; Philip Malana; John Ravuzepo; the late Albert Samo and his dear family; Ethel Suri and her late husband Ellison Suri; Sir John and Lady Ini Lapli; the Society of St Francis; Sisters of Melanesia; and the Sisters of the Church who have provided prayer and sanctuary in Solomon Islands and the UK.

In the writing of this book I would like to thank Brother Damian and Brother Robert SSF who provided a welcoming home, and space to write and walk on Holy Island while completing the book. Many people read parts oe drafts of this story and encouraged me: Bishop Derek Rawcliffe; Fr Peter Hosking; Felicity Rousseux; Dave Friswell; Carolyn Kitto; Sister Patricia Marie Kellam; Kerry and John Fieldhouse; The Community of Jesus' Way; Margaret and Richard Deimel; Fr Nicholas

Stebbings CR; Dr Petà Dunstan; Annie Hargrave; Richard Barnett; Joanna Woodd; Fr Timothy Radcliffe OP; Charles Montgomery, whose questioning led me to clearer understanding of all that took place; and Elizabeth Garsten who corresponded and affirmed throughout. I would also like to thank the Revd Nicholas Holtam and the clergy and congregation of St Martin-in-the-Fields for their support.

In helping to get the text ready for publication my very special thanks go to Revd James Minchin, Revd Brian Macdonald-Milne COMB and Daniel Carter who devoted so much time to patiently editing and correcting my original text and offering many valuable suggestions. I am deeply grateful to them. My gratitude also goes to Christine Smith, Mary Matthews and all at SCM-Canterbury Press for their advice and support in bringing the book to publication. Where possible I have tried to acknowledge photos not taken by myself, and special thanks go to Mike Lewis for his photos of the Passion Play; Richard Toke, Carolyn Kitto, Daniel Carter and Jim Rosenthal. I am also very grateful to Andrew Carter for his beautiful drawing of the map of the islands.

I would also like to acknowledge Monica Attias and the Community of Sant'Egidio in Rome, where on the 22 November 2006 the seven Melanesian Brothers were remembered in the Basilica of St Bartholomew at the shrine of modern martyrs in a thanksgiving service conducted by the Archbishop of Canterbury.

I would like to acknowledge here my own brothers and their families and my mother and late father, whose love and support is unconditional. In particular I would like to thank my brother Daniel who visited me in Solomon Islands in the midst of this crisis and understood my love for Melanesia – his indefatigable encouragement has helped bring this book to fruition. I would also like to acknowledge those who have shared some of this faith journey with me through friendship and prayer: Revd Juliette Hulme; Brother Benedict SSF, Nicolette Wade; Sister Marion OHP; Sister Mary Julian CHC; Fr Simon Holden CR for his wisdom and spiritual guidance; and Fr John Hovell whose literary correspondence and perceptive eye have been a constant eye opener to all things Melanesian. Thanks to Bishop William Pwaisiho, his wife Kate and family who have included me as one of their own family since my first arrival in Melanesia, and also the unconditional support of Barbara Molyneux and the prayers and support of all the many Companions of the Melanesian Brotherhood. I would also like to acknowledge my dear friend Jeri Eggleston who has a heart open for the lost and has always cared and understood.

I would like to thank Archbishop Rowan Williams who came to Melanesia, and whose acknowledgement of the faith and witness of the Melanesian Brotherhood was a sign to us of the international community of faith and prayer that has upheld us through the conflict.

Finally I would like to acknowledge the late Julie Wilson, Brother Tristam SSF and James Ilifanoa, from whom I learnt so much about love and friendship.

A note on language and spelling

The language most frequently used between different island and tribal groups in Solomon Islands is *pidgin*. In some of the conversations in this book I have tried to capture the descriptive flavour of this language, which has its own character and richness particularly in the telling of stories. I do apologise, however, that I have been advised to anglicise the spelling and construction in order to make it intelligible to non-speakers of *pidgin*. My apologies to those working to standardise the spelling of this language and for any inaccuracy or disrespect for this vibrant language.

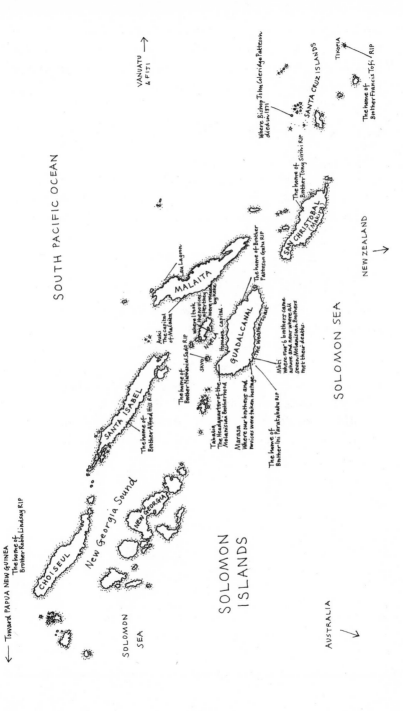

SOUTH PACIFIC OCEAN

VANUATU & FIJI →

Where Bishop John Coleridge Patteson died in 1871

SANTA CRUZ ISLANDS

TIKOPIA

The home of Brother Francis Tofi RIP

The home of Brother Tony Sirihi RIP

SAN CRISTOBAL (MAKIRA)

NEW ZEALAND →

The home of Brother Patteson Gatu RIP

Lau Lagoon

MALAITA

Auki The capital of Malaita

Where I took the novices at Hautabu. We were ringed by police.

The home of Brother Nathaniel Sado RIP

SAVO

Honiara capital

GUADALCANAL

The Weather Coast

Maki Where our 6 brothers came ashore and near where all seven Melanesian Brothers met their deaths.

SOLOMON SEA

Tabalia The Headquarters of the Melanesian Brotherhood

Marasa Where our brothers and novices were taken hostage.

The home of Brother Ini Paratabatu RIP

SOLOMON SEA

SANTA ISABEL

The home of Brother Alfred Hill RIP

New Georgia Sound

CHOISEUL

NEW GEORGIA

SOLOMON ISLANDS

SOLOMON SEA

AUSTRALIA ↓

← Toward PAPUA NEW GUINEA The home of Brother Robin Lindsay RIP

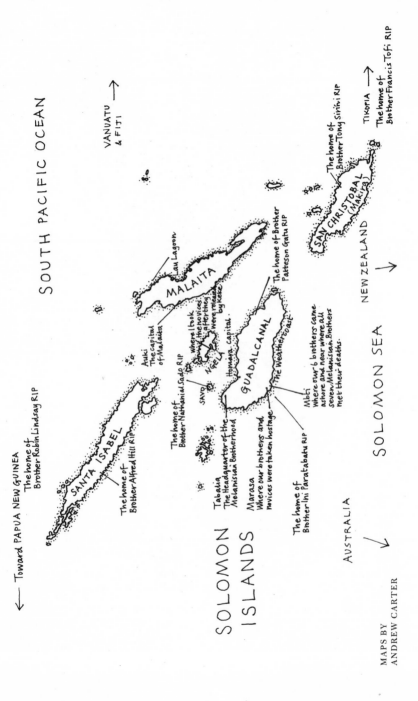

SOUTH PACIFIC OCEAN

← Toward PAPUA NEW GUINEA
The home of
Brother Robin Lindsay RIP

VANUATU
& FIJI →

SANTA ISABEL

The home of
Brother Alfred Hill RIP

The home of
Brother Nathaniel Sado RIP

Auki
The capital
of Malaita

Lau Lagoon

MALAITA

where I took
some of the novices
to Auki after they
were released
by Keke

NGELA

SAVO

Honiara, capital

GUADALCANAL

The Weather Coast

Tabalia
The Headquarter of the
Melanisian Brotherhood

Marasa
Where our brothers and
novices were taken hostage

The home of
Brother Ini Paratabatu RIP

Mbeti
where our 6 brothers came
ashore and near where all
seven Melanesian Brothers
met their deaths.

The home of Brother
Patteson Gatu RIP

SAN CHRISTOBAL
(MAKIRA)

The home of
Brother Tony Sirihi RIP

TIKOPIA →

The home of
Brother Francis Tofi RIP

SOLOMON SEA

NEW ZEALAND →

AUSTRALIA ↓

SOLOMON
ISLANDS

MAPS BY
ANDREW CARTER

PART 1

Prophets

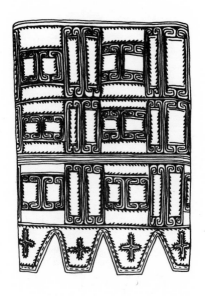

1

So that the human family may widen.

Brother Roger of Taizé

Lord Christ, you remain unseen at our side
present like a poor man
who washes the feet of his friends.
And we, to follow in your footsteps,
we are here, waiting for you
to make us into servants
of your gospel. Amen.

Brother Roger of Taizé

'What is the grace that you most long for in your life?' Brother Emil of the Taizé Community asked me. It was during a silent retreat at the Taizé community in France in the autumn of 1986.

'I would like to be able to teach, and to be a Brother in a community, and to work in the developing world, and to be a priest and still to direct dramas . . .'

There was a long silence and then he spoke: 'You long for many things. Perhaps you need to let go of some of them, in order that others may be fulfilled.'

I did not really want to let go of any of them, in fact I was unsure at that time of how to go forward. I had left Indonesia after four years of working there and I could not imagine any future that would fulfil me as much, because I was grieving for the place and the people I had got to know and a life I had experienced, which seemed so impossible in the Western world. It was hard to look forward, for I longed to go back.

'I want you to think of Mary when she receives the news that she, an

3

unmarried woman, is to have a child. In my French translation it reads she "ran off" to visit her cousin Elizabeth. That word "ran" has always struck me. She has received news that most women would fear, she is not even married, and yet we are told she hurries, she runs and when she meets Elizabeth she proclaims not her troubles but the greatness of the Lord and her joy. I would like you to meditate upon that response "ran".'

And that is what I did. And I remember after that in my prayers I found that my grief at the loss of people and place was breaking open and being released, and instead of a dark, bitter pain trapping inside me all that I felt I had lost, a new Word was coming to me: 'You will love again.'

The Solomon Islands at this time were practically unknown to me. They are a group of islands that often get lost in the folds of the map when you look at the South Pacific Ocean, above Australia and New Zealand, an arc of islands stretching from Papua New Guinea in the west toward Vanuatu and Fiji to the east. When up close we often cannot see the workings of God, or the answers to our prayers but when we step back it is different. When I step back twenty years I can see.

I went back to Taizé in 2005, two weeks after Brother Roger had been killed on 16 August. That night I sat by his grave. It is a simple grave beside the church where his community began in prayer. A candle burns. There seems no bitterness or resentment in the community after the traumatic murder of its founder, as though death is not such a big step for one who was already living God's eternity. Brother Roger's last words to be written down on the afternoon before he died were: 'To the extent that our community creates possibilities in the human family to widen . . .' and he stopped there.

I had come here to give thanks to God because those many requests I had made to God all those years before had been fulfilled, and more, much more than I had ever imagined possible. And, of course, the one grace that incorporated all my other needs: 'You will love again.' Yes I had experienced God's love widening beyond place and culture and time and even beyond this life. As I sat by this grave I was filled not with sorrow but peace. I realized that actually what I was giving thanks for was resurrection, the resurrection of Christ.

When I accepted a position with the Melanesian Mission in 1987 it had seemed one of the most remote places in the world that one could ever think of going to. The foreign students whom I was teaching at the language school in Bournemouth found it very amusing when I tried to find the place for them on the map. I remember my first meeting with the Melanesian Mission UK in 1987. They seemed a rather peculiar lot, each of whom had their own particular relationship with Melanesia about which they wanted to tell me, to the exclusion of the others. I remember that I was informed that Melanesia was 'a thief of hearts' and I was 'a very fortunate young man' to be going there. It was the last thing I believed at that moment, for one of my main reasons for going then was so that I could stop off in Indonesia on the way. They were, however, more right in what they said than I could ever have known. The place, which seemed so far away, has become my spiritual home and a major part of my life. I now know the meaning of what those committee members had tried to express and, as I too try to express my love and gratitude for this place, I will probably seem just as peculiar to the uninitiated. Yet I believe the story I am about to tell does not belong to one place or one culture. It is, in fact, the story of how God's love is at work again and again and again. It is the story of God searching for the lost.

2

His life was taken by those for whom he would gladly have given it.

Words written on the cross in Nukapu,
where John Coleridge Patteson died

Right from the beginning of my work for the Melanesian Mission I became aware that the first Anglican missionaries to Melanesia were men and women with whom one could feel proud to be associated. Today the word 'missionary' often conjures up many negative associations in the Western world – men and women who crossed continents and oceans in the name of God and left behind the very conditions in which material interest, colonialism, exploitation, and white superiority could flourish. Yet in Solomon Islands the islanders themselves still talk with love and pride about their early missionaries who established a model of sacrificial service which still inspires the young and old. Bishop George Augustus Selwyn, who in 1841 became the first bishop of New Zealand, believed there should be 'an episcopate of love as well as authority'.

I can speak from observation ranging over nearly half the Southern Pacific Ocean, that wherever this law of religious unity is adopted, there the gospel has its full unchecked power. Missionaries must be ready at a moment to put their lives in their hands and to go out and preach the gospel to others with no weapon but prayer and with no refuge but in God.[1]

---

1 Sermon of George Augustus Selwyn delivered at the University of Cambridge, 1854.

Selwyn had called upon young men from England to follow that path of love and missionary service:

> The Spirit of God is ready to be poured out upon all flesh, and some of you are his chosen vessels. Again I say offer yourself to the Primate of our Church. The voice of the Lord is asking 'Whom shall I send, and who will go for us?' May many of you who intend, by God's grace, to dedicate yourself to the ministry, answer at once: 'Here I am, send me.'[2]

In all of this, there was a passion for evangelism which has never left the Church of Melanesia, and yet it was also an evangelism which was broad, catholic and inclusive so that in Brother Roger's words 'the human family may widen'. Selwyn believed that this family,

> scattered over the wide ocean, are objects of the same interest to me as Apollos was to Aquila. If in anything they lack knowledge, it seems to be our duty to expound to them the ways of God more perfectly and to do this as their friend and brother, not as having dominion over their faith, but as helpers in joy.[3]

There was this sort of romance about mission work in the South Pacific and yet it came from missionaries who lived tough and practical lives and who were not deluded about the difficulties and dangers they faced or the hard sacrificial nature of their calling. This quality has continued and I can remember my own father saying that he used to read the *Southern Cross Log*, the journal of the Melanesian Mission, when he was at school and, at that stage, not even particularly Christian, but he said that the mission in the Pacific always seemed so exciting and full of adventure.

A student at Cambridge, John Coleridge Patteson, from Feniton, near Ottery St Mary in Devon, heard Bishop Selwyn speak and his message inspired him. Patteson had not been a particularly outstanding student at either Eton or Cambridge and in fact, apart from moderate success at cricket, his youth seemed quite unexceptional. Once Patteson joined the Melanesian Mission as a young priest his gifts were seen to flourish. He

---

2 *Ibid.*
3 *Ibid.*

was noted for his sailor's gift for enduring hardship, his Christian gift for deep friendship, his compassion and his linguist's gift for being able to master many different languages of the Pacific. We sense a man who had become animated and fully alive in this mission. The Revd R. H. Codrington, a fellow missionary, wrote of him:

> I remember noticing how different his manner was in the islands. His eyes were cast all about him, keeping a sharp look out, and all his movements and tones were quick and decisive. He thoroughly enjoyed the heat, he liked the food, which gave him no trouble at all to eat, and he liked the people.[4]

What was remarkable about his ministry – something that emerges in all his writings – is the quality of his love for the people of Melanesia and the genuine trust and respect he gave to them: he developed a relationship with the indigenous people that challenged the whole foundation of colonial prejudice. He writes:

> I have for many years thought that we seek in our mission a great deal too much to make English Christians of our converts. We consciously and unanimously assume English Christianity (as something different from the doctrines of the Church of England) to be necessary . . . Evidently the heathen man is not treated fairly if we encumber our message with unnecessary requirements . . . We seem to denationalise these races as far as I can see; whereas we ought to change as little as possible; only what is incompatible with the simplest form of teaching and practice . . . Christianity is the religion for humanity at large. It takes in all shades and characters of race etc.[5]

> I dread the imposition from without of some formal compliances with the externals of religion . . . Anything better than turning heathens into Pharisees![6]

---

4 C. E. Fox, *Lord of the Southern Isles*, London, Mowbray, 1958, p. 14.

5 Charlotte Mary Yonge, *Life of John Coleridge Patteson: Missionary Bishop of the Melanesian Islands*, Vol. 2, London, Macmillan, 1874, pp. 164–7.

6 *Ibid.* pp. 372–3.

Patteson also began to question the whole position of the European missionary in relation to potential converts. He believed that any missionary really unable to understand the native people, to love them and live with them would be 'wholly destructive of success in missionary or in any work':

> The pride of race which prompts a white man to regard coloured people as inferior to himself, is strongly ingrained in most men's minds, and must be wholly eradicated before they will ever win the hearts, and thus the souls of the heathen.[7]

His sermons express this inclusiveness: a God who loves without prejudice irrespective of colour, tribe or creed, a God whose love knows no boundary:

> And this love (of God) once generated in the heart of man, must need pass on to his brethren; that principle of life must needs grow and expand with its own inherent energy . . . No artificial or accidental circumstances can confine it, it recognises no human ideas of nationality or place but embraces like the dome of heaven all the works of God. And love is the animating principle of all.[8]

While Patteson may question the way in which the Christian faith is expressed, he never doubts the relevance of the Christian message itself. In all of his letters there is a constant longing that Melanesians may know Christ and experience God's promises. Charles Fox notes 'the spirit of prayer' and 'thanksgiving' that pervades all his writings. He is rigorous in his faith too, fearing sentimental attachment which would patronize the converts and overlook the need for 'true religion, sound learning and useful industry'.[9] Neither does he glamorize Melanesian culture or overlook the reality of blood feuds, tribal wars, head-hunting, and pagan

---

7 *Ibid.* Vol. 1, p. 405.

8 *Ibid.* Vol. 1, p. 297.

9 Fox, *Lord of the Southern Isles*, p. 19. The motto for St John's College New Zealand.

practices: he remains totally committed to the mission to 'convert the heathen'.

What becomes increasingly obvious, however, is how personally and intimately he becomes involved in and respects the lives of those he seeks to convert and teach: his missionary methodology is the result of that intimacy. We sense in his letters how much he depends on their recipro-cal love and affection. He painfully struggles to make sense of tragic events and his own responsibility for them and to reconcile this with his faith. For example, in 1863 while he was training Melanesians at St Andrew's Kohimarama, New Zealand, there was an outbreak of dysen-tery, which took the life of six Melanesian students and made twenty others seriously ill. Patteson attended the sick day and night and his struggle between grief and faith is captured in his letter to his sister:

Sosaman died at 9 am this day – a dear lad, one of the Banks Islanders, about ten or twelve years old. As usual I was kneeling close by him, closing his eyes in death. I can see his poor mother's face now! What will she say to me? She knows not the Christian life in death. Yet to him, the poor unbaptised child, what is it to him? There is another world! There is a God, a Father, a Lord Jesus Christ, a Spirit of holiness, a love and glory.[10]

Even harder for Patteson to accept was the death of two of his most devoted Norfolk Island assistants in 1864, when they were fatally wounded in an arrow attack while returning with Patteson from the shore to the ship in Graciosa Bay, Santa Cruz. Patteson describes in his letters the tragedy of Monday 15 August:

When the boat was about fifteen yards from the reef, on which crowds were standing, they began (why I know not) to shoot at us . . . I had not shipped the rudder so I held it up, hoping it might shield off the arrows that came straight, the boat being end on, and the stern, having being backed into the reef was nearest to them. When I looked round

10 Yonge, *The Life of J.C.P.*, Vol. 2, p. 45.

... I saw Pearce lying between the thwarts, with the long shaft of an arrow in his chest, Edwin Nobbs with an arrow as it seemed in his left eye, many arrows flying close to us from many quarters. Suddenly Fisher Young, pulling the stroke oar, gave a faint scream; he was shot through the left wrist. Not a word was spoken, only my 'Pull! port oars, pull on steadily.' Once dear Edwin, with the fragment of the arrow sticking in his cheek, and the blood streaming down, called out, thinking even more of me than of himself, 'Look out, sir! Close to you!' But indeed, on all sides they were close to us. How any of us escaped I cannot tell.[11]

Patteson himself drew out the arrow from Pearce's chest and bandaged him. Then he tried to extract the arrow from Fisher's wrist:

I cut deeply fearing much to cut an artery, but I could not extract the wooden arrow head. At length getting a firm hold of the projecting point of the arrow on the lower side of the wrist, I pulled it through: it came out clean. The pain was very great; he trembled and shivered: we gave him brandy and he recovered. I poulticed the wound and went on to Edwin. Atkin had got the splinter from his wound; the arrow went in near the eye and came out by the cheek bone.[12]

Although the arrows were not bone headed and did not seem to have been poisoned, Patteson dreaded the possibility that the two men would develop lockjaw. Everything seemed to be going well for the first five days and Patteson writes how much he admires Fisher's calm composure.

I kept on poultices, gave light nourishing food. But on Saturday Fisher said to me 'I can't make out why my jaws feel so stiff.' Then my heart sank down within me, and I prayed earnestly, earnestly to God ... I never saw in so young a person such a thorough conscientiousness as

---

11 *Ibid.*, p. 101.
12 *Ibid.*, p. 102.

for two years I witnessed in his daily life, and I had long not only loved but respected him . . . By Saturday the jaws were tight locked. Then more intense grew the pain, the agony, the whole body rigid like a bar of iron. Oh how I bless God who carried me through that day and night. How good Fisher was in his very agonies, in his fearful spasms . . . He never for a moment lost his hold upon God. What a lesson it was, it calmed us.[13]

At 4.00 a.m. on Monday 22 August Fisher passed away with Patteson at his side. Five days later Edwin Nobb's jaw began to stiffen:

On Friday, September 2, I administered Holy Communion to him [Edwin] and Pearce. He could scarcely swallow the tiniest crumb. He was often delirious . . . The death struggle at 1.00 am September 5, was very terrible. Three of us could scarcely hold him. Then he sank back on my arm, and his spirit passed away as I commended his soul to God. Then all motionless.

Only Pearce recovered from his wound. Patteson was broken by grief and his letters return to thoughts of these two again and again:

I never felt so utterly broken down, when I think of the earthly side of it . . .

I long for the sight of his dear face, the sound of his voice. It was my delight to teach him, and he was clever and so thoughtful and industrious. I know that it is good that my affections should be weaned from all things earthly. I try to be thankful. I think I am thankful really; time too will do much . . . God's grace much more.[14]

Patteson contemplated having to meet their families:

And now I must land in at Norfolk Island in the face of the population crowding the little pier. Mr Nobbs will be there, and the brothers and

13 *Ibid.*, pp. 102–3.
14 *Ibid.* Vol. 2, p. 106.

sisters of Edwin, and the uncles and aunts of Fisher. Yet God will comfort them . . . It is hard to seem thankful that I was left. But God in his great mercy, took those who were most ready to go.[15]

It is as though he was in dialogue with his own despair which he feared was an inner cowardice and failure of faith:

It is a sore temptation to wish have done with this weary world. All the more do truthful, manly, generous thoughts help one to resist such unworthy cowardice, such meanness, such disposition to shirk work. It has been a relief for me to write this, though I am not man enough even now to do it without feeling my cheeks wet . . .[16]

Oh how I think with such ever increasing love of dear Fisher and Edwin. Oh how I praised God for them on All Saints' Day. But I do not expect to recover spring and elasticity yet awhile. I don't think I shall ever feel so young again . . . and I feel very tired and indolent. No wonder I seem to 'go softly'.[17]

Patteson's words could be my own 140 years later. How strangely history repeats itself.

It was relationships of genuine love and concern that had the power to convert. George Sarawia, who was to be the first Melanesian priest to be ordained, in 1868, describing Patteson and his missionary example, wrote in his autobiography:

This is what they [Patteson] did for the sick. They were not ashamed to carry the bucket of waste matter and take it to the sea, they washed out the bucket and brought it back into the sick room. Then I thought they were doing what the Bishop had taught us in the school, that we should love one another and look after each other with love, without despising anyone, we should help the weak. All this they did to those

---

15 *Ibid.* Vol. 2, p. 107.
16 *Ibid.* Vol. 2, p. 122.
17 *Ibid.* Vol. 2, p. 123.

who were sick. Then I thought it was true, if anyone taught . . . the things that Jesus did he must follow it himself and humble himself.[18]

Patteson believed passionately that the initiative for mission should come from the Melanesians themselves and committed himself to their preparation and training, which must involve equality and mutual respect. Patteson was convinced that Melanesians could not only become priests but better priests than many of their European counterparts:

> I solve the difficulty in Melanesian work by saying 'Use Melanesians.' I tell people plainly: 'I don't want white men!' I have no intention of taking any more (clergy) from England, Australia or New Zealand. I sum it up thus: They cost about ten times as much as Melanesians (literally) and but a very small portion do the work as well.

In Patteson's later writings we find how he struggled with despair. He never returned to England. He seemed to find it increasingly difficult to feel comfortable in Western company and we see his real difficulty in coming to terms not so much with the cost of his own sacrifice but the cost of the sacrifice for those he loves.

Patteson's own death became a parable for the people of Melanesia, and his influence even more powerful after his death than before it. Before he died there was the sense of premonition of the event to come. On board the mission ship the *Southern Cross* he is said to have been teaching about the death of St Stephen and to have said: 'This might happen to any of us, to you or to me. It might happen today.' They reached the island of Nukapu near the Reef Islands in Temotu where Patteson requested to go ashore. It was 20 September 1871. Four men rowed him ashore, but the tide was too low for them to cross the reef in the boat so the bishop got into a canoe and went on without them, although they tried to persuade him against this. He lay down to rest in the canoe house almost like a sacrificial offering. While he was lying there

---

18 George Sarawia, *They Came to My Island* (translated and first published in 1968), Melanesian Press.

he was beaten to death with a club used for making bark cloth. His body was wrapped in a mat and put into a canoe. Across his breast was laid a palm branch with five knots in the leaves, which led to the belief that his death was carried out in vengeance for five native men that the 'black-birder' slave traders had carried away from the island. Indeed in accounts of the event we are told that Patteson's body received five wounds, like the wounds of Christ, and only his face remained untouched.[19] It was also said that after he died darkness covered the islands and people went about with torches even at noon.

Some men then attacked the four others in the boat who were anxiously waiting for Patteson just beyond the reef: Joseph Atkin was hit by an arrow in his left shoulder, John Ngongono by one in his right Stephen Taroaniara had six arrows in him. On reaching the *Southern Cross* Joseph Atkin immediately requested 'I am going back for the Bishop. Who will come with me?' Then Joe Wate, a boy of fifteen, stepped up and said 'Inau' (I), and also Charles Sapi, another fifteen-year-old. They discovered the body of the bishop floating in the canoe, one of the boys crying out 'those are the bishop's shoes'. The body of John Coleridge Patteson was buried at sea. Atkin wrote:

> It would only be selfish to wish him back. He has gone to his rest, dying as he lived, in his Master's service. It seems a shocking way to die; but I can say from experience that it is far more to hear of than to suffer. In whatever way so peaceful a life as his is ended, his end is peace. There was no sign of fear or pain on his face – just the look he used to have when asleep, patient and a little wearied. What a stroke his death will be to hundreds! What the mission will do without him, God only knows who has taken him away. His ways are not our ways.[20]

Patteson's followers, we are told by Yonge, 'had deeply to drink of the cup of agony'. Atkin was to die on 27 September from tetanus 'his whole

---

19 Margaret Cropper, *Shining Lights: Six Anglican Saints of the Nineteenth Century,* London, Darton, Longman & Todd, 1963, pp. 50ff.
20 Yonge, *Life of J. C. P.*, Vol 2., p. 572.

nervous system being jerked and strained to pieces' and his last words 'I want nothing but to die.' Stephen lingered on in agony with an arrow wound in his lung, dying from tetanus on 29 September. Bishop Patteson was 44 years of age, Atkin was 29 and Stephen about 25.

It was the news of the martyrdom of Bishop Patteson that stirred the British Government into passing laws to control the labour trade for the Queensland and Fijian plantations in the South Pacific.[21] Professor Max Muller predicted in a letter to *The Times* in 1872: 'In the distant future, depend upon it, the name of Patteson will live in every cottage, in every school and Church of Melanesia, not as the name of a fabulous saint or martyr, but as the never to be forgotten name of a good, a brave, a God-fearing and God-loving man.'[22] This was not to prove an exaggeration, rather Muller had underestimated the legacy of his friend. Today, hundreds of Melanesians name not only their children after him but also their churches. Thousands attend the celebration of his feast day and by the people he is remembered as both saint and martyr. The cross in Nukapu, which marks the place where he was killed, reads 'His life was taken by those for whom he would gladly have given it.'

As I re-read the accounts of this story I am struck by two things. First, how prophetic Patteson was to predict the indigenous growth of the Church and second, how closely the shape of this story of these missionaries' deaths is to be repeated 140 years later, this time by a group of indigenous missionary Brothers. Their death will also be an offering: there will be first the death of one and then the still more agonizing death of those who risk their lives for him. There will be sacrificial courage, and a tragic and seemingly futile loss of innocent lives. It will seem that prayer has failed, and that even God has abandoned them. Their deaths will also rock the Church and the nation, and shock all with the sacrilegious brutality of the murder of men of peace. Their deaths will seem to defeat everything they have striven for – and yet these men will also become catalysts for peace and symbols of hope. 'God's ways are not our ways.'

---

21 In 1872 the British Government passed the Pacific Island Protection Act controlling the unregulated recruitment of labour.

22 Sir John Gutch, *Martyr of the Islands*, London, Hodder and Stoughton, 1971.

Is it simply the way we tell the story that gives it meaning and creates its shape, or can we see something more? Can we see here the marks of the incarnation, and that the shape is the shape of the gospel – not a story forced to conform to what we would like to believe, but Christ, his death and resurrection, revealed even in our own lives?

3

And who are my brothers?

Matthew 12.48

On 20 September 1987, while teaching at Selwyn College on the island of
Guadalcanal in Solomon Islands, I was invited to visit Bishop Patteson
Theological College. The College was celebrating Bishop Patteson's
Day, the day set aside by the Church in memory of the death of John
Coleridge Patteson. It was at the Feast Day Eucharist that I first came
across the Melanesian Brotherhood. At least fifty of these young men,
aged between 18 and 30, dressed in white shirts, white *lavalavas*[23] and
with bare feet and medals around their necks, were filling the central seat-
ing area of the church. Some of them wore red sashes, a sign that they
were Novices, others wore a black and white sash as a sign that they had
made promises of poverty, chastity and obedience, and were Brothers in
the Community. I remember the first impression vividly as they began to
sing. It was a huge response to God: the roaring vibrancy and energy of
their voices, the *tete* seed rattles, the bamboo drum keeping the urgent
rhythm and the Melanesian custom tunes with their four-part harmonies,
which rose and twisted and swooped like frigate birds and then faded
away into a soft, long final note and then silence. The way they sang in
worship, and the way they responded seemed both powerful and yet
humble at the same time. Brave humility: it is a quality that remains and
is a unique expression of this community. They were not singers, and yet
when they combined together the sound had the depth and power of
the sea. Each one was dressed in washed, sun-dried, white cotton, but it

---

23 A strip of cloth bound round the waist and coming to below the knees,
Polynesian in origin, similar to a South Asian *sarong*.

wasn't just their clothes, there was something more that seemed to shine here. As I watched them going up to receive the Eucharist, one after the other, with such simple devotion, it seemed to me that their faith was not something extraneous but from within. Grace was part of them, like the grace of movement in an athlete who can run like a cheetah. And this impression of the Melanesian Brotherhood's faith has never left me in the seventeen years I have worked with them, even though, of course, I have had plenty of time to see all the human struggles and failures, for they are very much ordinary men too.

On that first day of meeting, when the service was over I walked down to the Melanesian Brotherhood's headquarters at Tabalia, for it is situated literally side by side with Bishop Patteson Theological College. I remember that the Brothers who showed me round told me the story of their Motherhouse with a great sense of reverence for the place. To me, a newcomer, it seemed a simple set of leaf and corrugated iron roofed buildings positioned around a grass square. To these Brothers, however, it was obvious that the place was sacred. Everything has a story: the coconut tree was planted by Brother Charles Fox, the coconuts around it are never collected, for they are signs that the community will be fruitful; behind the dormitories is a ditch dug by Brother Charles Fox and still dug today as a discipline for those Brothers or Novices who miss prayer; coming down the side of the square towards the chapel, everyone removes their sandals, if they are wearing any, for this is holy ground. Outside the chapel is a grass square surrounded by a neatly cut hedge and, on the east side, a large white cross and white altar on a red (for the martyrs) cement step. This is St Simon and St Jude's Square where their founder made his promises in 1925. Brothers still make their promises in this same square today, to live while they are brothers in poverty, chastity and obedience:

Most High and everlasting God,
accept me now as I come before you in love.
In the sight of the holy angels
and all the company of heaven,
I dedicate myself to the service of my Lord Jesus Christ.

I want to live the gospel.
O Lord, give me grace.

And the Archbishop of Melanesia blesses their lives saying:

Lord God and heavenly Father,
look with kindness on these your servants:
we send them forth as messengers of salvation and peace,
marked with the sign of the cross.
Guide their steps with your mighty arm
and with the power of your grace strengthen them in spirit
so that they will not fall.
Make their words echo Christ's voice
so that those who hear them
may be drawn to obey the gospel.
May they be brave, holding up the weak,
helping those who are in trouble,
giving honour to all people, loving and serving the Lord,
full of joy in the power of the Holy Spirit.[24]

Only the Brothers, they tell me, are allowed to enter the square.

The Melanesian Brothers' Chapel of St Mark is simple too: a rectangular building which focuses on a heavy wooden altar, made from *tubi*, a local hardwood. The altar maintains something of the tree from which it was cut; it is solid, simple and strong. The floor of the chapel is cement, polished like marble from the constant footsteps of the community who come five times a day for prayer. Behind the altar is a standing cross with mother-of-pearl inlay, like a rising sun, and on the walls behind spears and shields which, the Brothers inform me, were the weapons that the Brothers faced in hostile villages when their missionary work began. To the east above the altar is a stained-glass window depicting the founder of the community Ini Kopuria in front of a cross, a 'heathen man' on his

---

24 *Irareta Tasiu Melanesia: Offices and Prayers of the Melanesian Brotherhood*, Solomon Islands, Provincial Press, 1997.

right, and a Companion of the Brotherhood, praying on his left. This chapel, the Brothers tell me, is at the heart of all the community does.

It is the response of the Brothers to this place that makes you grow still and silent and want to enter into its life and rhythm. The grounds are full of birds, frangipani, hibiscus, mango trees; even the stray dogs seem to want to come to pray and sing out when the bells are rung. There is a simplicity and prayerfulness here, no division as it were between the inner life and the outer. I remember when a film crew from Hollywood came to this place. They were making a film called *The Thin Red Line*, directed by Terrence Malick. The film is about the American battle with the Japanese on this island of Guadalcanal during the Second World War. It is a meditation on life and death, upon the barbarity and cruelty of war – this juxtaposed with the creative but often cruel beauty of the natural world. A Frenchman, Claude Letessier, came to Tabalia to record the music for this film. He stayed for three days, and did not seem to want to go away. He had been living in Los Angeles. I thought perhaps he had not found the music he was hoping for. He kept on going into the chapel and then walking outside again, watching and listening. Finally, I asked him if this was the music he wanted or should the Brothers sing something different. He answered 'I've waited all my life to hear this. This is harmony.' In the visitors' book when he left he wrote 'for the place where I found harmony'. He told me he had travelled all over the world as a sound recordist, but this was a place to which he wanted to return. I felt that too. Tabalia and the prayer of that chapel drew me in. It was not like something new, it was like coming home.

At 5.30 in the morning the community gathers in the dark, then the pumped-up oil lamps are brought in with their white light refracting around the chapel, illuminating the white uniforms of the kneeling community. As prayer begins you can see the light of the sun rising; it streams in rainbows of colour through the stained-glass window and onto the altar. Outside, the songbirds and parrots arrive and bounce on the flowering trees. And the chapel is filled each day with a community of more than one hundred men who are not pious or overly religious, or fanatical, or narrow, and as human and diverse as anybody else; they are ordinary and yet extraordinary. It is as if the doors and windows are all open and there is no division between the holy and the secular. There is just this sense of presence going up and coming down, inside and out. As though God is still walking in the garden. If you doubt me, as Jesus said: 'Come and see.'

Brother Ini Kopuria, the founder of the Melanesian Brotherhood, was a Solomon Islander born on the island of Guadalcanal in 1900. He was baptized as a child and grew up in the Anglican tradition, attending the Church missionary school at Pamua and then St Barnabas College, Norfolk Island. After leaving school his teachers wanted him to become a catechist to his own people. Instead he joined the native police force in the service of the British Colonial Government of that time. His work took him all over Guadalcanal, his home island, both around the coastal areas and up into the inland bush villages. Kopuria, however, badly injured his knee while making an arrest and it was during several months of inactivity in Tulagi Hospital that he received a vision of Christ that made him question the work he was doing and led him to a life of missionary service. He wrote to the Bishop of Melanesia, John Manwaring Steward, describing his calling 'to declare the kingdom of God among the heathen . . . God made me remember: "Your life is mine and God can do what he wishes with his own."'[25]

In 1925 Ini Kopuria founded a Brotherhood for Melanesians and, in consultation with the bishop, prepared a rule of life in which he dedi-cated his life and land to God and made three promises of Christian poverty, chastity and obedience. The following year six brothers also took promises and joined him, and the Melanesian Brotherhood con-tinued to grow. The purpose of the Brotherhood was evangelistic. Ini believed that the gospel should be taken out and lived in the remotest islands and villages. He saw the white European missionary model as often drawing converts away from their traditional way of life. He wanted Melanesians to be evangelized but in a Melanesian way.

---

25 John Manwaring Steward, *The Brothers*, Auckland, New Zealand, The Melanesian Mission, 1928, p. 2.

He thought it all wrong that every Melanesian because of his colour should feel inferior to every white man because of his colour. He thought that there was this feeling even within the Mission and the Church itself.[26]

Ini chose a radical approach. He sent his Brothers out two by two on mission to all parts of Solomon Islands. Arriving unarmed, with no food or possessions, in often hostile villages, they aimed to stay and, if they were accepted by the chief and people, live the life of the people in that place: talking, sharing and working together before moving on. He believed that the standard of life of his Brothers should never rise above the standard of life of the people they served. It was not long before their reputation began to grow. These Brothers were prepared to come and stay. They were not frightened of devils and ancestral spirits. Their prayers could drive away fear. People began to speak of their miracles of healing and of the signs they had witnessed.

Another characteristic of the Melanesian Brotherhood that made it different from European models of religious community, was that Brothers took only temporary vows which could be renewed. Brothers who wished to leave the community after a period of service were free to do so; in this way the intention both honoured and respected the call to married life and affirmed that the period of religious formation and service would not be wasted when the Brother was released from the community and could return like leaven to his people.

Upon Ini Kopuria's death in 1945, Brother Charles Fox described him thus:

I think he was one of the ablest Melanesians I have ever known. What things stood out in his character? First I think his spirituality. Prayer was a real thing for Ini: he was the most reverent Melanesian I have ever met and that is saying a lot. God was in all his thoughts. Second his joyousness. He was almost always in high spirits, full of fun, full of joy of being alive: it was good to live with him. Third his deep under-

26 Charles Fox, extract from *The Southern Cross Log*, January 1946, Vol. 52, no. 1.

standing of the thoughts of Melanesians. At Brothers' meetings when disputes were often hot, Ini always knew who was really in the wrong and generally got that brother to say so. Fourth, his common sense. He always knew what was practicable and kept discussions to that.[27]

The stories of Kopuria reflect this same vitality and joy for life rooted both in prayer and a down-to-earth commitment to the people. He led by example: 'Two by two into every town and place.' He walked the roads, shared the life of the people, was unafraid of ancestral spirits or hostile heathen villages where he went and stayed, he even dug the pit toilets himself. There are stories of the Brothers praying with the sick, carrying the sick down from mountain villages to clinics, driving out fear and evil spirits, preparing people for baptism, fishing, planting, building leaf houses and visiting everywhere. To pick one of many examples, here is one recorded by Charles Fox:

> I remember coasting along the shores of New Britain in the mission ship looking for somewhere to land two brothers and receiving a refusal at each 'heathen' village until we found one where the people allowed them to stay. I took them ashore and I rowed back to the ship. I watched these two young men standing there with nothing but their haversacks, among a heathen people of whose language they knew not a word, who might easily kill or starve them after we had gone. They were a thousand miles from their own homes and knew that the mission ship would not come back for a year. A year later we called again and found them standing there once more, this time with twenty of the people prepared for baptism. After some years there were several hundred Christians there.[28]

Yet the last years of Kopuria's own life were not happy ones. In the Second World War the Japanese occupied the area of Tabalia, the cross in the square was broken, the Community was forced to scatter, hiding

---

27 Charles Fox, extract from *The Southern Cross Log*, January 1946, Vol. 52, no. 1.
28 Charles Fox, *The Melanesian Brotherhood*, London, The Melanesian Mission, n.d.

the Community's chalice and paten in the plantation. One of the Brothers was shot and died as he tried to escape across the Tanaemba river. Kopuria himself seemed to lose direction. Charles Fox with great compassion describes these last years:

> In the end, in the early days of the war Ini left the Brotherhood. On his travels he met a girl and fell in love with her and asked to be released from his life vows and was released by the bishop. Then came the Americans in their thousands. It was a time of great unsettlement for everyone; and for a time Ini went, as the bishop wrote, 'into a far country'. There followed soon the sickness from which he died, but not before he had come back to full communion. The last period of failure was perhaps needed for the final lesson of humility, so hard for men of great gifts. The failure did not last long. It was as though God took his hand away for a moment in order that he might hold Ini for ever.
>
> So on June 6th 1945 this brilliant, wayward, valiant leader of men found final happiness. As for us of the Brotherhood, he always held our hearts and can never be forgotten.[29]

Ini had two children, but both of them died in infancy. The Brotherhood themselves never talked about those last sad years in Ini's life. It was as if those years would tarnish the reputation of the founder, his failure to keep his life vow a flaw in his inspiring life which was better left untold. But for me it made him more human. It is, as Charles Fox describes, God's lesson for us in humility so that he might hold us forever. This was the true Christian story, but it was different from the stories of the superheroes that people like to create.

A mythology and a mystique began to grow up around these Brothers, or *Tasiu*, as they became known in Mota language. People began to talk of their miracles and to say that the Brothers or *Tasiu* had *mana* and spiritual power. Robert Codrington in his book published in 1891, *The Melanesians,* defined *mana* in this way:

---

29 Charles Fox, *The Southern Cross Log,* January 1946, Vol. 52, no. 1.

This is what works to affect everything beyond the ordinary power of men, outside the common practice of nature; it is present in the atmosphere of life, attaches itself to persons and to things. But this power, though itself impersonal, is always connected with some person who directs it . . . All Melanesian religion consists . . . in getting this *mana* for oneself or getting it used for one's benefit.[30]

Stories circulated that Brothers could part rivers with their walking sticks, protect villages with their prayers and holy stones, stop cyclones, defeat magic with their holy collects, even ride on the back of crocodiles. But the spirit of these stories reflects a similar message: that these local missionaries had a power of goodness to heal, to help, and protect and they were loved by the people, even those from different churches. The Melanesian Brotherhood belonged to the Melanesian people and also to God. They bridged the gap between the old *kastom* religion of ancestral spirits and magic, and the Christian faith based on love and service and Christ's victory over the power of evil.

The rule of life that the Brothers followed was simple but disciplined. They prayed seven short offices a day, dedicating each part of the day to the service of Christ. They met each month for a Confession Meeting in which each Brother was called upon to admit any difficulties he was facing or disagreements he had with his fellow Brothers. The rule forbade Brothers to complain about one another outside the Brotherhood. The following extract from some of the Brothers' Rule captures this contextualized spiritual discipline and desire to live the gospel:

> The love of Jesus must be shown in and through us. We must take the lead in showing this love for one another and all people everywhere at all times.

> Do not show love to only those you like most. Treat all people the same.

---

30 *The Melanesians: Studies in their Anthropology and Folk-lore*, Oxford, 1891.

If any person is around at meal times we must call him or her to join us. We apologise when there is nothing to offer.

If we catch some fish or fresh meat, we must first remember to share with the old or sick even when we have not got enough.

When we are at someone's house respect is required. We must not tell stories long at night. Measure your time and stop when you think you must. Too many stories will make you sometimes tell lies. Try to get enough sleep for the next day's work.

It is good to help someone doing or carrying a heavy load.[31]

The Melanesian Brotherhood was not restricted to Solomon Islands or to one race. By the 1930s they had begun working in Vanuatu and Fiji and in 1955 began a mission among the tribes in New Guinea Highlands. From 1975 to 1994 they worked among Australian Aborigines and Torres Strait Islanders in northern Queensland, Australia and in the 1990s set up two households in Palawan in the Philippines. By 2000 the Melanesian Brotherhood numbered about 450 Brothers and 180 Novices, and had established three regions in Papua New Guinea, Solomon Islands and Vanuatu, they were also being invited to lead Christian missions for the Anglican Church in other parts of the world: New Zealand, Australia, United Kingdom and Canada.

---

31 Extract from *The Principles and Rules of the Melanesian Brotherhood*, Honiara, Provincial Press, pp. 10–11.

4

For we walk by faith.

2 Corinthians 5.7

I began to ask myself why this Community was flourishing whereas religious life in the West seemed to be in decline. Perhaps it was because the Melanesian Brotherhood provided excitement and a way out of the village. It also gave free education and training for many of those who had been deprived of education above primary school level; it provided a chance to travel and to broaden experience; it also provided a sense of purpose and status – families would talk with pride about the member of their family whom they had given to serve God in the Melanesian Brotherhood. Yet it was also known to be a calling not to be embarked upon lightly. Poverty, chastity and obedience make radical demands on any young man's life. Christianity in the secular world has often tried to soften the demands of the gospel in order to become more attractive to its target membership. The Melanesian Brotherhood has always maintained the sense that Christ's calling is actually a sacrificial call. How I shy away from using that word. Like so many in the West I have a picture in my mind of French fields filled with crosses, of Jews forced into cattle trucks and gas chambers, of fanatical faiths legitimizing mindless allegiance and of the graves of seven Brothers at Tabalia. And yet if we abandon the concept of Christian sacrifice are we not abandoning the very nature of the love which is at the heart of our Christian gospel?

Why do so many want to join? Why did I want to join? The fact is that the life of this community inspired us. It had a simplicity and humble courage that reached the hearts of all age groups. We sensed that this was what the Christian Church should be like. These were real evangelists: good news people. This was not paper evangelism, this was not about lists, aims and procedures, budgets, modules, offices, committees, coffee cups, and endless administration and high maintenance. These were not 'super' evangelists and experts, cloned from USA and flown in from overseas with huge amplifiers. This was living the life of Christ, unsung, unfinanced, and undocumented. This was a ministry of presence without judgement or competition. These evangelists, whom the people could welcome in their own homes like a returning son or daughter, walked the roads with bare feet and no money. These Brothers would share whatever food there was, sleep on a mat and help hoe the garden, catch the fish or repair the leaf roof. They would come, whenever they were called, to pray for the sick, solve a village dispute, calm down a husband who was drunk and have a drink themselves when they had the chance. They would be there in feast and in famine and, what's more, they could bring God to both.

Ini Kopuria believed the Brotherhood must be prepared to share everything. The vow of poverty is very real. Within the Community resources are limited. More than forty Novices, for example, share each humid dormitory, sleeping on mats; they have no shoes, no watches, no possessions. They own a few tattered clothes usually passed from one to another, and their Brother's or Novice's uniform. Towels are usually shared and threadbare, t-shirts and shorts are borrowed from the washing line; most have no 'luxuries' such as razor blades, soap, washing powder or toothpaste. Most can fit their possessions into one bag. The Community eats twice a day: root crops like kasava, swamp taro, or kumara and some vegetables. Sometimes there is a little fish. In the bush areas they can usually find fruit, and always there are coconuts. At times there will be feast days, pigs will be killed and major fishing expeditions will go out, then there will be plenty; at other times when the floods and rain come, there may be only potatoes or perhaps nothing. The days when there is no evening meal the Brothers call 'find your own way home'. It means everyone must fend for themselves or simply go to bed. Yet, in all of this, I have very rarely heard any complaining. But despite their lack of resources, the Brotherhood aims to take special care of any guest who arrives at the Community. Portions are divided and divided again as guests arrive; often you will notice those who quietly go without and this is done with no resentment. When overseas guests arrive bearing gifts of bread, milk and even cornflakes, they usually get fed back to the guests. The Community is not advocating deprivation, neither is it glorying in a spirit of fasting. (When there is plenty the Community will eat as if there is no tomorrow.) Yet the Brothers will tell you there is freedom in this way of life – a freedom to accept what the day provides. Less is more. The most simple things can seem like a feast day. I was from the West, and a culture that increasingly demands a hundred choices for everything. Yet few things can compare with cold water when you are thirsty, or fresh fruit and a coconut to drink after you have walked through the sun, and washing in the water gushing from the roof gutter after the drought ends and the rain comes. Less is often much much more.

When the Australian-led intervention force came to Solomon Islands in 2003, one of their written objectives was 'to end the *wantok system*'. By this the Australians meant they wanted to help stamp out corruption and nepotism and the way public finance can be siphoned off by the extended family. '*Wantok*' means literally 'one talk': those who speak the same language and are thus in Melanesia (where often on one island as many as three or four languages are spoken) one tribe. It made those who know the country laugh. The *wantok system* is the community, the way one shares with his tribe and language group, it is those bonds of family, kinship and culture and interdependence which bind people together. The Melanesian Brotherhood sought not to end the *wantok system* but to extend it beyond the barriers and prejudices of tribe and island and even nation. That was the aim for our Community, not to destroy . . . but, as Brother Roger of Taizé said, to create 'possibilities in the human family to widen'.

Part of this extending of the *wantok system* will be being open and ready for others when they come, however inconvenient. And of course it is a system that can be abused and that is costly and must ultimately depend on a mutual reciprocity. But it does not always work that way, and so is ultimately costly. Yet is that not what the gospel is? We may think it does not fit in with modern work ethics and assertiveness training, but does not Christ teach about going the extra mile, giving your coat as well, forgiving not seven times but seventy times seven, turning the other cheek, giving everything to the poor? It may be inconvenient but it does seem fairly central to the Christian message.

I send a message to the Sisters of Melanesia asking to borrow a book that is in their library. The following morning two sisters arrive at my house for breakfast. They have walked fifteen miles through the night to bring the book. Our driver has just returned from Honiara at one o'clock in the morning. He has been driving all day and he has missed his evening meal, but there is a crowd of people from the village gathering round the truck supporting a woman who is in great pain and just about to give birth. He turns the truck round and drives back to the hospital in Honiara. The trip will take another three hours; usually there will be no one to pay for the fuel and so the money must be borrowed from what has been set aside for another purpose. This happens most days. Is this a misuse of funds? Perhaps a mother's life has been saved and that of her new born daughter. We are widening the *wantok system*, there is no other way. Solomon Islanders do not have savings and bank accounts or expense accounts like the advisers who have been flown in.

'To the extent that we create possibilities for the human family to widen . . .' I remember an old man died near the village of Vila. He was a lonely man who had arrived from the Weather Coast on the other side of the island with no family with him. The village was suspicious of him and the children were frightened. High grass was growing around his home and he never seemed to eat or wash. For some reason or problem he had been rejected by the community but now the Melanesian Brothers visited him and shared food with him. When he was found dead in the grass by his house no one would touch him. He had been sick; perhaps they would get sick too. They called two Novices who carried him back to his home, washing and cleaning his body and preparing him for burial, wrapped in a bed sheet. In the evening more Melanesian Brothers and Novices arrived and prayed and sang around his body through the night. The villagers, no longer afraid, came and joined them. In the morning the body of the old man was buried. It was a lonely death, but one that had been transformed. There are many such examples. In London I have never known how to respond to the homeless: whether to give them money or to walk past. Both alternatives fill me with guilt. Yet it was with the Melanesian Brothers on mission that I saw an alternative. They sat down with the homeless and spent time with them, just as they would have spent time with a bishop.

Luluwai, the chief of Surapau village in the mountains in the west of Guadalcanal, is complaining. He has heard that some people want the Brotherhood's household on his land to move to a different place. 'If they want to move the Brothers they'll have to cut my neck first,' he says, 'I'll go back to my heathen ways and so will the whole village,' he threatens. When the South Sea Evangelical Missionaries came, they came only once and then went away: 'I don't want to join a church which comes and runs away,' says Luluwai. 'When the Brothers came they stayed with us. I was suspicious at first. I told the children to keep away from them, but they always seemed to find their way back to those Brothers and I heard them learning songs and laughing and playing. I thought that our ancestral spirits would soon frighten them off, but they stayed and I let them plant their gardens and I gave them food. I helped them. I gave them the land to build their house. It was a hill where no one else wanted to live because of the lost spirits of some children who died there; I thought that this would test them, but they didn't seem afraid and I began visiting them; we smoked my tobacco and shared betel nut and told stories.'

Luluwai says that before the Brothers brought the Church there used to be much fear: 'If there was a problem, like you broke a *kastom*, if you didn't sacrifice a pig, the devils would take revenge and kill one of your children or bring sickness.' Luluwai hedged his bets. He had several wives and he did not want to lose any because of a new religion. Yet he was attracted to the way these Brothers lived and the peace they brought. When his wives died and he was left with only one, he saw this as a sign and decided to be baptized and to make sure everyone else in his tribe was baptized too: 'Now problems can be settled in the church. We have forgiveness. This time we are not frightened to welcome strangers. Those devils and spirits from before have no power now. We love the Brothers. But don't send us any Brothers who misbehave and have come here to find a wife!' Luluwai is under no illusions about the problems of maintaining the vow of chastity.

Tabalia is preparing for the Brotherhood Feast Day of St Simon and St Jude. For two weeks people have been arriving from every part of the Solomons to join the celebration. The Brothers and Novices have vacated their rooms and dormitories. These will be for their visitors and they themselves will sleep anywhere they can find – verandas, sheds, even down at the piggery. More than 5,000 people will arrive in time for the weekend of the feast day. The taps dry up. No one complains, water is carried half a mile from the river. No one is bossing, no one is shouting; there is an atmosphere of joy and celebration. The Community is working together with a harmony that remains a mystery to the overseas guests. No one pays, no one is quite sure where it has all come from or who is feeding whom but, like the feeding of the 5,000, again and again there is enough for everybody. It is the miracle of reciprocity.

A young Novice Manasseh Paulo is dying from cancer in Honiara hospital. The doctor has told us he does not have long to live. I go to celebrate the Eucharist for him. For the last twelve hours he has been in agony but now the pain has left him and he seems to radiate a sense of peace.

'Mi givem hem *kastom*,' says his father pointing to the magic cure in his son's hand. The doctor tells me 'I have given him some morphine to help him cope with the pain.' The Brothers tell me 'We have been praying for him and God is helping him.' Here are three different perspectives on healing. What strikes us all is the sense of peace that now emanates from this young man, and seems to illuminate him so that we feel we are standing in a holy place. He sits up with great effort. 'No, it's all right', I say, 'you can lie down.' But he will not let me begin until he has prepared properly.

'I must wear my Melanesian Brotherhood medal,' he says. They put it round his neck. His devotion is moving. We are all quiet now. His father says, 'After you are better we will take you home.'

'No,' says Manasseh, 'my home is with the Brothers at Tabalia now.'

Later he asks some of the Brothers to buy a chicken for him at the market – 'Tonight I want to have feast with all of you'. They have been sleeping on the hospital floor for many days at the foot of his bed.

'Don't forget the feast' he reminds them.

They go out to buy the chicken and to cook it. When they return Manasseh has died. But the divide between life and death does not seem so great: the feast they prepare on earth will be celebrated in heaven. And for Manasseh, and for many others in the Brotherhood, God is no stranger. The family stretches outwards but also above and beyond.

The Melanesian Brotherhood did create opportunities for the human family to widen and I too found myself included, captivated by the goodness of this life. I found those possibilities I had prayed for all those years before at Taizé becoming part of my life and it seemed so right that I had hardly even realized it. Yet here I was on the other side of the world in a Community I had known nothing about, which had enabled, like a gift, all those things I had longed to be: a priest, a teacher, living in a Community, part of the excitement and vitality of the developing world in Melanesia, working on adapting the gospel into Melanesian dramas with casts of up to 120, yes and almost a Brother myself. In 1993 I became chaplain to the Community. My job was to help develop the spiritual life, the training and the mission of the Community in all the countries where they were working.

My house is always full. There have been at least twenty Brothers and Novices who have been sitting, or sleeping on the floor, or cooking pots of sweet potato in this room this morning. There are enough people to empty the numerous containers of water in the fridge every hour and of course fill them again. The water is not even cold because the refrigerator is not working because there is no electricity; water is never in there long enough anyway to get cold. But that is what they have come to share, for there is nothing else in the refrigerator, although they keep on having a peek to see if it has been supernaturally restocked in the few minutes since they last opened its door with all the insulating rubber peeling off, and tried to get it closed again. There is no sense of crowding or disturbance. There is a harmony of living, presence without conflict. So somehow there is space, even in a house that is full. I have often thought that in Western cultures we could not live together like this; we need to control and organize. But here it is different. This is company that does not require word or attention and yet upholds. Wherever you walk or work or pray there are people willing to walk, work or pray with you. There is always company. There is no old people's home, or people living in physical isolation, there is no single person struggling to do everything alone. There are at least ten people to carry the baby. I do not think God intended us to spend our lives trying to manage alone, forever in competition to show our standard of self-sufficiency.

It has become a joke among the Brothers:

'Have you eaten today?'

'Not yet, I am living by faith.'

This life is also to be struggled with, at times it weakens but it does bring an awareness of God in all things. There is an awareness of dependence on God in the storms, floods and cyclones that can so easily destroy the people's livelihood and homes, an awareness of God as you set off in overloaded boats for other islands with no life-jackets and no money for extra petrol and only flip-flops to use as paddles when the engine breaks down. There is faith needed by those who go out to fish in small canoes far from shore in rough seas. There is awareness of God in his creation when the rainy season comes and the taps silt up and there is thick mud everywhere, and the brown swollen river, which can move bridges, is the only place to wash. There is a prayer in the head of Brothers as two by two they walk the hot roads with bare feet and hope that a truck will stop to give them a lift. And yet no Brother will ever look back or hold out his hand to stop anyone. And so we walk and we listen and we hope for the sound of a slowing truck and then sit precariously on the back among the market produce. There is faith too as a Brother with often little formal education gets up to preach in a church, or teach, or stand at the side of the sick to pray for healing. Here living is not about profession, income or property, it is about *life,* and God cannot be taken out of the equation of life easily. But does this faith keep us passive, waiting for signs and divine intervention rather than shaping our own futures? Perhaps. We are not so driven; we do not rush to change; we wait for the tides and the flooding rivers to recede and then begin again. All is provisional, all is passing, except the land and spirit and God. A Brother may be poor in material possessions, but in Christ he is seen as rich. Life is a gift of God, and ultimately in Melanesia the one who can intercede with God is needed during the decisive moments of our lives, just as much as the rich are needed to provide food for feast days and funerals and transport to hospital and corrugated iron for the church roof. For all those who live in the developing world know the vulnerability and fragility of human life. They have feared sickness, they have all witnessed death in their community, dug graves, gathered round bodies and heard the wail of relatives and the smell of the departed. For those who know the poverty of death and do not try to hide it from their young, is it not far more wise to prepare for eternity than for that which will be taken away? And perhaps it is those in the Western world who are really living in poverty when they fail to realize that life is a gift, but see it as their private possession, thus in death they are cheated and lose, whereas in this Brotherhood it is as if life has moved just beyond sight and the dialogue continues.

Yet how easy it is to idealize this way of life from a distance only to realize close up that its goodness is not without great frustration, wound and struggle. In 1962 Charles Fox described how the Melanesian Brotherhood was sometimes looked upon by the priests as 'cheap labour'.[32] If there was any job to do, which no one else could be found to do, then the Brotherhood would be asked: rebuilding churches, moving schools, transporting, acting as caretakers and security, taking messages and so on. In the recent ethnic conflict many private businesses and church properties relied on the Brotherhood as night security to prevent break-ins and looting. The Community would often be too widely stretched and fragmented. They could be used like foot soldiers but, once released from the Community, they would return to obscurity, anonymous and powerless. I still feel that many of the Brothers who suffered in the conflict did so with very little acknowledgement for what they personally suffered.

There is increased temptation for Brothers to abandon their difficult vows of poverty, chastity and obedience. When one Brother transgresses the rules, it is often the whole Brotherhood that is blamed. Just as I have

---

32 C. E. Fox, *Kakamora*, London, Hodder and Stoughton, 1962, p. 76.

seen the beauty of community, I have also seen its failure. The individual who is different or who does not conform can be rejected. There is greater loyalty to the group than to the person, initiative is sometimes stifled and talents remain wasted. Traditions, which are often held onto defensively, can lose touch with their original meaning or intention and can repress the spirit and become barriers to growth and new understanding. Community is sometimes threatened or challenged by individual initiative and creativity. Community can seek scapegoats, gossip about leadership, divide in jealousy, feed on rumour and prejudice, fail to defend an individual's rights for fear of creating a precedent, or because others are projecting their own fears and defensiveness. Yet when the individual abandons the Community he finds, instead of freedom, a loss of direction and opportunity.

There has always been the danger that the Brotherhood itself, respected for its spiritual *mana* or power, can be tempted away from a Christ-centred approach into cultic practices that reinforce superstition and fear rather than liberating people from it. Has not there always been the danger of using religion contrary to the very spirit of Christ, who rejects those temptations in the wilderness? A mythology has developed in which the people start trusting in the use of Brothers' intercessions, collects and holy objects: stones, walking sticks, holy oil and water, and prayers for binding devils etc. They are seeking the person who can control and direct God's power and even use it against their enemies. Thus the holy man must prove his power by the miracles he performs, his ability to bring divine intervention for one's own side and even direct God's curse and judgement. This kind of religion may sound primitive but many in our world today are still using the name of God to attack their own enemies and fears. Is there not in all of us some of this kind of longing, to try to make God conform to our own needs and causes? How often is our prayer nothing more than an effort to change the future and bring us good fortune?

Although I see all of this, I am still captivated by the good. Is it possible to live with this spirit of the Beatitudes? And why do I, who have witnessed this truth, still shrink from it? I think it is because like many I fear the powerlessness of having no money and no escape. I fear being cut off from my own family and those I love. I fear losing my independence and self-sufficiency. I fear my sins and weaknesses and being unable to express my desire for love. I am concerned about hunger and sickness and becoming a burden and being unable to get out if the going gets tough and missing the luxuries at the end of the hard journey. I wonder about feeling vulnerable and trapped, oppressed by poor leadership, dispossessed, even exploited or forgotten, no longer in control but controlled. For this is also the experience of poverty in the developing world. And yet I deeply long for the freedom of those vows, the freedom of those I have seen coming to God, ready to serve him and their neighbour in all things, so uncluttered – a poverty where service for others becomes pure grace, where everyone can become your brother, your sister, your mother, a way of life where you can walk lightly and simply in the way of Christ as I have seen Brothers walk. Can this vision of Christ-like poverty be true? And quietly, humbly, the Brothers and Sisters who embrace this call seem to say 'Live the gospel and you will see.'

At Tabalia in Solomon Islands I prepare to take my vows as a Brother – vows of poverty, chastity and obedience. It is that call to live by faith and in thanksgiving for the blessings of God I have received and for the Love and Truth I have witnessed. It is a symbol too of my solidarity with the Community with whom I have shared so much. To take this step, the tradition is that I must climb a steep mountain, which the Brotherhood has named *Pentecost*, and spend a night of prayer on the top.

Four of us reach the summit. I am dehydrated and exhausted by the climb, but glowing. The bottle of water is delicious. I cannot stop drinking. We pray together on the top, singing our evening office. We sit in silence as the thick black darkness surrounds us. I feel anaesthetized with the exertion. I lie back and look up through the darkness. There is no moon, just the glow from the smouldering fire. We have made a shelter with branches to protect us from the rain. The night is noisy with insects and the patter of rain dripping through the leaves. I feel so still, so at peace. The darkness is soft and black as velvet. I long for this night to last forever. In the early morning light, with the low sun filtering through wet leaves, we celebrate the Eucharist on an altar we have made from branches. These are timeless actions, within time and location and yet for all time and all people. I watch these beautiful actions set against the trees and the sun and hear the familiar words joining the sounds of this mountain, and know that we are not alone but part of something much greater than we can ever understand. We light a fire so that the smoke will be seen by the Community and set off back down the mountain.

When we reach the road a man calls out to us. There is fear in his voice. There has been a terrible accident, the church truck has stalled while climbing the hill to the Community. A man has been crushed and is dead, four others are injured. There is shock and trauma. I see the mangled truck on the hill, the blood on the cement where they laid the dead man's body. My Brothers in the Community have washed and prepared his body for burial and taken him back to his village where he will be buried. And in the midst of this tragedy we prepare for St Mark's Day: Mark, the evangelist of the Good News whose gospel again and again tells us 'Do not be afraid.'

On that following day I go into the square where the founder of the community stood seventy-five years before and, with my knees really trembling, make my promises:

Most High and everlasting God,
Accept me now as I come before you in love.
In the sight of the holy angels and all the company of heaven,
I dedicate myself to the service of my Lord Jesus Christ.
I want to live the gospel.
O Lord, give me grace.

A simple offering, because I believe God to be the God of the living and of the dead and we must make him present both on the mountain and 'in the valley of the shadow of death'.

5

When you hear of wars and insurrections . . .

Luke 21.9

Solomon Islands, known as 'The Happy Isles', had not witnessed any major conflict or violence since the Second World War when Guadalcanal had been the scene of major land and sea battles between the USA and Japan. The ethnic conflict and near civil war, which broke out in 1999, came both as a shock and a tragedy for a group of islands that, on the surface, seemed to have established a harmonious relationship between different tribal and island groups and a strong and balanced sense of community and tradition, despite the pressures of modern development.

The conflict developed on the island of Guadalcanal to which, ever since the Second World War, there had been a steady migration of people from other islands especially around Honiara, the capital of the Solomons. A large proportion of those coming to settle were from the island of Malaita. It was the Malaitans who began to make up a large proportion of the labour force on Guadalcanal. They provided many of the construction workers, the work force for SIPL (Solomon Islands Plantation Ltd), crew for the Japanese tuna fishing fleet, and workers for the logging companies, plantations, small industries, factories and shops. Many Malaitans became successful at setting up their own small businesses. Malaitans also became the dominant island group within the Royal Solomon Islands Police Force.

Many Malaitan settlements began to be built not just within Honiara but within a thirty-mile radius of the capital. Some of those coming from Malaita bought land from Guadalcanal landowners, others simply came and settled. At first, when land seemed plentiful and relationships were harmonious, the Guadalcanal people gave their land generously and agreements were often undocumented. Over a period of twenty years these settlements grew in size as members of extended families from Malaita came in search of work, and also as the result of a high birth rate. Malaitans began to take up an increasingly large number of places at Guadalcanal schools. Often, because of their industrious, entrepreneurial approach, they were more materially and financially successful than their Guadalcanal neighbours. In many ways there was much integration and harmony in the relationship between the people of Guadalcanal and Malaita; there were intermarriages, sports competitions, shared feast days, and a common Christian faith. In schools, church, and community activities, there was often a rich and joyful sense of cultural diversity with different ethnic groups sharing worship, songs, dances, customs and traditions from their home islands. Yet beneath the surface there was, among some Guadalcanal people, a growing resentment: the prejudice that Malaitans were increasingly encroaching on their land, taking advantage of their generosity, failing to respect Guadalcanal custom, sometimes causing violence and conflict within the community. They believed Malaitans were using Guadalcanal land to become richer than the indigenous population, and that their domination of the land would increase until they eventually took over completely. Into this equation was added a new source of suspicion and grievance when in 1998 Gold Ridge Gold Mine was opened by an Australian Company in East Guadalcanal. Many Guadalcanal people felt aggrieved that such a small proportion of the rumoured massive profits were going to the people of Guadalcanal themselves, and such a large proportion to what they saw as financing an increasingly Malaitan dominated government and public sector.

At the end of 1998 a militant group on Guadalcanal emerged. They have been known by various names: initially the Guadalcanal Revolutionary Army (GRA) and then later the Isatabu Freedom Movement (IFM). They began by demanding SI$2.5 million compensation for the

Guadalcanal people they claimed had been murdered by Malaitan settlers over the years. They demanded state government for Guadalcanal and that all Malaitan settlers go back to Malaita. Although many believe that the movement was politically motivated by certain opportunistic politicians, it quickly became a popular young peoples' movement on Guadalcanal. It began with almost a sense of excitement that harnessed the energies of a lot of disenfranchised young men from the villages. For the group aged between 14 and 30, who had little status within the village, little education or stimulating work prospects, IFM provided a common cause behind which to unite. This Guadalcanal army quickly grew in size. There was a syncretic mixture of influences: a return to traditional warrior culture and *kastom* mixed with a militarism adopted from a diet of Hollywood war videos. They dressed in any bits of khaki uniform they could find, often 'Rambo'-style headbands mixed with *kapelatos* (the traditional bark cloth loincloths). The group began military-style training in bush camps and carried an assortment of hunting rifles, home-made guns, bows and arrows. They dug up old ammunition left behind by the Japanese and US at the end of the Second World War. At first it was almost as if they were surprised by their own success. Malaitan school children in the Guadalcanal Weather Coast schools, feeling threatened, were evacuated. Then slowly members of the IFM, empowered by the fear they generated and the new status their weapons helped them command, began their move against the Malaitan settlements east and west of Honiara. The IFM quickly developed a cult-like status. There were rumours that it was adopting heathen practices from the past, sacrificing to ancestors, using magic and *kastom*,[33] to gain power and the movement was surrounded by secrecy. Those who may have initially had sympathy with the movement now became frightened to speak out against what was happening, for fear that they would be targeted or forced to pay compensation.

Between 1999 and 2000 some 25,000 Malaitans were driven off the land in Guadalcanal back into Honiara, many fleeing from there by ship

---

33 *Kastom:* customary practices often linked with ancestral religion and traditional beliefs which incorporate the spirit world including the use of *kastom* sacrifice and magic.

to Malaita. Most of their homes were burnt. The government rapidly tried to organize customary ceremonies to pay compensation and restore justice. But in fact they were a travesty of true customary practices and failed to reconcile anything. Instead this encouraged the thinking that the government was ultimately responsible for paying compensation for militant atrocities. It was to prove a costly and dangerous precedent.

At first, the Malaitans seemed to do very little to resist this huge displacement. But, with increasing violence and destruction of property, there were rumours that payback time was coming. Towards the end of 1999 the Malaita Eagle Force (MEF) came into operation after a raid on Auki Police Station in Malaita in which automatic weapons and ammunition were stolen. The MEF set up roadblocks in Honiara on the pretext of defending Malaitans and began armed raids against the IFM on the outskirts of Honiara from which there were fatalities. The violence escalated. By pushing the Malaitans from that land the Guadalcanal militants had effectively cut themselves off from the capital, Honiara, and thus from the resources and infrastructure of the country: access to banks and finance, fuel, provisions, medical supplies, the hospital, and transport. The Honiara police force became increasingly compromised as the many Malaitan policemen were seen as supporting MEF. In 2000 many of the weapons held in Honiara police armoury found their way into Malaitan hands and these automatic weapons gave them a lethal advantage over the IFM, who themselves had acquired some automatic weapons from their raid on Gold Ridge Mine and, it was rumoured, from Bougainville in Papua New Guinea, where an armed conflict had also taken place. The hostilities now took on the character of payback and revenge, resulting in brutal acts of retaliation. After the headless corpse of a Guadalcanal man was found dumped in Honiara market, the head of a Malaitan was impaled on an IFM road barricade to the east of Honiara. Militants on both sides were later to allege that they were 'manipulated by politicians'. Both IFM and MEF had a similarity about them. They were armies of disenfranchised youth who had been stirred up by marginalized 'big men' for their own political objectives. These armies that they unleashed were ultimately to become difficult for them to control or direct, and would ultimately turn on those who had sought to use them.

According to these militants, 'the very people who started the ethnic tension are just sleeping next door to you or driving cars around Honiara'. These, the real conspirators who manipulated others, 'changed their colour as fast as an octopus so that you did not notice them'.[34]

In June 2000 the MEF, claiming the Prime Minister Ulufa'alu (himself a Malaitan) and his government had done too little to protect their interests and, demanding the payment of compensation for the land and property they had lost, attempted a coup to oust the Prime Minister. Though he was reinstated a week later, the damage was done and there was no longer any confidence that either he or his government could restore order. He was later deposed by a parliamentary vote. The coup, and international condemnation that followed, led to the exodus of most expatriates from the country and the withdrawal of economic aid.

The two opposing factions now faced each other in bunkers across a no-man's land on both sides of Honiara. Fighting went ahead with loss of lives on both sides. MEF sought to isolate IFM from the resources of Honiara while IFM continued to surround Honiara with the hope of driving the Malaitans off Guadalcanal. There was complete economic collapse in the country with neither the government nor the police force providing any credible alternative to the factionalism which had developed. The *kastom* of 'paying compensation', traditionally used to weave together the fabric of community and reconcile disputes, was now being used to justify extortion. There were atrocities on both sides with reports of torture, beheadings, rape and casualties. The MEF-controlled government patrol boat shelled Guadalcanal villages, and two wounded militants were even shot dead while in hospital. The Happy Isles had developed into a place of violence and war that few had imagined possible.

The actual direct conflict was comparatively short-lived. By October 2000 both sides had agreed to meet in Townsville Australia, where a peace agreement, which ended direct hostilities, was signed. New national elections were held in 2001 and, despite setbacks, there was an

---

34 Sethuel Kelly (former militant) quoted by Jon Fraenkel, *The Manipulation of Custom*, Victoria University Press, 2004, p. 64, see also p. 78.

uneasy peace. But the aftermath of the ethnic conflict brought lawlessness, further economic collapse and a host of other social problems. The amnesty offered to the opposing faction meant that none of the issues of the violence were addressed and the guns stayed in the hands of the militants despite their agreement to disarm.

The Melanesian Brotherhood, the Society of St Francis, the Sisters of the Church and the Sisters of Melanesia are all Anglican Christian religious communities. Each member of these communities takes the religious vows of poverty, chastity and obedience. All the Anglican religious communities have their headquarters in the area of rural Guadalcanal controlled during the conflict by Isatabu Freedom Movement (IFM). They also have households in Honiara that came to be controlled by the Malaita Eagle Force (MEF). Thus the religious communities found themselves bridging the war zone, divided by the broken bridges, road-blocks and check-points of the two opposing militant groups. Throughout the conflict, schools, colleges, villages, even families divided against each other on ethnic lines. In contrast, each of the religious communities managed to maintain its unity. Malaitans lived, worked and prayed side by side with Guadalcanal Brothers and Sisters on both Guadalcanal and Malaita. What is more, it was only these Brothers and Sisters whom the militants did not judge according to tribe.

The first response of the religious communities was a humanitarian one. As Malaitan villages were destroyed and the Malaitan settlers were displaced, Tabalia (the headquarters of the Melanesian Brotherhood) to the west of Honiara and Tetete ni Kolivuti (the headquarters of the Sisters of the Church) to the east of Honiara, became places of refuge for Malaitans driven from their homes. IFM respected the sacredness of these places. The communities were able to safeguard the Malaitans seeking refuge and transport them to Honiara.

During the height of the tension it was only the religious communities to whom the militants allowed freedom of movement – the trucks of the religious communities passing freely through the road-blocks and check-points of both the MEF and the IFM. The religious communities were able to help the displaced Malaitans get safely to Honiara and therefore prevent some of the violence that could have developed. At the same time they tried to be impartial and not to take sides. It was not long before the IFM needed help from the religious communities and sanctuary when their own villages and homes were threatened by MEF and they were unable to get medicines and important supplies through the Honiara road-blocks.

In the capital, Honiara, our religious communities remained places of sanctuary where the Brothers' authority was respected and those who ran away to these houses were safe. Therefore, both in rural Guadalcanal and Honiara, the religious communities became the only places that people felt were safe and could be trusted to help either side.

Hundreds of requests were made to the religious communities. Brothers and Sisters were stretched to the very limits. People needed them to search for relatives and to reunite divided families. They were asked to look for children, to pick up property and possessions they had left behind in the displacement, to protect those who were threatened, and to transport family members to safety. Many families and marriages were divided by tribe or island, and once again it was the religious communities to whom the people turned for help to reconcile these divisions and disputes.

Eventually the communities, especially the Melanesian Brotherhood, decided that they must become more directly involved to prevent further violence, killing and suffering. At the Melanesian Brotherhood Great Conference at Tabalia in October 1999 we elected a Malaitan Head Brother and an Assistant Head Brother from Guadalcanal. In the middle of this tension it was an important and symbolic move. The new Head Brother Harry Gereniu expressed the belief that the community and ethnic unity of the Brotherhood must move out from Tabalia and be taken into the conflict zone. In May 2000 the Brothers chose and commissioned a team from among their number to work directly for peace; these Brothers moved into the no-man's land between the road-blocks of the opposing militants and spread out to visit and to try to pacify those directly involved in the growing violence. Their message was a simple one and the following is an extract from a letter they took to the militants on both sides:

> In the Name of Jesus Christ we appeal to you: stop the killing, stop the hatred, stop the payback. Those people you kill or you hate are your own Solomon Island brothers. Blood will lead to more blood, hatred will lead to greater hatred, and we will all become the prisoners of the evil we do. Stop this ethnic tension before more innocent people suffer.[35]

The Brothers continued to camp between enemy lines for the next four months, moving backwards and forwards between the militant groups, talking to them, trying to calm them, praying with them, trying to lessen false stories and suspicion generated between factions. And they forbade, in the name of God, either side to advance beyond their barricades. Similarly, the brothers visited the camps of both the MEF and IFM where the training was taking place and prisoners were being held and tortured. By their words and presence they sought and were often successful in reminding the militants to use peaceful ways and to awaken Christian conscience to stop torture and violence. The Melanesian Brothers also became involved in negotiating the release of hostages taken by the rival factions, most notably a Solomon Islands' Airlines pilot who had been taken prisoner on the Weather Coast of Guadalcanal.

The Sisters of the Church also worked very bravely trying to get supplies through the road-blocks to families and children. They also carried the displaced, the wounded and the dead. Brothers carried the corpses of victims across the check-points to return them to grieving relatives for proper burial and investigated the deaths of those missing, even digging up the bodies so that they could be identified and their remains returned.

When the Townsville Peace agreement was signed, the Melanesian

---

35 'Letter to all those involved in the present ethnic tension. May 2000', *A Resource Book for the Training and Mission of the Melanesian Brotherhood*, ed. Richard A. Carter, Honiara Provincial Press, 2005, pp. 80–1.

Brotherhood and the other religious communities shared in the celebrations. But, as they were to learn, the problems were far from over. The Melanesian Brotherhood was asked to work with the Peace Monitoring Council, but withdrew after only three months as it seemed to be undermining their community life. In 2001 increasingly the religious communities were being called upon to become the security guards for commercial property and people, a role that depleted their manpower. Those who felt threatened requested Melanesian Brothers to stay at their homes. Qantas Airlines wanted Melanesian Brothers present for their aeroplanes to land at Henderson Airport.

In hindsight, after the events of 2003, it is easy to say that the Melanesian Brotherhood had become too involved in protection and security of people and property, but at the time there was no one else for people to turn to. The Brothers were called upon by both sides to become intermediaries and messengers because they were trusted. Even the new British Police Commissioner William Morrell requested Melanesian Brothers to accompany him on his tour of familiarization throughout Solomon Islands, for he felt they could help build trust with the grassroots Solomon Islanders. It was a trust he greatly needed after the assassination of a former police commissioner, Sir Frederick Soaki, by a member of the police force, which many believed to be 'a chilling message to the new Commissioner'.

At Pentecost 2002 in a meeting of the Brothers at Tabalia it was decided that the Melanesian Brotherhood must help with collecting guns, for the guns were causing such injustices and social unrest in the nation. The Melanesian Brothers decided with one mind that there could be no chance of true peace in the nation unless the guns were destroyed. The Brothers issued a call for all guns to be returned. During the next five months there was a huge response to this call. The Melanesian Brotherhood worked to disarm all sides and this included guns held illegally by members of the police force, Malaitan and Guadalcanal militants or anyone else holding weapons. The many guns, bullets and bombs handed over to the Brotherhood were taken out to the deep sea and, in the presence of the Police Commissioner, sunk so that they could never be used again.

Yet there was a cost to this initiative. Some of the militants believed that the Brotherhood was being manipulated by the government. The handing over of guns was a divisive issue, for no militant wanted to relinquish his power without adequate protection. Guns had provided both militant groups with power and influence and the freedom to extort at whim.

Many of the former militants suspected that the new government was duplicitous and that while the government demanded disarmament from the people, they were concealing their own stash of high-powered weapons and maintaining their own private militias as 'security'. In July 2002 two Melanesian Brothers visited one of the Malaitan gang leaders, Jimmy Rasta, to request that he disarm. They were badly beaten outside his home, one Brother requiring many stitches in his face. Jimmy Rasta himself was contrite and angry with his men, but it was a sign of potential danger as no Brother had ever been attacked previously by either side.

By 2003 it was increasingly obvious that the situation on the Weather Coast of Guadalcanal was growing worse. Harold Keke (the IFM leader) and his followers had not given up their guns, and many Malaitans used this as their excuse for refusing to hand over theirs. There was a culture of fear in which few were brave enough to speak out, but rumours of the atrocities taking place on the Weather Coast of Guadalcanal reached Honiara, including the murder of Father Augustine Geve, the Member of Parliament for South Guadalcanal and Roman Catholic Priest, whom Keke accused of corruption. Many of those whom Keke suspected of complicity with the government or betrayal of his cultish cause were tortured or executed, including his own followers. The Royal Solomon Islands Police Force were poorly equipped and lacked the trust and expertise to deal with the Weather Coast situation. They had enlisted the support of Keke's opponents led by a former leader of the IFM and now bitter opponent of Keke, Andrew Te'e, and this joint operation was causing its own problems. There were accusations of the burning down of villages and human rights abuses on both sides. The majority of the Weather Coast people, including women and children, were confused and afraid, caught between Harold Keke's militants and a joint operation militia which many did not trust.

Brother Nathaniel Sado, the first of the Melanesian Brothers to be murdered, had gone to visit Keke in February 2003 with another Brother and a parish priest. They took with them a letter from the Anglican Archbishop, Ellison Pogo, to try to open up a dialogue for peace and to bring an end to the atrocities in which so many innocent people were suffering. It was obvious at this stage that the Royal Solomon Islands Police Force did not have the numbers, capability or support to re-establish the rule of law and order. Brother Nathaniel knew Keke well and had worked with his brother during the disarmament period. He naively believed that he could help bring peace. When the other Brother and the parish priest were unable to meet with Keke, they returned. Against their advice, Brother Nathaniel decided to stay. We do not know Brother Nathaniel's motivation for staying, but certainly he made the mistake of believing Keke would not harm him. On Easter day one of Keke's followers deserted and ran away to Mbambanakira. He reported on Solomon Islands Broadcasting Corporation (SIBC) news that Brother Nathaniel Sado had been murdered. When the Brothers heard the news of this death they were deeply shocked and unsure whether it was true. This was a period of rumour and exaggeration where news such as this needed to be verified. The Melanesian Brotherhood had always tried to intercede for others; now there was no one to do likewise for them.

On 23 April 2003 six Brothers led by the Assistant Head Brother Robin Lindsay from Oro Province in Papua New Guinea, who was responsible for the welfare of the Brothers in the Solomon Island Region, left Honiara by canoe for the Weather Coast. Their mission, as author-ized by the Archbishop of the Church of Melanesia, was to visit the Brotherhood households on the Weather Coast to find out what had happened to Brother Nathaniel and, if his death was confirmed, to try and bring his body back for burial. The other five Brothers who went with Brother Robin were Brothers Francis Tofi from the island of Tikopia, Tony Sirihi from island of Makira, Alfred Hill from the island of Ysabel, Patteson Gatu and Ini Paratabatu from the island of Guadalcanal.

PART 2

Good News

6

Water that became wine.

John 2.1–11

All stories need a beginning. In John's Gospel Christ's ministry begins with a wedding. So I too will start with that wedding which is, in many ways, the overture for everything that is going to happen. It will introduce themes to which it will return to develop, play out and bring to fulfilment. John begins with a party, a stage on which his protagonists are present. Christ is present, so is his mother, and disciples. There is the master of ceremonies and there are the guests who will fail to recognize the miraculous drama taking place in their midst. There are also the servants who will do and see all that Christ tells them and thus participate in this sign of salvation.

I have decided that this story will be the theme for a drama I am preparing with the Melanesian Brothers and Novices to celebrate our feast day. We begin discussing this scene by asking what, for Melanesia, is the major dilemma this story poses: not *how* does Christ turn water into wine but *why*? In Melanesia alcohol is a major social problem. Most of the Brothers who are working with me on this drama, have direct experience of seeing alcohol leading to serious domestic abuse, drunkenness, the squandering of money and violence. These are social issues which the Church has had to stand out against, and alcohol carries with it the taint of scandal and sinfulness. Yet here we have Christ not just seen making wine, but literally gallons of it. The discussion leads to the idea that wine is a symbol. From our knowledge of the Bible, we discuss what it might mean within a Jewish and then a Christian cultural context, and how this might relate to a marriage. If wine in this context is a symbol of *covenant*, or relationship, then we must look for a cultural equivalent within a Melanesian context.

'Pigs!' one Brother volunteers, 'and strings of shells to pay the bride price!'

'How essential are these things to a wedding ceremony?' I ask.

'Too important . . . a marriage for the people of Malaita without the boy's family presenting pigs and shell money would be impossible.' They discuss why:

'It is a sign of the marriage contract between the two families . . . it binds them together . . . shows that they have become one . . . it is a sign of honour . . . generosity . . . reciprocity . . . the gift is essential as an outward sign of respectability . . . it shows them they can't run away from each other for ever and ever amen!'

'What would happen', I ask, 'if the pigs did not arrive and the shell money was not enough?'

'Impossible! A family must give more not less!'

'It would bring great shame – shame to the boy and the bride in the eyes of everyone.'

'The marriage would be considered worthless . . . cheap!'

'What if in the middle of the ceremony we tell the bride's family that the shell money has run out and that we have brought no pigs only a few chickens and coconuts?'

'Impossible! They couldn't do it. It's too shameful. There will be no marriage. It is an insult . . . there would be a feud . . . fighting between the families!'

Our drama has begun here and now.

'What happens if the girl's family is from Malaita and the boy's family from Guadalcanal and there was this insult?'

'Someone would die!'

First of all we need to develop the dramatic and cultural context in which Christ's miracle will be set. Our wedding of Cana becomes a wedding between these two different tribal groups. There is already hostility between these two tribes. When a young boy from Guadalcanal falls in love with a girl from Malaita we know that our drama has an instant sense of conflict and danger. We begin with improvisation, an improvisation which will later be written down, sharpened and focused and later prepared for performance. First we see the boy trying to tell his parents that he has fallen in love with a Malaitan, and then the girl trying to tell her family that she wants to marry a boy from Guadalcanal. There is shock, and then prejudice and then growing hostility. But the young son is persuasive, and finally, with both families, things have gone too far to escape a scandal, a bride price is arranged between the two sets of parents much to the disapproval of the extended family who predict the worst.

The day of the wedding arrives but the bride price fails to materialize. The boy's extended family have all promised to bring pigs and shell money. Instead they arrive empty-handed making excuses or, worse still bringing even more insultingly inappropriate gifts, a pile of coconuts, a skinny chicken, two possums on a stick. The audience roars with laughter, as the groom becomes increasingly desperate. In the other village the extended family are preparing the bride for marriage, dressing her and decorating her according to *kastom*, offering her advice and warnings. But as the bride's family wait they grow increasingly impatient and angry. Then gossip reaches the bride's family that the bride price cannot be met. They are insulted and incensed, it seems to be confirming their suspicions and all their prejudices about the other tribe; some of the uncles talk of taking revenge.

In the Guadalcanal village the groom is in total despair, torn between love for his bride and the humiliation he knows the wedding will bring. The groom's aunt turns to her son, 'Do something! You must do something!'

'Mother . . . this is not our business,' the cousin replies.

'Whatever he tells you to do, do it!' his mother pleads with some of the villagers.

Now the son does give instructions: 'Take those six wooden drums for pounding yam,' the young man tells them. 'Go to the beach and fill them with sand.' To another group he says: 'Go to the chicken coop and bring back all that you see inside.'

The first group do what they have been told.

'Now take the drums and pour them out in front of the groom's father.'

As they pour them out centre stage the crowd gasp in amazement.

Beneath the sand emerge strings and strings of shell money, the most valued and respected possession in Melanesia, worth thousands of dollars, still more – beyond the value of money, the signs of covenant and social binding going back to their earliest ancestors, treasured beyond any other possession, holding a cultural power words can never possess. These are beautiful polished shells shining in the firelight held up in trembling hands by the astonished groom.

'Why?! Why?!' he says to his equally astonished family, 'You have saved this greatest gift until last!' But now there is whooping and shouting because the second group has arrived back. In the chicken pen they have found seven pigs. These are now strung screaming on poles between them. The audience is cheering now; they cannot believe their eyes; a miracle of huge cultural proportions is emerging in front of them.

'Get the panpipers. Music!' the father calls. The village panpipers and dancers stream in, dancing and swaying with the vibrant music, and begin a huge procession carrying the strings of shell money, swinging pigs, with pallets of food hoisted on their shoulders, and thus they lead the Guadalcanal boy and his parents to meet his bride. The Malaitan village hear them coming and stand dumbfounded, dropping the bush knives and sticks they had taken up in fury. They rush for woven mats instead, which they lay out in front of the bride. And so the bride price is paid, far more than is expected; it is an astonishing act of generosity and the bride's parents are overwhelmed by the beauty and quantity of these shining strings of polished shells and all that they symbolize.

The bride and groom step onto the mats, bound together by a miraculous gift which has transformed mourning into dancing, conflict into peace. The audience are roaring their approval, whistling and encouraging the couple for their wedding night. The whole crowd is dancing now. No one is quite sure where this bride price has come from, no one, that is, except a very proud ageing aunt, some stupefied servants, and the aunt's son, a young man of great authority, standing humbly and slightly apart from the crowd, smiling as the couple make their vows to the cheers of the audience.

We performed this drama on the night before our Community's Feast Day of St Simon and St Jude in 1998. About a thousand people had gathered to watch, villagers from all tribes, many of them from Malaita, and many from Guadalcanal. It combined elements essential to powerful dramas: simplicity, conflict, a sense of danger and powerful symbols. And there was a sense too of transformation and wonder, that somehow a divided people, as divided as the audience who watched, had been transformed by a miracle in their midst, a gift, a free and overwhelming act of grace. No one would forget the Wedding of Cana. It was, as it is in John's Gospel, the perfect overture for the festival. The same audience shared the Eucharist together the following day, and some of us glimpsed a little more of the wonder of the miracle of this wedding too. Perhaps others, who tasted the bread and wine, the joy and unity of the celebration, and later the pigs of the feast, felt divisions dissolving like guests at Cana, and similarly did not realize where this new wine had come from. It was of course only the beginning. The wine would become blood. It would take several years of bloodshed and ethnic conflict and the death of seven Melanesian Brothers before some of those who watched that night would be able to learn its meaning and the islands could feast in peace together again. But those of us who performed this 'action' knew who the Saviour was, and believed in him, and when the conflict came we remained bound together by his same grace.

7

Every kingdom divided against itself is laid waste, and no city or house divided against itself will stand.

Matthew 12.25

I had never believed that this kind of violence could happen in Solomon Islands. It could happen in Rwanda, or Bosnia, or even Papua New Guinea but not Solomon Islands. 'It can happen anywhere,' said Father Jim Nolan, my Catholic friend from Ireland. They have always called Solomon Islands the 'Happy Isles', now it is a reminder of what once was.

My mind goes back to a time in 1999, when the tension had just begun. I had helped Ethel and Ellison Suri to evacuate from Selwyn College in West Guadalcanal. All the staff and students had been told they had three hours to evacuate by ship. We rushed to fill boxes with their possessions but it was obvious there was not enough time. Ethel suddenly just said 'Let's leave everything behind. It's not important. The only important thing to me is that my family is safe.' So they left and, of course, she was right.

It all seemed like a game at the beginning. I remember walking along the road to Selwyn College with Brothers and Novices the afternoon before that evacuation. It is a fifteen mile walk from our community to Selwyn College. We had been asked to go to the school by the church, as there had been threats by the militants against some of the students and it was felt that they were no longer safe. I remember hearing a sharp, fast banging. 'It sounds like the banging of planks of wood', said one of the Novices. That was the nearest sound association – timbers slapping against each other in a succession of loud cracks. 'It's not timber, I think its automatic gun fire.' We looked down the road and saw two Sisters running towards us at great speed, holding onto their veils. It looked so comical that everyone laughed. They were shortly followed, however, by two trucks of Field Force police in military fatigues and helmets, lying flat in the open-back trucks with an armoury of weapons, including a tripod and machine gun, pointing over the side. This was where the gunfire had come from. They even had a flame-thrower, which was setting fire to all the temporary roadblocks that the militants had formed along the road. They stopped and asked us where we were going and when we said to Selwyn College they asked if we wanted a lift. I told them we would prefer to walk. It was the last thing I wanted to do, go along a Guadalcanal road with a truckload of heavily armed policemen spraying bullets into the bush. The following day I preached at Selwyn trying to encourage the students. Outside we could see the Field Force had taken up positions round the school, supposedly to defend the place from militant attack. It looked as though they had been watching too many war videos, but both the SR88s and the bullets were real. It all seemed so bizarre, such a massive over-reaction. The headmaster had not wanted to close the school, but had been ordered to. As he addressed the students and explained that everyone must return to their dormitories and pack as quickly as possible, he suddenly broke down in tears, and I was aware of the stress he had been under trying to protect his students as well as maintain workable relationships with the young Guadalcanal militants, now so much in evidence around this area. We helped them load up the dinghy and ferry out to the boats waiting offshore. There was a sense of sadness that the school was closing, but also of adventure and that things would soon be back to normal.

I looked round and realized that the Brothers and Novices and I were the only ones left. We had helped the school evacuate and there we were standing on the beach. I realized that on one side of us was the Field Force while on the other side the IFM were preparing an ambush, and we had to get back through all of this on foot. We started walking along the road as quickly as we could. The IFM had taken up positions along the hills with a collection of hunting and home-made rifles, bows and arrows and even home-made crossbows. They had erected a huge steel gate across the road but they opened it to let us through. We walked along the centre of the road, the militants watching us in silence. We were known to all of them. We had walked this road many times before and usually they were our friends; they would wave to us and call out in greeting, but no one was talking to us now, yet neither would they stop a group of Brothers who were considered 'Man blong God'. There was an uneasy silence. Then some older men came towards us and asked us not to cross over the bridges. They said they had put *kastom magic* on them to 'target' anyone who crossed. They suggested very politely that we cross upstream. I was not sure what they were talking about because obviously they did not want to talk openly about their use of magic. I kept straight on across the bridges. Later I was to hear that they had accused me and the *tasiu* of breaking the spell.

'Spell for what?'

'Magic him makem ball blong man big too much!'

'Ball blong me, him same same yet!'

The fact that our testicles had not been affected had been proof of our holiness, and we had also apparently had the effect of exorcising the spell and thus saving the manhood of the Field Force who came after!

I do not joke. It was not long after that the firing began. The Field Force had brought in the patrol boat which was shelling the hills from the sea. There was a helicopter, owned by an Australian tourist company, hovering above, which had been hired to spot militant positions. As we walked there was the crack of single shots from the hills.

'Don't worry,' I told the Novices, 'they are not firing at us.'

There was another loud crack of gunfire.

'But I feel the air moving close to my ear' said one of the Novices. After the whistle of that bullet our speed increased. The bridge just before our headquarters at Tabalia had been sabotaged, all the planking and some of the supports pulled off. It was sagging precariously. The Police Field Force truck could not cross and a confrontation was in progress. Our group of Novices and Brothers clambered across the bridge supports, the helicopter flying low overhead, the Field Force watching us from their positions of cover.

We turned up the path to Tabalia, relieved to be out of the firing line. Reaching the top of the hill there was a group of about fifty of our Community waiting for us. They cheered as we approached. We felt like returning heroes and yet the whole experience had not been one of courage but one of pure fiction, as though we had walked through a film set. A few weeks later I met the helicopter pilot in Honiara. 'You are one of those mad missionaries who walked through that gun fight!' he laughed. 'Yes,' I replied, 'I think it was a bit more dangerous than we realized.' 'Yes,' he replied 'those were real bullets, but you missionaries don't worry about stuff like that, do you mate?' He bought me a drink and then another.

It had begun like this. There had been a sense of excitement among the young militants. In those days they seemed like a group of adrenalin-charged football supporters getting into a riot. I remember seeing a truck-load of militants driving past me on the road. More than thirty of them crammed into an open-back truck waving their collection of home-made weapons in the air and shouting. Some of them were no more than thirteen or fourteen. That day they were going to fight the Police Field Force. Before anyone died, it had seemed more like one of those video adventures the kids and young people loved to watch at night, on a TV screen with an audience of at least a hundred, powered by a roaring petrol generator.

I remember the day things changed for me. I was saying goodbye to the Malaitan families from Tabahau village, being evacuated from a playing field by helicopter. It had made about five trips. The women and children had been evacuated first. It was the teenagers and young men who had been left behind until the last trip at half past one. I went back to my house for some lunch. Suddenly, behind my house I heard the noise of someone running. I looked and saw the rush of someone go past. I looked out of my back door. It was not how someone usually runs, but a run of total terror, not just running but running for his life. He was being hunted down. One hundred metres behind came a group of IFM militants chasing the group of Malaitans. They stormed into Tabalia. I watched as they slashed at the posts of our guesthouse with their bush knives. They were like men possessed. They rushed into our dining hall

61

where one of the Malaitans was cornered. I ran towards the dining hall. Brother Thomas grabbed hold of me, pulling me back. 'He's one of our aspirants', said Brother Sam, lying. I think Sam's quick thinking saved the Malaitan boy's life.

The leader of the IFM group arrived, bringing his men under control. He was the brother of one of our Brothers, whom I knew by sight. He apologized that they had entered Tabalia in this way. 'This place him holy place and me fela respectem this fela place' he said. 'But you no letem any Malaitan hide long here.' They left. I later heard that one of the Malaitans had shot at them the night before.

The Head Brother called me to his room where he had told the Malaitans to hide for safety. The group hid at Tabalia until nightfall. We told them we would transport them to safety in Honiara, but they did not listen, or were too frightened. That night they left without telling us. We were later to hear that one of the group never made it. He was slower than the rest and had been picked up by the militants and taken back to their camp. I heard he was executed with a bush knife, but I did not want to believe this, for these were people I believed were incapable of such an action. His body has still not been found. I began to see that a threshold had been crossed. It was no longer a game. Once people have been murdered, it is impossible to go back to that former state of innocence. And we too began to change. Our voices dropped to a whisper. We became careful who we spoke to, more watchful, less trusting. Fear is insidious, it begins like a virus, hardly noticeable at first, but it spreads and infects and it destroys faith in humanity.

8

What have you done? Listen, your brother's blood is crying out to me from the ground!

Genesis 4.10

From the diary of May 2002

There have been traumatic changes on Guadalcanal as a result of the ethnic tension, and beneath Solomon Islanders' brave and cheerful resilience I see pain and suspicion. Of course, the problems are mostly confined to Guadalcanal and areas of Malaita, and on many of the other islands life continues almost as normal. And yet, it is Solomon Islands' 'fall'; things can never be totally the same again. It is Cain and Abel with all the resulting experience of guilt and betrayal, and the memories of those who experienced the violence will not easily heal. Politicians have lost credibility, crime goes uninvestigated, the most obvious casualty is the police force, which no one trusts. The road to Tabalia, thirty miles to the west, right out to Maravovo and Selwyn College is a dramatic illustration of all that has taken place: houses, agricultural projects, villages, Tambea resort, completely burnt out, now nature taking over so that one would scarcely know what was once beneath the bush that has reclaimed these places. There is a silence along this pot-holed track with its sagging and broken bridges. There are only two or three trucks that now travel this road. I remember only three years ago how our Novices and Brothers went out two by two walking to villages all along this road, people waving as they passed. Now it is lonely and deserted. It had always made me joyful to see the Brothers and Novices out on the road – it seemed good news was being spread and I knew every one of the homes and villages they visited would be pleased to see them. Now there are no

Malaitan villages or settlements for them to visit. People now do not look up as you drive past, or they quickly disappear into the bush as though ashamed or afraid. The undergrowth on either side narrows the road and threatens to cover it completely.

Many of the Brothers involved have told me their stories. The news which reached UK was of the courage and bravery with which the religious communities faced this tension and how they did so much to prevent violence and bring peace. This is indeed true, and a testimony to their costly and courageous faith. And yet, for those who tell their stories and witnessed terror at first hand there is no sense of glory in the events that took place. They live with painful memories in which they saw events that were dark, sickening, and evil, and which they will never forget. Brothers have told me of what it was like to be shot at, to transport mutilated corpses back to loved ones, to try to find where those who died were buried in shallow graves and dig up the bones at the request of grieving relatives, and to search for the lost. One of the Brothers had to carry a decapitated corpse wrapped in a plastic sheet back across the road-block with a young Novice. How can you forget?

A Brother who was positioned at Alligator Creek between the two militant camps told me of the deaths he witnessed on the road – a man shot through the chest, another whose throat was slashed. 'Why had they done these things? I was suspicious of everyone. I could not forgive what I saw. I was unable to eat. I did not want to tell anyone when they asked me because, when I remembered, it was worse. I still feel frightened to tell anyone . . . I don't like talking. I feel the anger inside me boiling and it comes out. I can't stop remembering. It rewinds in my memory like a video . . . playing over and over again.'

Both sides bear responsibility. It has been over a year and a half since the peace agreement was signed, but you can still see the pain this Brother is carrying. He asks me not to disclose his name. He believes they will come and get him because of what he witnessed. These stories do not go away, however much we want to believe in 'the Happy Isles'. This ethnic conflict was brutal and destructive and that needs to be heard. It can take place in any country of the world when prejudice and hatred and violence gather momentum and run amok, unchecked. It is not surprising that so many of our Brothers wanted to be released from the Community after these events and found it hard to settle, or sought to forget by drinking alcohol. For the ex-militants and perpetrators the reintegration is far harder. One of the crucial issues at stake is how to disarm those who still have high-powered weapons and who have derived their power from them.

The same Brother who told me of the deaths he witnessed comes to see me during a retreat I'm taking. I am reading Ezekiel 36.23–9 (Revised English Bible):

> I shall give you a new heart and put a new spirit within you; I shall remove the heart of stone from your body and give you a heart of flesh.

He says he found meditating on the passage helpful. He tells me about how, after the horrors he had witnessed, he came back to Honiara, to the Brothers' household at All Saints. He says he was tired, not just physically, but 'tired in my heart'. He said he lay down on the floor and as he was lying there he heard a woman crying and calling to him '*Tasiu*! *Tasiu*, please help me. They have taken my son away and I need your help.' He said he pretended not to hear but she kept on calling him again and again and her crying did not stop. And the Brother thought to himself 'Why doesn't she call someone else? I have seen enough, done enough, had enough!' and he continued to pretend to be asleep. But the mother kept begging '*Tasiu*, please help me. The MEF have taken my son. There is no one else to help me.' And then this Brother began to think 'What if this woman was my mother?' And he could no longer block out her crying. So he got up and listened to her story. And she told him how the MEF had 'arrested' her son and she had heard he was going to be punished and she was frightened they would kill him. And this Brother said that, as he had listened to her story, he suddenly felt so angry and with the anger came a new courage, and he said that at that moment he had no longer been afraid, or at least his fear didn't matter any more because he knew he had to do something. He had gone alone to the MEF where her son was being held and demanded his release. They of course refused, saying that this boy was to be punished for some crime or betrayal. But the Brother was burning with a righteous anger because here they were, claiming judgement over this boy, when he himself had seen what was happening and some of the brutal things they themselves were doing. He told me 'I said, "Release the boy *now*. I am taking him back to his mother." It was as though God just gave me that authority. They made excuses but I was so full of anger that I ordered them "Give me the boy now, not later – in the name of God. Give him to me now!" And they did. They obeyed me or God. And I took the boy back to his mother and then I slept.'

I have also been struck by so many people's goodness and inner strength in times of great difficulty. I remember how so many of those who were displaced in the conflict gathered together a few possessions and just carried on despite losing so much. I remember the older refugees who arrived at Tabalia sat around selling the cabbages and betel nut they had managed to harvest in the few hours they had to evacuate their houses. There is courage here. Solomon Islanders are survivors and they can pick up and carry on with so little. The links of family and tribe you carry with you, and as long as these links are maintained there is still a sense of identity and connectedness. It is when this cultural and corporate identity is lost that the real alienation and disintegration begins.

Our Brotherhood has more applications than ever from those seeking to join. Many of those applying to the Brotherhood have been involved as militants in the tension and are now looking for a way to find peace and forgiveness. One of our Novices seems highly disturbed. He comes to see me again and again. He was a former militant and he tells me of the 'magic' they used on him. 'They made me swim in blood' he tells me. He is haunted by these memories and he needs psychological professional help, of which there is practically none. For many of those who have been involved it is the Brotherhood that can provide them with the chance to turn wrongs into right and exorcise some of the evil they have experienced. It is indeed a mark of grace when you hear their stories and see how happy they are to become part of a Community that tries to live out its gospel of forgiveness and God's special love for the poor. There are fifty-seven Novices in our second-year programme. There are not enough tables for all of them and some are writing their notes on the floor.

I enter the gates of Honiara Hospital known as *Number Nine* and a young man called Kevin is rushing into the hospital carrying a plastic bottle full of drinking water. He looks no more than about eighteen but tells me his wife has just given birth to a baby, 'Kevin Junior'. He is grinning from ear to ear with pride and I congratulate him as he hurries past me down the corridor, then stops and comes back and gives me a crumpled $10 note 'Dis one for you now Tasiu!' he says with joy. It seems a blessing for us both!

In the hospital ward one of our former Brothers, John, is sitting at the end of his wife Joycelyn's bed. She is thinner than ever, her limbs are bone and stretched skin and above her knees there are painful swellings. The sore, which for months would not heal, has now led to other lumps. John is massaging her legs to help her. Her eyes are heavy and hooded and she fights hard to open them. She is much weaker than when I visited only a week before. I hold her thin hand and wonder whether she doubts God's love for her and our past prayers for healing. She tells me her leg is very painful. I mention her two-year-old little daughter Siobhán, named after my sister-in-law. When I visited last week she had been playing under her mother's hospital bed. I know the mention of Siobhán will bring happiness, and I see this mother's face flood with light and love. 'Him gift blong you. Him beautiful for good.' Three years ago we prayed that she would have this baby when it seemed impossible for her to conceive, and now Siobhán is their blessing. John tells me how Siobhán is so sensitive to her mother, she seems to instinctively know her mother's needs. There is a Trinity of love here – father, mother and daughter – and they are ministering to each other and to me: no struggle, no bitterness, not even a demand, simply a to and fro of love into which I am drawn. They are perched on the edge of the unknown, no grip, no clinging, balancing together on the brink of eternity.

To see the three of them is an insight into Solomon Islands at this time. For they are visible signs of a people who trust in God and in values not immediately graspable, but real and of great truth. This is what the

Church is really for, to make Christ present, something vitally necessary to all our lives, and to make God's love known even when the future is so unknown.

With the $10 I and a hungry Novice decide to buy fish and chips, but the shop is closed so I give him the $10 for supplies. 'Its my pleasure,' I say. It is. He is setting off on a thirty-hour journey by boat with twelve other Novices and seems excited.

In the morning before they leave, we celebrate Holy Communion around the long table at Chester Resthouse. The service feels transparent. There is a charged silence, everyone is listening and focused. Afterwards, each Brother brings and explains to the others a list of needs: domestic disputes, conflicts, sickness, problems that the Brothers have been requested to pray about.

9

They shall beat their swords into ploughshares, and their spears into pruning-hooks.

Isaiah 2.4

From the diary of July 2002

A lot is happening. The Melanesian Brotherhood has become very much involved in the disarmament programme. The Brotherhood leaders all felt it was important for the whole Brotherhood to support this work and to pray about it before we began. We wanted this mission to be independent from political interference and for the Brotherhood to maintain its own way of life. We began this on Pentecost Sunday with a real spirit of unity among all the Brothers who came to Tabalia to be commissioned. A group of seven Brothers was chosen to co-ordinate this mission and moved into Bishopsdale, next to the archbishop, where they are now based. I was appointed chaplain to this mission and will visit them for two days each week to pray together and take Holy Communion in the small chapel. Our aim is the collection of all the weapons both high-powered and home-made.

The house is empty apart from three beds; the rest of the group will sleep on mats on the floor. One of the bedrooms has floor to ceiling cupboards down the whole of its length and I joke with Brother Jude that in a week's time this will be filled with the ammunition and guns that we have collected. The group of peacemakers is young and enthusiastic. There is a World Cup satellite link-up and we have been lent a small television around which we crowd at night to watch. The football is keeping the Honiara drunks off the streets for a while. Brother Albert Tanimana leads this disarmament initiative but communicates little about what is going on. It is Brother Jude Alfred who is his bright and fearless assistant who seems to be the source of dynamism and ideas. They sit outside the house on the balcony overlooking the sea, chewing betel nut, discussing the plans, while Brother Basil and Brother Baddley smoke Winfield cigarettes, flicking the butts over the low wall, and the huge Brother Matthew Taonia cuts tobacco. His room at night will become known as 'the engine room' because of his snoring. No one has any experience of a disarmament programme and they will make decisions as they go along. It is decided that Brother Jude and I will visit the Solomon Islands Broadcasting Corporation, and put out a message to be broadcast on radio six times a day. The message will announce the following:

A MESSAGE FROM THE MELANESIAN BROTHERHOOD

We all hope and pray for peace. But lasting peace will only arrive when there are no more guns and weapons in our land. We want to make Solomon Islands a land safe for our families, our children and our children's children.

In the name of Jesus Christ the peacemaker we call all those who still hold guns to hand these over now so that they will never be used again.

Guns cannot bring true protection. They make us a target and an enemy of others.

The Melanesian Brotherhood is now beginning its mission to collect, clear, and destroy all guns and weapons. If you still have a gun or weapon in your home, truck, or any hiding place, please contact any member of the Melanesian Brotherhood now. The Melanesian Brotherhood has households throughout the Solomon Islands . . . You can visit us or telephone or tell any Brother, and we will be happy to come to your home. The handing over of guns can be done privately with no identities disclosed. It is between you and God. We will pray with you and your families for protection and peace.

This is a call for our whole nation whatever our tribe or island or church. Let us make Solomon Islands a nation of lasting peace.

It seems a naive attempt, and yet it is based on certain important realizations. First, the fact that many holding onto their weapons want assurance from those they can trust that the weapons really will be destroyed or put out of use and are not going into enemy hands. Many have also been holding onto weapons for their own protection and they do not want their names disclosed for fear of reprisals. They feel a deep need to be reconciled with God. Many are deeply troubled by what has taken place and the actions in which they have been involved. They are searching for forgiveness. They do not want this to be an act of surrender to the police or to an international peace monitoring council whom they do not know or trust. If they are going to give over their weapons, it will be for God and an act of faith.

We began with the police force itself for, since the tension, many of the police have been holding onto weapons privately, and there was the suspicion generated by the tension that many of these weapons were used by the Malaitan militia or Eagle Force. There was deep distrust and division among the police force, and officers mumbled that the corruption and suspicion went to the very top. The Assistant Police Commissioner agreed that we should address the whole police force. About 150 assembled in the run-down police club, scraping chairs across the floor, or standing behind in the shadows. The electricity had been cut off and the hall was growing darker. We were not experts and were not there to deal with the causes of the division. That was their job. We were there in faith to help facilitate a move towards reconciliation, and it was like opening the floodgates for it was the first time they had collectively had the chance to discuss their concerns and fears. There was great anger towards those leaders and politicians they felt had betrayed them. They knew that many of their own police leaders were duplicitous and, though calling for weapons to be returned, had their own arsenals and agendas. There were those who argued that religion should stay out of this process and that disarmament was political, and yet none of the anger was directed towards us. 'What about Harold Keke on the Weather Coast and his men?' He had not disarmed. What about the Prime Minister himself, Alan Kemakeza, and members of his cabinet who had called for this amnesty period for disarmament? Had they handed over the weapons they were known to be holding? There was fear that once the police handed over their weapons they would vulnerable to attack, and become the scapegoats for crimes committed during the tension. While they had guns they commanded power and authority. That was the faith that we demanded of them. We had made our case, given the chance for a decision to be made and opened the can of worms, now we wandered off into the night, feeling that we had been pulled into something far greater than we had power to reconcile.

Two days later there was an official parade at Rove where we were called upon to witness the weapons handed over. But just before the ceremony was to begin the opposition faction took off noisily in their police vehicles. At the weekend there were rumours flying around – what Solomon Islanders call '*coconut news*' – that the opposition to this disarmament process were planning to attack the central police station. A group of Brothers with their walking sticks sat on the lawn of a deserted police station to keep watch. Taking courage from their presence, slowly members of the police force emerged and joined them on the lawn. The Brothers prayed all round the station and everyone sat outside talking until morning. No attack came.

Miraculously, after a week the police force approached us to hold a service of reconciliation at St Alban's Church. I preached, taking for the text Christ the Good Shepherd and our need to listen to his voice and not that of the thief 'who comes to steal, kill and destroy'. Then leaders and representatives of different groups within the force got up and publicly apologized to each other. The police advisers from Australia were astonished, for I think there had been some expatriate scepticism about the involvement of a religious community in the disarmament process. But this is Melanesia. The following day there was a public parade in which they returned their weapons and washed their hands clean in holy water. The Brothers prayed over the weapons and poured litres of holy salt and water over them (we prayed that they would rust!) and returned them to the armoury. Over the next few weeks there was a constant flow of guns being returned, an amazing assortment of lethal weapons: dark, heavy, oily, each perhaps with its own dark story. Perhaps the Brothers are treated a bit like the hobbits in *The Lord of the Rings*, the only ones trusted not to become corrupted by the new-found power these weapons bring. Our prayer is that they will be able to maintain this spirit of transparency, for like 'the ring', these weapons exert a sinister influence. The key to the armoury was also given to them for safekeeping. The police cannot trust each other or even themselves when pressure is put upon them, for who can refuse a *wantok*?

Brother Jude shows me the cupboard again. The others are watching the World Cup on the TV. The sliding doors are pulled back to reveal an armoury of weapons which has been handed over. There are army issue pistols, 2.2 hunting rifles, plenty of the SR88s and SLRs assault rifles, and many lethal-looking home-made guns, grenades and ammunition, which seem as if they could well do as much injury to the user as the target. There is even a machine gun on a tripod from the police patrol boat, with belts of ammunition that had been used by the Malaitan Eagle force when the boat was commandeered during the conflict to shell the shore east of Honiara. I have to sleep in this room and it is not easy. The back door of this house is held shut only by a bent three-inch nail. There are no curtains on the windows and the outside lights shine through the frosted glass. Throughout the night I can hear the Brothers' disarmament four-wheel drive Hilux going in and out for what they call 'patrol', the headlights sweeping into the drive and across the ceiling, and sounds of talking and laughter. They are collecting weapons from every quarter, fearlessly picking up on leads, and directly confronting those who are known to be concealing guns. What a lethal supply of weapons to sleep with, if anyone were to decide to break in here. I want the Brothers to get these weapons destroyed as soon as possible. I suggest dumping them at sea. Yet I am not in charge of this mission, only here each week to celebrate the Eucharist, and to listen, talk and pray with the Brothers. It is they who have been out day and night, searching for weapons, visiting homes, persuading, following up on requests and tip-offs they have been given. They have placed their lives in considerable danger in this process and trusted God. They seem to have implicit faith that these weapons are now safe and no one would target this house. By arguing that we must destroy the weapons immediately I seem to be doubting the spiritual authority of their mission. For them this is not their work but God's, and they believe that if God is helping them to collect these weapons he will also protect them. There are stories everywhere that the *Tasiu* have spiritual power. People say that when the Brothers come to houses and people refuse to hand over weapons, the guns turn into snakes and come out of their hiding places. I ask Brother Jude if he believes this is true and he shrugs. They are certainly not denying these stories for this spiritual *mana* or power has had a tremendous effect. Yet how does this fit with my Christian faith, which speaks to *me* of incarnation, God within mortal human flesh, who refuses to turn stones into bread and jump from the highest building to prove the angels will protect him? But don't these Brothers have an equal right to believe in the miraculous, for there are plenty of miracles in Christ's ministry too?

The International Peace Monitoring Team (IPMT) is here, many of them Australians with every kind of equipment and financial backing; they frequent the Honiara Hotels and carry satellite telephones, survival packs, life-jackets, and rehydration tubes hanging from their necks. They have four-wheel drives and practise helicopter evacuation drills, and yet most Solomon Islanders treat the IPMT as a joke. Even the Brothers seem to believe that most of the guns the IPMT has collected are of the home-made type that no one wanted anyway. Each night the radio trumpets news of the Peace Monitoring Team's success, but even this seems to be working against them, for in the culture here there is a deep aversion to the honouring or promotion of oneself, completely contrary to the competitive individualism of the West. One of the Brotherhood's mottoes is 'If I honour myself, my honour is nothing.' The members of the IPMT keep on approaching me with their clipboards requesting details about the weapons which the Brothers are collecting. They approach me because I am white, but I keep on pointing them towards

Brother Albert and Brother Jude for it is they who are in charge. The IPMT seems unable to grasp this. They seem innately suspicious of our collection, although it is more successful than their own. When they ask for the serial numbers of the guns we have collected Brother Matthew reacts angrily 'Olketa useless man ia! Tell them to find the serial numbers of those bits of pipe they have been collecting!' The IPMT does not have the trust of the people.

It is 2 a.m. A couple of young men are crouching in the drive outside. I can see the ends of their cigarettes burning as they talk to the Brothers. I go outside and sit down on a piece of timber. One of the visitors says he wants to talk to me. He is aged about 30. He says he has a wife and two children. He says he has a gun hidden at his house that he wants to hand it over. I tell him the Brothers will go with the Hilux to pick it up. He seems nervous. He says he needs the gun for protection. I tell him having a gun in his house makes him a target. He seems to be listening to me. The next day he comes back. He says he wants to change, to be free of the things he has done. He says he wants me to pray for him. He says he can't sleep at night. We are sitting on the floor in the middle of the empty sitting room and, in a matter of fact way, suddenly his story is spilling out. He talks about a time in the conflict when they had cut off the head from a corpse of one of the militants and had kicked it about like a football. He said it had seemed like nothing at the time, 'everyone was just kicking it' and he had done it too, but that now he just kept on remembering. It was the most terrible thing he had ever done to kick this head, but at the time it had seemed part of the conflict, something you had to do to show you were part of everyone else and not frightened.

What response can there be to such a violation of human life? It isn't just the corpse that has been violated, it is his own life. We go over to the chapel and I pray for God to have mercy and I pray that the handing over of his gun will be the beginning of change. And there is holy water on the altar of the chapel, and I pour it on his hands and head, for words cannot cleanse him and nor can I take him out of this nightmare, but nothing is outside the forgiveness of God. And as the water runs down and forms a puddle on the cement floor of the church it is a sign: ultimately forgiveness can only be a gift from beyond us. I tell him he must hand over the weapons he is holding. The next day he brings them.

They come seeking forgiveness, not directly, but you can see that is why they have come. They can be guilty of unspeakable horror, and yet they are so recognizably human. They are both perpetrators and victims, the crucifiers and the crucified, for they have violated the divine in themselves. And we are filled both with a sickness at the violence and a longing for them that somehow they may come back from the darkness, back into the light. How much more is *God's* longing for all of us? Have we grown so sceptical of human nature that we can no longer live the central premise of the Christian faith, that no one is beyond the redemptive power of God? I reflect upon my reaction to those who come. I feel humbled by them, by their honesty, and I feel full of compassion. But are we offering them cheap grace with no accountability? No, we are not offering them anything; it is God who offers again and again 'seventy times seven'. 'Father, forgive them, they do not know what they are doing' – costly forgiveness, as costly as the horror of these deaths. The resurrection is not ours to give away, but it is within the possibilities of God's love. If we do not believe that, then Christ's death was for nothing.

Today we received a message from the Sisters of the Church that an old man urgently needed to see us before the last day of the weapons amnesty. We drove out along very muddy tracks to his deserted village, where he welcomed us with much enthusiasm. Then calling together the three generations of his family, he began to tell us the story of how he had made a whole collection of home-made weapons, bombs and shells. He claimed he had learnt his expertise in the Second World War and knew how to make explosive out of glycerine and sand. As he told his story he paused at strategic moments to send a son off to collect the described weapon or shell, and presented it to us with some pride. Even at the height of the tension he had refused to move from his home, although all the other villagers had run away. He wanted us to know that his whole family had never missed saying morning and evening prayer together. He wanted to surrender these weapons now but only to the *Tasiu*, that is why he had called us. At the end of his story he called his sons to make their final offering of two well-oiled high-powered military automatic rifles, which certainly were not home-made. Brother Albert prayed for him, a wonderful prayer for forgiveness and peace and God's protection for his whole family, and as he prayed the old man began to weep, deep heart-rending sobs. Finally, when his crying had ceased I told him that he would feel free, now that he had returned his guns. His whole face lit up in the most wonderful smile: 'me feelim! me feelim!' Indeed it was difficult for all of us not to feel it, it was as if a dark cloud had lifted.

It has not all been so blessed or easy, and there have been setbacks too. Not all will give up their guns, and there have been violent exchanges between militant groups and more deaths. There is the fear that this will lead to further pay-back, but the mood of the majority is that they have had enough of this now and want peace. And so there is hopefulness even despite setbacks. In much of this I have been overwhelmed by the incredible courage and faithfulness shown by some of our Brothers. In faith they have gone out and continue to go out to the very centres of conflict and need, and meet face to face those involved. I am reminded of Bishop George Augustus Selwyn's words as he began the Melanesian Mission in 1854: 'Missionaries must be ready to put their lives in their hands and to go out to preach the gospel to others with no weapon but prayer and with no refuge but God.' This is indeed the case at the present time, but it is also important to temper the Brothers' idealism with the need for realistic care and caution, for all courage must be motivated by compassion for human life and the desire to save and protect, and we must never senselessly put ourselves in harm's way. Nevertheless, I have still much to learn from the faith of these Brothers.

10

I have set before you life and death, blessings and curses. Choose life so that you and your descendants may live.

Deuteronomy 30.19

From the diary of July 2002

On St Alban's Day I am invited to preach for the Patronal Festival and prepare a sermon about the sacrificial nature of Christian service which has lately seemed so sadly lacking from public life, with many looking after their own self-interest and demanding compensation from a bankrupt nation. I use the text from St Paul: 'Offer yourself as a living sacrifice to the Lord and dedicated to his service' (Romans 12.1, Good News Bible). I talk about the sacrificial nature of Christian service, and speak out against corruption and profiteering, which seem so endemic. Politicians are trying to distance themselves from the militant leaders they previously manipulated and pandered to. The state coffers have run dry, but the militant appetite for compensation has not. The politicians are nervous because the militants know too much. Reconciliation can never bear any fruit while this spirit of double-dealing and duplicity continues. It is too obvious to everyone. The same politicians who are calling for total disarmament are also suspected of telling certain militia leaders to hold onto their weapons, and others are certainly holding onto weapons themselves. Minutes before the service I hear that the Prime Minister and the Deputy Commissioner of Police will be attending. I wonder whether I should abandon the sermon and preach something less controversial, but decide to go ahead anyway.

Side by side with the drama of the disarmament the simple daily life of our Community continues. I love best of all teaching the Novice classes from 8.15 to 12.00 each morning. I have never enjoyed teaching more. They are so eager to learn, crammed in the makeshift classrooms. Our lessons have complete freedom to become discussions, or debates, or prayers or acts of worship or move into song, role-plays, dramas and dances. Teaching here is like making music. But there are practical difficulties: when you write on one side of the blackboard the Novices on the other side have to stand up and come over, perching their exercise books on the long windowsill to write. This week for the first time at Tabalia the Novices are being provided with lunch, after the generous donation of rice and tinned fish from Nicky, the Chinese-Thai boss of a fast-food restaurant in Honiara. She is a Buddhist and says in Thailand she always gives to the Buddhist monks; here she gives to the Christian Brothers. It is the same, she says; it brings good karma. We have been able to provide lunch for the Community at Tabalia. Previously, after two biscuits and a cup of tea at 7.30 a.m., most of our Community did not eat again until 6.30 p.m. Perhaps some of the more traditional Brothers think we have gone soft, especially since on the first day of lunch, the church-keeper forgot to ring the bell for afternoon prayer and so nobody turned up for prayer or the afternoon work session. The Brothers love to recount stories of the hardships they faced when they were Novices. 'In our day . . .!!': human nature has much in common the world over! But the Novices themselves are very enthusiastic about the new arrangement, and so is the nurse who believes in better nutrition and blames the poor diet for the stomach-ache, ulcers, boils and lack of resistance to sickness, especially the malaria, that many find hard to get out of their systems.

Back at the disarmament house at Bishopsdale the Brothers believe they need to confront the former commanders of the Malaita Eagle Force who are known to be holding onto weapons and ammunition and show no signs of surrendering them: Lusibaea known as Jimmy Rasta, Moses Su'u and Leslie Kwaiga. Leslie is an extremely influential lawyer. He also happens to be an Anglican, known personally to me over ten years ago when he was studying law in Papua New Guinea. I know he receives Holy Communion at his house each week, and Brother Jude Alfred telephones him to say I will celebrate at his home this week as we wish to talk with him. He agrees. As Brother Jude and I arrive at his home Leslie welcomes us both. He then calls me aside and tells me that his whole family will be attending the communion service and I should not use the sermon as an opportunity to attack him. He says he is tired of that, and that is why he has stopped attending the cathedral. 'I am always being attacked by priests who know nothing of the conflict or my position.' He speaks with a smile but I know he is serious. He promises that after the service we will have time to talk. His children respond to the presence of the Melanesian Brothers – children always do. They are gathering round us and wanting to help us set up the altar, and I know the family is pleased we are here.

I preach, basing my address again on the Good Shepherd, in contrast to the thief and the hired man. I keep it general, but the inference is clear. After the communion Leslie tells all his family he wants them to stay. He tells us that he knows the *Tasiu* have come for a reason and this is our chance to speak to his whole family.

After the warmth of the Eucharist there is now a tension as I begin to speak. I say that I have known Leslie a long time. I say that I know he has influence and commands authority. I also say I know him to be a faithful member of our Church and thank him for the opportunity he has given us to voice our concerns. Brother Jude now takes over. He explains about the disarmament mission. He talks about the need to surrender guns to end the climate of fear and extortion. He appeals to Kwaiga to hand over the weapons he is still holding and to use his Christian influence to get other MEF members to hand over their weapons too. Kwaiga listens attentively, giving us a free chance to present our case. He then stands up to respond. He begins by telling the story of how long he has known the Melanesian Brotherhood. How our Community became a home to him when he was a small boy and how he has always loved and respected the Community. He then recounts how the Brothers opposed him during the tension when the MEF were manning the barricades, how they tried to take supplies through his road-blocks which he believed would go into the hands of his enemies. He says that at times those confrontations were angry, but he had never stopped respecting the Brotherhood. 'I know your Community condemns me and what I was doing, but today I have listened to you and now I want you to listen to me.'

He tells his own story of the way he grew up on Guadalcanal, bought and developed land, and as a lawyer initially supported the IFM claim for compensation and land rights to stop Malaitan encroachment. But then he goes on to describe how Malaitans like himself were pushed off the land and lost everything they had developed. 'I had lived all my life on Guadalcanal, I had never lived on Malaita, but now we were told to go back to our own land.' Still, he claimed, he was patient with their grievances. This, after all, was ultimately their ancestral land. As a lawyer, he had even agreed to provide them with legal representation in land rights cases. But then, he said, he had watched as hundreds of Malaitans fled to Honiara and camped at the Sports Centre. He saw them panicking to get on overcrowded boats back to Malaita like rats running for safety. They were full of fear and there was no one to defend them. And then he said he began to hear stories about violence and aggression against his people including the abuse of Malaitan women. As he tells this I can see him harden, and there is anger and hatred in his voice. It is a physical violation of their custom and honour. It was this he says that forced him into action. He began to see that the government was incapable of doing anything to offer real protection. Kwaiga goes on to describe the way in which he and a small group of supporters formed the Malaita Eagle Force to protect his people.

He recalls the excitement and audacity of planning their first operation to rob the Auki armoury, and how simple it was and how quickly their army and membership grew. He tells of the desire to create a disciplined and trained force that would defend his people, protect them against further attack and seek justice for the violence against his people. He describes their first operations against IFM positions either side of Honiara, how he felt when he first heard that one of his operations had caused fatalities, but how this had strengthened his resolve; this was the cost of the violence that the people of Guadalcanal themselves had begun. Kwaiga is intelligent, articulate and convincing. He is telling the story from his perspective and his story contains much that is true, for I too witnessed it. And yet, if we were listening to the cause of Harold Keke and IFM, I am sure too there would be parts of their story with which we could empathize. It is the truth but it is not the whole truth. Defence became revenge. The MEF were unable to control their more thuggish supporters. There were operations that even shot people in hospital and civilians in Visale. There were beheadings, executions and acts of pure brutality. And now there is extortion and theft in the name of compensation against those who have no involvement whatsoever in this original conflict. Violence has continued after the peace agreement. Pay-back time has not ended. 'Blood will have blood', as Shakespeare knew. Kwaiga does not mention or take responsibility for any of this. He is seeking to justify himself to us, and I wonder why. Perhaps he needs us to believe he is innocent to alleviate his own guilt. Why else would he invite us here? The *Tasiu* still represent a moral authority for him, his better self, his conscience, the time before he became involved in all of this.

Then suddenly he turns to the Melanesian Brotherhood. He tells us how we are being manipulated by a corrupt government, to front and conceal their double dealings. He says we are being used. 'The Brotherhood should stay out of politics. Your job is to bring spiritual healing, not collect guns for the government.' He tells us that the government and Prime Minister are in the hands of the MEF. 'We can bring the Prime Minister down at any time and he knows it. This government uses the *Tasiu* because you lend them your reputation of integrity. The Brothers are innocent. They do not know they are being used, but you will lose the trust and respect of the people.' Kwaiga is growing forceful. 'We are not going to give up our guns while Keke is holding on to his. The government know this. Members of cabinet are holding weapons despite their public announcements. These guns came at a price. Why should we hand them over?'

Kwaiga is winning the argument and knows it. He knows much more than we do. They say the Prime Minister fears him. We can only appeal to his better conscience. 'We are not here for the government, or for money or for any other ulterior motive. We decided to take part in the disarmament process not because of the government but because that is what we believe Jesus Christ demands. We believe that there will only be peace when we have the courage to put an end to violence.'

'You have the power to influence your members from the top down. Leslie, if you wanted to, you could really make a difference. Think of Nelson Mandela; he was a lawyer too. He believed in the armed struggle, but now he has become one of the greatest peacemakers this world has ever known. You have the opportunity and the ability to do the same.'

Brother Jude says, 'We respect all you have told us,' and then adds with great simplicity, 'but we still believe you must hand over your weapons.'

The dialogue is over. It is night. Kwaiga says he has an appointment with the Prime Minister. It is strange, but it seems as though the whole family is on our side. They have lived with their father's cause. They have seen the MEF gatherings, the visits of the commanders, the politicians, the discussions, the guns, and the drunkenness. They know this fear and they are longing for it to be over. They are so pleased we have come. They know me from when I have visited their school and led pro- grammes and the dramas we have performed, and they come out to say goodbye asking us to please come and visit them again, and they mean it. Kwaiga and I talk about the time he was at university with James Ilifanoa who also trained as a lawyer and was my best friend. James died tragically before all of this. Had he been alive I wonder where James would have stood. He had so much potential, insight and brilliance. I never saw any violence in him, but would he have been led into it too? He was *of* his Malaitan culture but had the imagination and humour to laugh at it, and rise above it. I remember the way he read nearly all the books in my book- case, even Samuel Beckett's *Waiting for Godot*. He loved to quote Vladimir and Estragon's '"Shall we go?" "Yes, let's go!" [They do not move.]' He never wanted to leave. What insight he had to be able to dance with perspectives and not be confined by culture. It was a rare and wonderful rainbow agility, so wasted by his death. He was from a remote village in North Malaita. His father would sit outside his shed of a house selling betel nut, fearing to leave lest someone break in and steal his shell money. And yet his son was so different – the uncontainable James, such a fluent and amusing communicator in English, playing with words and phrases and alive with ideas and good intentions. He was the hope of the whole village, the first one to reach sixth form and then university overseas. At least four of his cousins were named after him and everyone loved it when he came back home to the village, a whole gang of them following him around, wanting to join him in his plans to build houses and yam and taro gardens and Creek Bird National Park!

Isn't life strange? One minute I am locked in this mortal argument with Kwaiga and then suddenly here we are talking of James and I am recalling the joys of those Christmases in Malaita. How we swam for more than a mile down that cold clear river near Takwa on Christmas day. No presents, no special food, but free, and the best Christmas I can remember. How we shouted and sang with all his extended family through New Year's night when Joseph cut up the goal posts as a joke and we rang the church bell as the gang called out 'Wake up and Happy New Year!' I felt more at home with him than I have ever felt. I love James, I love this country, I loved these times in Malaita. There is so much goodness here, but goodness is so easily destroyed. For James it was alcohol that took him away from us. We lost him. It does not necessarily begin with the will to destroy, but destruction has a momentum of its own and, once begun, it can take an incredible amount of strength or grace to break free from that recklessness which is leading to death. Change is possible, but you need God. It's hard to save yourself once you have trapped yourself. God must break in. It is God's love which can bring hope and change. Once we have recognized the love of God and what his forgiveness can bring, can't we live the same love and awaken others to it, even beyond death?

I remember the day of James' burial in North Malaita. I travelled for twenty-four hours to get there as soon as I heard, by boat, and then I hired the church truck. Willie, the diocesan driver, agreed to take me. He could see it was important to me. It was seven hours along broken roads through the pot-holes. When I arrived, the funeral was over and it was pouring with rain. I walked through the bush to the clearing and the mound his father had been preparing for his own burial ten years before and we had laughed at his father's *kastom*. The rain was heavier now. When I reached the area I saw James' grave, which had been filled in only two hours before, awash with mud, and his fragile mother kneeling and weeping by its side. We knelt there together holding onto each other crying as the rain poured down. James' wife saw me and rushed over and joined us. Three of us holding onto each other, holding to this wonderful man whom we had lost, washed by the rain. Remembering this, I am deeply aware that somehow it is those who live on who must fulfil the potential of the departed. Somehow I must live James' goodness and a life worthy of both of us. I do not have his speed of mind or reckless brilliance, but perhaps I can balance him. I smile as I write this, for he was such a joy to be with and even after all these years and the tragedy of his death, I still feel that happiness when we used to be together. He is redeemed and healed beyond this life. '"Let's go!" [They do not move.]' James is like a messenger from the world beyond, calling upon me to live what I believe, not just for myself but for him too.

I wonder whether Kwaiga will think any more about what we have shared. Brother Jude and I return like children, as though we have been given an insight into a conspiracy beyond our depth, and yet I cannot stop believing that it is our very freedom from intrigue and deception which is our strength and what Kwaiga longs for most. 'Father, Lord of heaven and earth, to you I offer praise, for what you have hidden from the clever you have revealed to the merest children.' The gospel which Kwaiga claims to believe is about renouncing the power of the world and the desire for pay-back and compensation. He is telling us as Brothers to do the very thing he himself is called to do. For he does have the influence to bring change, far more than I. There is intrigue far beyond our knowledge, but is there not also the hope that you can rise above that, rise as Christ rose above the traps of the plotters? When there is repentance and the desire for change there is hope but when there is self-justification how can there be a breakthrough? The renouncing of the armed struggle involves an even greater courage; it involves the recognition of the failure of violence, and that involves facing up to the horror of what he has done himself. I feel no condemnation for Kwaiga, just a longing that he may be brought back from this death in life into the life of God, for he could do so much. It is the only way forward for him and this nation. But I fear he is not listening to God yet.

It is sad to report that Solomon Islands is economically in dire straits. In the last two weeks the exchange rate has changed from SI\$8 to the UK pound to almost SI\$12. There is no water at all in Honiara because the government has not paid the landowners for the water supply and so it has been cut off. There are constant power cuts. The teachers are on strike because they have not been paid for months. Solomon Islands College of Higher Education has not received a grant to start its new semester, and the students are still waiting. There are no medicines, and last week the paramedics went on strike because they have not been paid, and so the hospital is in chaos. I sat at the Central Hospital all morning with the Brotherhood tutor. He has a very painful suspected tumour on his knee and has waited since March to receive the results of a biopsy sent to Australia. Today we were lucky to meet Dr Oberlie, a wonderful Swiss doctor, who continues to work in Solomon Islands despite all the problems. He seemed understandably very preoccupied at first but later came back to say he had paid out of his own money for a lab technician to work on the results, and told me to come back next week when he hoped to be able to give us a proper diagnosis. Our tutor has been so patient despite many sleepless nights of pain. His name is Father Dixon Nakisi.

The economic future looks bad because there is no income to support government ministries and the public sector. Much overseas aid is still being withheld as donors will no longer accept the way aid packages have been diverted to pay compensation to former militants and government salaries, which are producing few tangible results. And there is still not enough security for any investors to want to commit money to this nation. Who can blame them when you see the total vandalism that has wantonly destroyed literally every income-generating investment outside Honiara? Solomon Islands Plantations Limited (SIPL) which boasted sophisticated driers and generators, roads and housing for its ten thousand workers, is literally a skeleton, stripped of every bit of corrugated iron, its generators pointlessly vandalized and smashed, its buildings burnt out and pulled apart, leaving only the cement base and a few charred frames. I believe the future will depend on the rural communities and their ability to find small-scale initiatives to generate income and to hold together, and it is in the role of grass-roots community care and development that the Church has such a vital role to play.

When I arrive at our disarmament house at Bishopsdale I can tell something is wrong. Brother Albert is on the telephone and sounds angry. The whole disarmament and peace process is in jeopardy. There is news that ten Kwaio mercenaries from Malaita have travelled to Keke's stronghold on the Weather Coast. They have been intercepted by Keke, apparently after running out of petrol and firing on one of Keke's boats. There is news that Keke has had them executed on the beach. The story is deeply disturbing, and there are many rumours claiming to know who put the money up for this ill-fated, reckless assassination attempt. It has blatantly destroyed any hope of building trust for disarmament. Perhaps that was the intention of its backers. The Kwaio relatives are refusing to believe rumours they are dead. The police will not go near Keke, they are already far too compromised. It is the Melanesian Brothers who once again have been requested to find out what has happened. The Brothers themselves realize how dangerous the situation has become, and are loath to get involved in a situation which is clearly so full of double-dealing and deceit. But who else has the impartiality at least to find out what has happened? And there are relatives too asking for information about the deceased, one of them, an Anglican priest, who is the father-in-law of one of the Kwaio mercenaries. The Brothers themselves do not want to go. They feel that the whole work for peace has been undermined. From this point onwards Harold Keke's paranoia and his conviction that the Prime

Minister and his cabinet are evil and corrupt will grow unbounded, as will our Community's fear that we are not being told the whole truth.

I later hear that Brother Jude Alfred has gone himself. Three days pass and he does not return. I lie awake worrying. Finally, we get a message that he has been prevented from returning by bad weather, but that he is safe and has been staying with Keke. He returns to confirm the story that all of the Kwaio mercenaries are dead with the exception of the driver from Bougainville, who managed to escape to the Brothers' household at Kolina.

The atmosphere of this disarmament has changed. We began with such hope and idealism. But it is impossible now that Keke will agree to disarm, for he believes that he has proof that the government is conspiring to have him killed. On the other side, the Malaitan militia leaders will refuse to disarm on the pretext that they need to defend themselves and Honiara from Keke and his men.

I arrive at the disarmament house. I have been teaching an adult group of lay preachers in Honiara. It's about 10.00 p.m. As I enter the house I see that the Archbishop is there with the Brothers. They stop talking and there is silence. The Archbishop greets me, but I can feel I have disturbed something tense and important. I can see some kind of discussion is in progress. I excuse myself and go through to the bedroom wondering what is going on. Not long after, I hear the Archbishop leave. Brother Jude comes into the room.

'What's going on?'

'I'll tell you tomorrow.'

'I want to know now.'

'I don't want you to worry.'

'I'm already worried.'

'We were attacked,' says Brother Jude, 'Brother Billy and me.'

'Where's Billy?'

'At the hospital. He has had twelve stitches in his mouth and face. He was cut with a ring when they hit him.'

'Who did this?'

'Jimmy Rasta's boys.'

'Are you alright, Jude?' I can see for the first time that he is not.

They had gone to meet with Jimmy Rasta, the MEF commander, at his bottle shop at Ranadi, in east Honiara, aiming to meet the militant leaders face to face. Outside there was a group of his men who had shouted at them, asked them what they wanted, and accused them of being police informants. They had started pushing them about and insulting them. They had grabbed Brother Billy's walking stick and broken it in front of him, and then they had started hitting them. The other Brothers had run away, but Brother Jude and Billy had been caught in the middle. Then Rasta himself appeared and called his men off, swearing at them and telling them they were stupid. He told Jude and Billy to get in the car and had driven them back.

'What did the Archbishop say?' I asked Jude.

'He said I should go back and meet with Rasta again.'

'What? Let him go himself!'

I sit with Brother Jude. He has shown so much energy and courage over the last months. He has confronted this violence non-stop with his tireless goodness. I have been amazed at him, how he has grown in wisdom, his initiative and such courage, while maintaining his warmth and Christian spirit. Everyone loves him. And now for the first time his spirit has deserted him. Brother Billy is taken back to Tabalia. His face is a mess, his eyes swollen and black, stitches in his cheek and chin. The wives from the Theological College come down to bring him food. He is treated like a hero, and everyone wants to hear what happened. But Jude stays in Honiara. He seems dejected, and I do all I can to encourage and to persuade him to come back to Tabalia and rest. He agrees to come with me to Tabalia but he is not himself and spends most of the weekend sleeping.

11

Were not our hearts burning within us while he was talking to us on the road?

Luke 24.32

From the diary of August 2002

Brother Francis Tofi is back from the Weather Coast for a few days. It is great to see him. Last Sunday was the Brotherhood fundraising, which went well. I spent most of the day with Brother Francis. It makes you feel so peaceful to be with him. He has been posted at Kolina, on the Weather Coast of Guadalcanal. It is only a few miles away from where Harold Keke and his supporters are based. The parish priest tells me Brother Francis is too brave. He has been preaching openly against the use of violence and speaking out against anyone who joins the militants. Keke heard about his ministry and sent a group of armed men to demand that Francis go and meet with him. He refused, telling them that he had no business with Keke and, as he was not a follower, no reason to obey Keke's orders. He also told them not to come to the Brotherhood again carrying guns. He said that it was a holy place and, as none of the Brothers carried any weapon, asked why was there any need for guns? Apparently they returned to their commander meekly. When you see how sycophantic everyone else is with to Keke you would appreciate Francis's courage. When Keke appeared at the Theological College last year the students were all rushing to shake his hands as if a saint rather than a psychopath had just arrived. Brother Francis tells me how their household at Kolina is so quiet at present. Few visit them but he says he loves sitting in the chapel by himself each day. It seems to rain ceaselessly and I imagine him sitting in the leaf chapel meditating with the wind and rain, the waves crashing on that violent Kolina beach below. When I have visited, the boat driver has to count the waves and after the seventh make straight for the shore. The villagers rush into the sea and literally lift up the whole boat, passengers, luggage and engine and charge up the beach so that the next wave will not smash you against the stones or flip the boat over in the surf.

I persuade Brother Francis to come and help count the money from the fundraising. His gentle presence does much to improve this horrible task. Our treasurer becomes increasingly officious as the money mounts and the buckets and baskets overflow. Francis has to get off. He has been asked to help try and recover a stolen Landcruiser from Moses Su'u, one of the MEF former commanders. I am wanting to get back to Tabalia now but, as usual, there appears to be no transport. I have important and difficult news for Father Dixon Nakisi. Dr Oberlie has contacted me to say that cancer has been confirmed and he needs to see him as soon as possible.

It is already nine o'clock in the evening and I really want to get back, but Honiara is eighteen miles from Tabalia. Brother Francis Tofi has arrived and offers to walk with me. 'It's too far', I tell him. 'No, if you want to go back, I can walk with you.'

We set off walking through Honiara and then out past Bishopsdale. We stop at Valbrose Garage where I buy some bread and *Ma-Ling* Chinese luncheon meat, for the journey, and something to drink. We leave the town behind, pass through White River market with its shacks and betel nut stalls and staggering drunks with dreadlocks and the stink of garbage, yeast and marihuana and blare of reggae. It feels like a dissolute shanty town after the deluge. Then on past Tanagai through the village where the fighting took place, which is now just the charred stumps of houses in the undergrowth. We wade across the river, where the American iron bridge once was, now jutting out into space, with a section of it lying broken off and rusting among the coconut trees. We continue out along the dark pot-holed road to the west. After a mile or so it is obvious that without a torch we will struggle. So Francis guides me down a track towards the sea where the family of one of our former

Novices, Wilfred from Bellona, lives. Wilfred throws his arms round us both. He smells of yeast from home-brewed alcohol, he is 'full drunk' and delighted to see us. We sit with his uncle while he goes off to borrow a light for us and returns with a large diving torch, which he insists we take with us for our journey. Francis and I set off again, the torch guiding us around the pot-holes. But now the moon is coming up and the trees no longer overhang the road, so we can see much better and it is a beautiful night. After two hours' walking we reach a bridge over another river and sit with our legs swinging over the edge and open the tin of meat and slice it with the lid onto the bread.

Brother Francis tells me he can still remember all his Novice classes with me when he was training. I remember him too. He was always so attentive and his answers so intuitive; he is the kind of person you always wanted to return to in a discussion to hear what he had to say.

'I always remember what you told us about violence', says Brother Francis. 'You were telling us about the Second World War and about the killing of the Jews in Poland. You told us that six million Jews had been murdered and that was twelve times the whole population of Solomon Islands. We could not believe how such a terrible thing could happen. You said that evil has a power of its own and that one of the Nazi commanders had said "It is hard to kill one person but once you have killed one it is easier to kill two, and once you have killed two there is no difference in killing five, and nothing between five and twenty." This is what is happening with Keke. They no longer feel any guilt for what they are doing. They kill as if it were nothing.' Francis has been there, two miles only from their camp. I have heard that he waded into a mob of the militants who were beating someone with the butts of their guns. He managed to stop them and saved the man's life. Francis does not mention any of this. I see him in my mind sitting in that Kolina chapel during the day praying, the wind and rain blowing against the walls. If evil multiplies, so too can goodness generate and grow greater than the power of darkness. This man is like a beacon of hope, like the light with which he guides me along this road. Somehow to be with him you feel safe. He has a rare quality of being both very gentle and very strong.

When you walk simply to arrive, this road seems very long, but tonight the company is greater than the distance. When you swim in the sea you can feel different temperatures of water like currents you swim through. It's the same when you are walking through the night. There are darker parts, and lighter parts, times of talking and times of silence. I do not realize, of course, that I will never forget this walk, nor that I will return to these memories again and again, because it will be one of the last times we are together before his death.

When he was due to be admitted as a Brother, Francis came to stay at my house. Tabalia was so crowded with people there was nowhere for many of the Community to stay. Francis and some of the other Novices slept on mats in my living room. His father had come to witness the ceremony. They are Tikopian. His father wore their custom dress, the custom mat, belted around his waist. He gave me that mat as a memory after his son died. Francis's first posting was in Malaita, and when I flew to Malaita to preach in Auki he was there waiting by the side of the grass airfield to meet me. He had walked all the way from Airahu and stayed with me until I left Malaita. When he heard I was becoming a Brother he wrote to me. I was in England when I received the letter and he was still serving in Malaita, and he sounded so joyful. I kept the letter: 'Brother Richard thank you so much for our company together at Auki . . . I really enjoyed and still remember your words of encouragement to me. About my new posting I feel settled and everything is running smoothly and full of Holy Spirit and fire . . . I hope God will make it possible for us to be together in any mission in the future. My best love and prayers for you Father and Brother Richard. Sharing great joy with you in your admission. God Bless and Peace be with you! From yours Brother Francis Tofi.'

On the road to Tabalia we talk about the present mission for disarmament. Francis is anxious about the Brothers' involvement. Francis says that it is essential that the Brothers remain completely neutral and are not seen to be siding with anyone, let alone any police operation against Keke. 'Olketa Brothers must stop simple.' Stay simple. More is less. It is only by being men of God, free of prejudice, impartial to all sides, that they can be peacemakers.

It's a long walk and now we are getting tired and beginning to stumble.

Brother Francis has bare feet and they are sore and bleeding, and although he is stronger and a much holier man than me, when I remember these things, it is as though somehow I have been called to walk the greater distance, to walk much further but to the same destination. After Francis' death I will recall Bishop Patteson's words 'God in his great mercy, took those who were most ready to go.' But how I hope he will still be walking with me.

A truck picks us up about two miles from Tabalia and takes us the last part of the journey. As we come up the hill to Tabalia we can see some-one making a fire in the kitchen to heat water for breakfast. It must be getting on for five o'clock in the morning. We wash squatting under the two stand-pipe taps behind the dining hall, the cold morning water splashing down over our heads, washing away the grime of the journey. There are the first signs of dawn in the sky over the black silhouette of the coconut plantation. I go back to my room and lie down, both refreshed and exhausted, and sleep, but it is only a matter of minutes before the morning bell is ringing for prayer.

12

For those who want to save their life will lose it
and those who lose their life for my sake, and for
the sake of the gospel, will save it.

Mark 8.35

From the diary of August 2002

I celebrate Communion for the Community, but I am feeling feverish and I have a bad headache. I also have the message from Doctor Oberlie for Father Dixon on my mind and I wonder how he will take it. I go over to Father Dixon's house and as gently as I can tell him and his wife the bad news about the diagnosis of cancer. He thanks me. I tell him Doctor Oberlie wants him to come into hospital as soon as possible.

Our nurse aid, the diligent Abraham Hou, lives next door with his wife and holy young son Septimus. Septimus loves to visit me with his best friend, my namesake Richard, in search of crayons and story books. His Dad takes my temperature and says I have malaria and must take the usual regime of four tablets of chloroquine a day for three days. It might sound too bad but eight tablets at once can kill a large dog; believe me, I've seen it! It's the way they put down diseased and unwanted strays.

I begin the treatment immediately, believing that the malaria will come under control as it usually does. On the second day, however, my temperature increases and there is frequent diarrhoea, thinner than water, and on the third day after my final dose I have never felt worse in my life. Everything I try to eat or drink I am violently vomiting out, and I am becoming frightened of dehydrating as I am losing fluids far faster than I am replacing them.

In all of this the Novices and Brothers are very attentive, coming to my room with so many coconuts and bananas that my small bedroom is looking more like a market stall. They are 'swimming' my head with cold water from a bucket to get my temperature down, and stand over me in their uniforms with hands pressed on my head whispering prayers and collects of healing. It is indeed comforting. Richard's mother brings me bananas she has burnt in the fire, which she says will help my stomach. She insists that I eat them while she waits with me. She says that 'burn burn banana now him good time you sicksick olsem, finish him now! You must finishem!'

I lie there from Sunday morning to Thursday with so little movement that my self-winding watch stops and I no longer know the time. On Friday morning I stand up, but my eyes and head are spinning and it is like being on the deck of a boat in rough seas. My chest is tight from suspected pneumonia, so now I must go through a course of antibiotics. But my trip to Honiara puts my own four days of sickness, juxtaposed with Father Dixon's diagnosis, into perspective. Poor man, he is now in hospital but welcomes me into his room with such hospitality. His wife has set up camp in the corner of the room on a woven mat on the floor so that she can be with him. He has his own room and shows me the bullet marks in the floor. It is the same room where the two patients from Guadalcanal were shot dead by Malaitans during the conflict. It does not add anything to the atmosphere, imagining how they died here.

I also visit the disarmament team, but they have disappeared. One Brother, looking a bit sheepish, is cooking a pot of rice for himself with a whole tin of corned beef.

Friday 10 August

A hard day. I couldn't sleep last night. It must be because I have been sleeping all week. I lay there wondering how I am going to get through the next months. This ministry is draining all those involved. I think of Brother Jude, with all his potential and idealism, being beaten up. He seems unsettled and needs to get away from Honiara. The peacekeeping group are being pulled in all directions and I am no longer sure who is influencing whom. The small signs of disintegration have begun. The group is no longer eating together. Individuals grab food, which has been left for them by different Mothers' Union groups, before rushing off on some new urgent mission of disarmament. But when I arrive only some make it to join the prayer, others are sleeping on the floor or just out. No one seems to know where the others are or when they will be back. There are others here who are not even in the Brotherhood, asleep or just coming in and out. In the bedroom there is a whole wardrobe of high-powered weapons. There are some photos of the Brothers taken with a cheap Kodak lying on one of the mats. They show the Brothers posing with the guns they have collected. What is the power that weapons exert? For in these photos these seemingly humble religious are transformed into something different: the slouch, the angled head, the gun held with one hand. It is an image so familiar from videos. Brother Jude used to hold this Community together but since being beaten up he has been absent, and his presence and motivation is so obviously missing from the house. Yet they have been under so much pressure night and day it is so understandable. The success of their disarmament programme cannot be underestimated; they have achieved so much but I worry they have lost the earlier discipline and focus. And they do not really tell me what is happening any more. I remember Brother Francis Tofi's warning: it is not just what we do, it how we are seen to do it. The other members of the Community see them rushing about in the four-wheel-drive like action men, and are beginning to resent them. I was told that other Brothers do not like visiting Bishopsdale any more. They used to go because there was always food there, but now they have been told by the Archbishop to stay away. He has put up a notice on the door saying visitors are not allowed.

Saturday 11 August

Another hard day. I am back at the mother house Tabalia. I feel real darkness. I stumble about getting ready for prayer. Some of the Brothers have put Brother Billy's broken walking stick on the altar in the chapel. 'What is that meant to mean?' I ask Brother Caulton. Brother Caulton shares my instincts for all that is cultish. Are we trying to bring down punishment or God's curse on his attackers? Brother Caulton confronts the Community and everyone agrees it should be removed from the altar. I put it away in a vestry cupboard.

One cassava for breakfast and one for supper, nothing else. The Novices and Brothers are out foraging in the bush and the place is deserted after prayer. I feel terrible, perhaps it's the antibiotics, or the aftermath of malaria or not smoking, or perhaps it's just the lack of a *wantok*. All spiritual books I pick up seem very good at diagnosing the spiritual crisis and very poor at dealing with it. The water is not working and the toilets are blocked. The bucket to carry water has disappeared. I have no toilet paper and the batteries of my torch have run out. Someone has borrowed my small radio. The years stretch out before me, I am whingeing vocally and I have no right to. The demons are out in force with a hundred scenarios of an alternative lifestyle: a home, walks along the river, visits to family, a regular wage and the dangerous desire for more physical intimacy, all of which are present impossibilities. Real poverty is not glamorous. It unlocks all one's selfishness and instincts for self-preservation. Yet it also opens windows of perception and empathy and one sees more clearly those, who, while struggling with greater deprivation, still have an instinct for the greater good, and still show acts of compassion and care for the needs of others while struggling to keep their own head above water. This is true generosity.

Last night, Alejandro Junior, the new Filipino Novice came with me to Matthew's house. Matthew is a theological lecturer from Shropshire and a good friend. Matthew is away but we can use his kitchen to cook. I am hungry for the first time in over a week which must be a sign that I am recovering. Junior boils eggplant and then dips them in egg and fries them. It tastes delicious. It's good to be with Junior. He is adapting well. I see his cultural mistakes as when he wears his sandals inside the house, or doesn't put on his uniform properly and the others laugh at him. I see his failed attempts to joke with the Solomon Island Novices and some-times his isolation. But he is growing more thoughtful, more sensitive to the spirit of the gospel, and they are beginning to love him. He grasps intuitively something of the poverty I am experiencing, and asks me if in England I have a house or a car. 'No', I answer. I don't even have an English driving licence. I think Junior is trying to understand why I should choose to live like this. Poverty in the Philippines is something to be fought against, not embraced. I am unable at present to explain to him. I admire Junior. It has not been easy for him, but there has been an openness to change. He is a deeper person than the one I met in Manila. How often it seems that when someone is thrown in and left without the distractions of the familiar then we are able to see the true life in them – God's life shining through their vulnerability. He has a Filipino gentleness. He is very loyal to me and will not go without me. When I was ill he came to sleep on the other bed in my room because he wanted to look after me. At night I heard him moaning and talking in his sleep. Like Abraham, he has set out on this journey far from home in faith.

On Saturday evening Sister Doreen takes me to Tetete ni Kolivuti (TNK), the headquarters of the Sisters of the Church. I have agreed to celebrate and preach for them. Doreen is, as always, full of non-stop chatter and encouragement:

'You need a break, Brother Richard. Think of all you have been doing. It is not easy Brother Richard. Everyone needs a break.' She chatters on. But I am preoccupied and distant. I am thinking about the disarmament group. They came to Tabalia today for something but none of them told me the reason. I feel alienated from their programme and unsure of their present objectives. There needs to be closure on this disarmament mission. We have done as much as we can do. It has been a time of adrenalin and fast living in which they have been much sought after. But now it seems hard to extricate them from their new-found status and associates who seem to be leeching onto them and using their good reputation and the trust they command.

On our way to TNK we visit the refuge Sister Lillian is building for women who are the victims of violence. There are already women and children there and also sandflies everywhere. Gentle Sister Lillian is sweating away planting taro in the swamp. She seems very dedicated and happy in this ministry. Since the conflict there seems to have been a rise in the violence against women. Ex-militants vent their pent-up anger in the home, and so often wives become the victims. It was Sister Lillian's idea to provide this sanctuary for women and their children who need time to escape from this violence.

TNK, the headquarters of the Sisters of the Church, is quiet and peaceful and very welcoming. It is a group of houses on a hill in the middle of a huge oil palm plantation, which has not been in operation since the conflict. The Sisters have built a new chapel and the place is surrounded by posts on which they have mounted hundreds of orchids. Their dogs always run towards you barking ferociously when you arrive. This is the Community's only security. It is good to be back at this place of retreats and so many happy memories. This was where my father led my ordination retreat. It was a time my mother still recalls as one of the happiest times of her life. This is the place where my friend Russ from America tried to teach the theological college students the spiritual values of fasting, without realizing the Sisters were supplementing the rations of dry biscuits he had provided with baked potatoes, fish and home-made bread. Russ kept up his meditation in the chapel, oblivious; he used to lie on his back while meditating because he had tendonitis. All the students thought he was just having a sleep.

I begin to feel better for the first time after finishing the malaria. I relax, wash, eat and prepare my sermon for the following day. TNK seems a relaxed and happy place. But it has had its share of trouble. Some of the ex-militants are camping in the plantation and Doreen says that some have been hanging around too closely, so that some of the Sisters feel threatened. Doreen is not afraid to confront them. She can be fairly militant herself when challenged.

The text for my sermon is the story of the Canaanite woman coming to Jesus saying 'Have mercy on me, Sir.' Her need disturbs and seems at first to be a nuisance, even to Jesus himself, and the disciples urge him: 'Send her away, see how she comes shouting after us.' Jesus' reply to her seems astonishingly racist and insulting: 'It is not right to take the children's bread and throw it to the dogs.' Yet he is awakened by her reply. Is Jesus testing her? Is he setting up a situation in which, by feigning opposition, he allows her the chance to witness to her faith, thus herself defeating the prejudice? Or is it that she has disarmed him, is it that the human Christ is repeating the commonly held prejudice among Jews, and yet is great enough to recognize truth when he sees and hears it, and thus to change?

'True, Sir, yet the dogs eat the scraps that fall from their master's table.' There is no status or honour to be won for helping her, and yet this woman's shocking self-denigration and yet persistence – not only in need but in the faith that Jesus can answer that need – breaks through. I think of the Novice who came to my room and disturbed me. He was trying to tell me he had not written his Bible study for homework and could not. He was trying to tell me that he had not had any schooling and he was struggling to read and write. He was wanting help and I was tired and trying to get rid of him. I think of Selwyn smiling and rushing up to me in Honiara still waiting for the chance to go to school. I think of so many people waiting, hoping, waiting for recognition. It happens all the time. Our Novices go to the hospital because they are sick. They wait outside in the sun all day and finally they see a nurse who gives them a handful of Panadol, which they could have received here. And they take this so patiently without even complaining. And these same Novices are themselves so willing to help anybody. An old man came to me today looking anxious: 'I may be attacked today because I still owe money that I have not been able to pay. You, Brother Richard, I know can help me!' I think of how I cut Novice Benjamin out of the drama I am preparing because he did not come to rehearsals. I know how disappointed he is and that this was the same Novice who brought me coconuts when I was sick. We have to go on giving, go on breaking through those prejudices, go on being re-orientated by the disarming goodness and humanity of those who need us and confront us and ultimately change us and fill us, in a way that preserving our so-called boundaries could never do. For what a privilege it is to be able to care and help and, when that is denied us and we are no longer able to give, then we truly experience poverty.

13

Behold how good and pleasant it is to dwell together in unity.

Psalm 133.1 (Common Worship Psalter)

From the diary of September 2002

I have broken my glasses. The only optician in Honiara has no lenses at the moment. The only other way to replace them is to go to a Chinese store and try on different pairs until they fit. Unfortunately this system is more helpful to the long-sighted than the short-sighted. I also have been having pain in my kidneys since the malaria and terrible pain urinating. It was so bad last week I had to go and lie down in the clinic in Honiara where they gave me an injection for the pain. The doctor thinks it may be kidney stones but there is no ultrasound to check this and the hospital x-ray facility is not in action. I will get all of these things done in Papua New Guinea where I have been invited by the Melanesian Brotherhood to attend their Regional Conference and to lead a retreat and workshop for the Brothers in Popondetta.

For a long time our Brothers in PNG have struggled to find a place for their mother house. At the last Regional Conference they decided to move out of Popondetta as the urban life was encroaching too much on the life of their Community. Looking around for land, the family of Brother Robin Lindsay offered them some about four hours' boat journey along the coast at a place called Deboin. It was an offer showing the generosity of Brother Robin, and his love and commitment to the Brotherhood. The idea was good: a place of quiet and prayer to establish a proper novitiate, free from worldly distractions. Unfortunately, it has not worked out as Deboin has turned out to be far too remote.

I visited Deboin to assess its suitability. Located high up in the hills, it is the derelict site of a logging company with all the resulting ecological devastation. The topsoil has been washed away. Huge deep cracks and gullies split the dry red soil. It is hot, dusty and the gardens the Novices have planted bear only stunted fruit, which are often ravaged by wild pigs. There is a sense here among the Brothers of feeling rather desolate and scattered. They have used some of the housing left behind by the loggers, but there is no centre to the Community and it is obvious that the spirit of the Brothers is not in this place. The chaplain told me that it had not been an easy year, and there had been a lot of time when there had been very little to eat. There had been bad cases of malaria too, with very difficult transport problems when they needed to get Brothers to the hospital in Popondetta. Yet I found a wonderful group of Novices and their lives expressed a different story.

Our arrival caught them by surprise but as our boat came into land I could see them engaged in different tasks along a mile stretch, cutting timber, fishing, working in the gardens. But they had spotted us and came sprinting excitedly along the shore to meet us. It was as if the adversity they faced had toughened them and increased their solidarity. At night we tracked down the mountain again to the sea and after many attempts they managed to get a diving torch working and they dived for fish to welcome me, while I paddled a canoe to pick up the catch. There is a great energy here, a kind of reckless enthusiasm and spontaneity. But despite Brother Robin's family's generous gift of land, it does seem that this place is too remote to be the Brotherhood's headquarters in PNG. There is no telephone or postal service, and the only means of communication involves at least four hours by boat with outboard motor.

The Brothers held their conference at Dobodoru, which I attended after my visit to Deboin. Dobodoru is about 17 miles outside Popondetta and situated on a deserted American airbase. Two years ago the Brothers were offered land here, and it quickly became obvious to me that here they had found the perfect place for their regional headquarters. As the Brothers arrived there was a tension in the air. Nearly all the Brothers were unhappy about the last four years in Deboin, which, for many of them, felt as if the Brotherhood had been moved out into the wilderness.

They had struggled to build, but their work now seemed pointless and wasted. To start again, to search for a new place to settle, seemed a depressing thought. And so we began our retreat with a spirit of desolation. Dobodoru, this old airbase, is on a massive plain stretching as far as the eye can see. The Brothers had built simple high leaf houses here, which caught the wind blowing. They had also built a leaf chapel with leaf roof open on all sides. Looking beyond the altar are miles of kunai grass and a wide open sky. The wind across the plain cut patterns and ripples in the grass. In the next few days of retreat the mood changed dramatically. Any tension there had been seemed to dissolve. 'We have been making decisions for our Community in despair,' said one Brother 'we must begin making them in a spirit of peace.' It suddenly seemed as if the last four years had not been such a disaster after all. This rootlessness had been painful and frustrating and yet it had been a time of learning too. And was not this very displaced homelessness reflected in the life of Christ and the life of so many of the world's poor? Could not the past be seen, not as a disaster to be forgotten, but as a journey to a greater and deeper understanding? How often our security comes from ownership, building a home which is also a defence and a visible sign of validity and belonging. How much we fear to face the risk of the wasteland, where the future is uncertain and nothing seems secure or permanent. And yet it is in that wilderness that a person is formed and faith becomes real, because it is here that our faith is not an appendage to life but the meaning of it. It is here that something is at stake. This kind of provisionality has always been a mark of the Melanesian Brotherhood, indeed a mark of discipleship.

And so, in a simple, beautiful way, God's grace unfolded. Here on this plain, the Brothers had found what they were looking for – a place far enough away from Popondetta to provide peace and quiet, and yet a place near enough for good communications and transport. There was a river and acres of flat, fertile soil, and this wonderful wind across the plain to cool from the hot sun. The landowners came to meet us. They told us that they had been keeping the land for the last fifty years because their great-grandfather had said that this land was for the missionary work. When the archbishop of PNG arrived they offered him the land and the title of the land to the Brotherhood as a gift. And suddenly the sky was clear and all tensions were gone and we held a conference with no hostilities, making good and wise decisions.

On the festival day I came back to Dobodoru to find they had surrounded our open chapel with black plastic. 'But why?' I asked. 'So that the candles won't blow out', I was told. A parable perhaps of what we do to our Church: we block out, we sacrifice the breadth and depth of God's miraculous creation to keep our familiar rituals alive, to keep our candles alight, while outside we miss the burning energy of an exploding sunset diffusing out to the corners of the sky. 'Please take the black plastic down', I pleaded. And my maverick Brothers, not seeming to worry at all that their day's work had been in vain, ripped the plastic down and let the wind and the beckoning kunai grass in again!

In Port Moresby I stayed with a tough and committed group of Brothers who are looking after a parish in Marata: an area of the capital that has been a criminal no-go area. No parish priest with a family will brave working here and so our Brothers man the parish. In the midst of stories of dumped corpses, murders and break-ins, they have created a wonderful sense of community. Celebrating the Eucharist here feels like you are celebrating on the front line. And what commitment among the faithful members of the parish who find in the Brothers a Community who are not afraid to come here and stay, walk about at night, and give them all courage and hope. I felt proud to be part of this group of Brothers and protected too, for they would not let me go anywhere alone but looked after me like a group of faithful bodyguards.

I was back in Solomon Islands for only two days before I set off for Vanuatu for the Melanesian Brotherhood's Regional Conference there. I visited our Brothers in Ambae four years ago. At that time there were fourteen Brothers and two households working in Vanuatu, and a feeling that the Southern Region was the poor relation of the Melanesian Brotherhood. In four years there has been a total transformation. Now there are forty-nine Brothers, over seventy Novices, and a new intake of thirty-five aspirants.

I held their retreat on a most beautiful beach against an ever-changing sky, with little shade from the sun. We slept on the sand lighting many small fires to keep warm. We drank from a sand pool that collected water filtering down from the surrounding cliffs. For meditation I swam with about twenty Brothers about a mile around the cliffs, looking up at thousands of bats circling. We saw a beautiful white owl suddenly attacked by a hawk fall into the sea, its feathers now sodden bedraggled and lifeless. Was it a sign for the future? The Brothers explored the caves, climbed the cliff and dived and jumped into the water . . . all in the silence of the retreat. I celebrated the Eucharist kneeling on the beach, the Brothers circling around a mat on the sand with the ocean behind me.

14

The Parable of the Talents

Luke 19.11ff.

From the diary of November and December 2002

And so back to Solomon Islands.

The drama I am working on for our mission is going well. I wanted to work on one of Christ's parables, to address the present situation. These parables are such open texts, they are puzzles that invite application and interpretation in Solomon Islands. I want it to be as hard-hitting as Christ's original parables, though deceptively simple. It must find a way through defences and, while winning empathy, proceed to turn expectation upside down. We have been asked to perform at the Police Club. The drama is based on the Parable of the Talents, a story of both potential and waste. A father, who is the chief of his village, calls the village together to make an announcement. There is joy and celebration for this chief; this father is greatly loved and respected, but he announces to the village that he has decided to leave the village and go away. He chooses three of his sons from his extended family and divides his shell money between them: five for one, three to another and one to another. He hands over his authority to these three. He points to the sea, to the plantation, to the community and calls upon these sons to use their talents wisely for the good of the village. And then, quite simply, he walks out on them.

And what is left behind? There is all the raw talent and possibility and expectation of Melanesia at this time. Yet, coupled with this, almost a sense of bewilderment and betrayal that the old order and securities have vanished, and there is confusion and lack of confidence and vacuum.

There are tremendous resources, and yet very little experience in leadership. There is memory of the old order, but few rules for the new. At the same time there is also a sense of liberation, excitement and possibility, and all the temptations and deceptions of a new world.

The three sons make their way to Honiara. The first son, John Paul, much to the anger of the village, seems to waste his talent by buying empty oil drums; they are disappointed when he returns because he has not bought any of the consumables they have longed for. The second son, Dicka, likewise, is a disappointment, buying a massive, empty, fibreglass ice-box, bigger than himself which he carries on his head. The third son Kaibo, however, makes friends with the militants and politicians. Their money flows, as do the women; he spends the night in the Honiara clubs and hotels and returns to the village dressed in military fatigues and dark glasses with a new status as a 'Commander', derived from the high-powered guns he is carrying. He tells the village that he will not spend but defend his inheritance, and will use the guns to protect their property from intruders and migrants.

The first son, John Paul, initially scoffed at by the village, builds a hot-air drier with the oil drums and slowly encourages the community to get the cocoa business running. The second son, Dicka, starts fishing; at first laughed at, he catches a huge fish (the size of a man) which he drags ashore kicking, and inspires the others to come with him to fill the ice box to feed the village. The third son, Kaibo, creates nothing but builds up a cult-like militia, stealing and destroying and extorting money and alcohol. The parody of present life in Solomon Islands is both comic and uncomfortable.

We plough on to the end of the drama to the final scene, which I thought would be so hard to direct, but now it begins to flow naturally and powerfully. Kaibo, drunk with his men, attacks the village store to get their hands on more alcohol. The store keeper, his first-born brother John Paul, and members of the International Peace Monitoring Team confront them, and Kaibo and his men start to shoot. In the ensuing pandemonium his father returns. The father now calls his sons to account for the gifts he has given them, but Kaibo turns his gun on his father shooting the beloved chief in front of all his people. The father crumples reaching out as he does so towards his sons. The first-born son John Paul runs forward to hold his dying father in his arms as his father tells him that he is the one fit to look after the village, and calls upon him to use the gifts of creation for the good of all his people. John Paul now turns towards his youngest brother, suddenly empowered, wise and brave. He rips the gun from his younger brother's hands, telling him that he has created his own hell and ordering him out of the village. Then, as the music changes and the Brothers begin to sing the beautiful *Let all the Islands rise and sing,* John Paul, backed by the whole village, looks up to the sky and calls out in love and gratitude to his father for all the gifts of his inheritance. Lighting a fire, he burns the guns that have murdered his father and caused havoc in the village. And above the mourning villagers the transfigured spirit of the father appears telling his people to listen for his voice and that they will hear him in the wind and waves and see his face in the stars by night and he will never desert them. 'My ways must live in you.' He calls upon the people of Solomon Islands to use the gifts of creation to build up their nation and promises that he will return. John Paul is a beautiful actor; tall, languid, open and now strong, he points the village towards the vision of his father and promises faithfulness and to honour the gifts of his inheritance.

We have booked the Police Club to perform. We practise during the day and by early evening a huge audience is assembling waiting to get in. It is then that we realize that someone has disconnected the electricity. The Police Club has failed to pay the electricity bill. Friends set off in search of portable generators and extension cables. I stand around talking with Brother Francis Tofi outside; he has come to watch. It is now dark and there is a packed hall waiting by candle-light. The Prime Minister and Minister for Peace and Reconciliation arrive and also sit in the darkness. Finally, a power line is connected across the football field to the police station. We hope they have paid their electricity bills there. We pray also that the drama will move some of the huge audience to a new integrity. The Prime Minister is visibly moved and keeps wiping his eyes.

Brother Francis watches with me with great concentration. In this present context it is indeed powerful stuff. He tells me we must play it on the Weather Coast and Keke and his men should see this, as should the Police and Combined Operation who are now are as mistrusted as Keke himself and in fact creating support for Keke by their own acts of violence. Francis tells me he is still not smoking . . . much!

On 3 December we ended the programme for disarmament with a service of thanksgiving at St Barnabas Cathedral. The Prime Minister, the Minister for Peace and Reconciliation, the Governor General, the Commissioner of Police are all there to thank the Brotherhood for the work they have done and all that has been achieved. In terms of weapons returned and a new sense of commitment to justice and law and order, the Brotherhood has indeed done much. I have to say, however, that this is not without cost to them personally or to our Community, for I fear that the more we are called upon by police and government the more we are in danger of becoming entangled.

The Brothers who worked from Bishopsdale on the disarmament programme have returned to other postings. Brother Francis Tofi has been appointed to take over at Bishopsdale. The focus of his new group will no longer be disarmament but peace and reconciliation. He is a good choice to lead this group. We climbed Pentecost mountain together for the Novice's retreat before their admission as Brothers. Again I am struck by his peacefulness and inner strength. Brother Caulton Weris says how much he respects him. He will be assisted by Brother Tony Sirihi. Brother Tony is a steady man too, with a heart of great kindness. I know him so well. When he was a Novice he was always at my house. His own father disappeared when he was a young boy in Makira. He left the house one morning to go and work in their farmland and never returned. They searched and searched but he was never discovered. I have watched Tony grow in confidence and stature. He will be a great support to Francis.

15

He sent them out to proclaim the kingdom of God and to heal.

Luke 9.2

From the diary of December 2002

We have decided to lead the Christmas Mission this year around Guadalcanal including the Weather Coast. We will be visiting the area where the police continue their fight against the militant leader Harold Keke. There are sixty of us, moving from village to village for over five weeks – two nights in some places and three in others. We receive the biggest welcome I can ever remember in all my years in Solomon Islands. It is a bit like being part of an army of liberation after the struggles and tensions these villages have faced. We are the first group to visit them since the conflict began, and what a huge group too! The villages have decorated the roads with flowers hanging from vines. They welcome us with warriors, marching bands and pan-pipers, and lead us in procession to village centres where there are long, elaborate ceremonies with newly erected flagpoles and solemn flag-raising rituals, and then speeches followed by at least 200 metres of hands to shake, so that our hands feel as if they have been sandpapered. Then we are led to the most delicious fruits, set out on bamboo tables in purpose-built dining shelters: bananas, and coconuts and oranges, water melon, masses of delicious pineapple, pawpaw and fresh limes.

In the village of Marasa the welcome party waited for us from 10.00 in the morning until 10.00 at night when our boat finally arrived. As we arrived, there were hundreds of oil lamps burning on the hillside in the dark; I said it was like the faithful virgins in Christ's parable. One mother ladled out cupfuls of the most delicious fruit salad in the dark, more delicious still because we were hungry, dried up and salty after a day at sea, and could not see what we were being handed until we tasted the thick sweet mix of juices.

Each night for most of December we performed in the centre of these villages, under an ever increasingly huge moon. I seek out the best locations for the drama. The group loves it when we act on sand because the running, jumping, chases, twists, turns, fights and falls of these Brothers and Novices become even faster, more frisky and spirited, and the laughter grows as does the speed and tension of the drama. Best of all is to see the drama with the sea and the reef as the backdrop, the *rain trees* and coconuts illuminated by our lights. On some nights the sound seems to travel crystal clear, and it as though the whole island is listening. On other nights there is a battle against the thick air, the waves breaking on the reef and the wind blowing the sound away.

On a mission of this size, where you sleep in leaf huts on mats on the floor, often with as many as twenty in each hut, everything is very communal including toileting in the mangroves, or along the beach. I try my best to find a hidden spot so I don't have to greet my congregation while squatting. You sometimes need to escape. I do this by going for swims in the sea with John Hovell, who is famous in New Zealand as a Maori artist and in Solomon Islands for his ability to float on his back and for writing the most wonderful letters to everyone. I've taken to swimming out to sea with him for ablutions, keeping my distance of course! There's more privacy that way, but at 5 o'clock one morning he told me he was almost washed out to sea. Strange to say I have much enjoyed reading *Portrait of a Lady* which John gave to me to read; it couldn't be further removed from sixty Brothers on mission in Solomon Islands. There again, one of the most popular videos among the Mothers' Union is the copy of *Pride and Prejudice* I brought back from the UK. Problems of marrying-off your daughters and unrequited love are universal and equally, if not more, relevant to village life in the Solomon Islands. Fr John is a wonderful person to have on a mission because he creates a sense of peace and space and yet has such a perceptive artist's eye for every detail and character. He records everything that is going on in both village and Community, and all this will become part of his correspondence. Each day he sits with different Novices helping them to prepare and practise their preaching.

When we perform *The Parable of the Talents* we know that many of those who watch have been directly involved in the ethnic tension. At Mbambanakira some of the audience are members of the Combined Operation against Keke. They claim to be protecting this area, but they are very unpopular in the villages. At the clinic some of the Brothers have met women who claim to have been beaten with metal wires by members of this Combined Operation force. They have come to the clinic for treatment for the sores they have sustained, which have gone septic. The Combined Operation forces carry their SR88s and strings of bullets across their shoulders, as if they are posing. They think we will be impressed by their weapons. To most of us it looks pathetic. They watched *The Parable of the Talents* and in one performance at the end of the drama an old man started shouting at them, 'You see now! Do you understand now? That's what happens. That's what your guns are doing! That's the destruction you are causing! That's *you* in the drama!'

But can a drama really change lives? In the final village in which we were staying, one of the members of Keke's militants, who had been part of everything from the beginning, escaped from them and came to join us. Frightened and ashamed, he followed us, keeping out of sight for fear he would be suspected. When we travelled on to another village by boat, we found he had followed us overland. On the final performance of our parable there was a new actor in the drama. It was this former militant. He had asked the Brothers if he could join them, and of course they accepted him. For him it was a moment of catharsis because as the play reached its conclusion he was among those stripping off the army uniforms and stamping them into the mud and smashing the guns against the rocks. When we left the Weather Coast he came with us.

At Marasa we performed the drama late at night as we had been waiting for the rain to stop. As the drama reached its climax, the rain came again sheeting down but the audience did not run for cover but stayed standing there under the open heavens as the ground rapidly became a river. In the final scene the tropical storm released new energies of freedom and movement. Kaibo, after killing his father, stripped off his military fatigues in the mud and lashing rain and smashed his own gun, begging for forgiveness from his brother on his knees in the slime. Father Lionel Longarata, drenched and standing on ground that was now a pool of water, spoke from his heart to all those present, calling for all violence on the Weather Coast to end. He said that Harold Keke claimed to be a man of God, but if he was a Christian then he and all his followers must end the way of violence.

Five months later the drama we had acted out would be performed in terrible reality. The whole village would witness brutal murder, and this village, which had welcomed us in the night with candles and cups of fruit and Christian love, would be burnt to the ground and Father Lionel would be bound on the beach next to the corpses and for three days awaiting his own execution.

Father Lionel Longarata and I discuss the possibility of a follow-up mission in this area of Guadalcanal. They have been through so much and Father Lionel says this mission has been important to everyone. They have felt abandoned by the Church. We discuss the possibility of the Novices joining him in this district for their Novice practical. They can spend one week in each of the villages over for a total period of three months preaching and teaching. Father Lionel says that he will take care of them, and it will be something that will encourage everyone.

As our boat, the *Ini Kopuria*, passes Kolina, we see two Brothers standing on the shore waving. I remember Charles Fox's story of setting Brothers down in these remote places and letting God do his work through them. I am aware of how cut-off this village is, and of their courage. We are very near to Keke's base here, but we have decided that the mission team will not go ashore. Sixty is too large a group and we do not want to inflame the situation. Neither is the captain or the ship's crew happy about waiting offshore in this area. Keke's men have often commandeered ships for their own purposes. But the captain stops the engines and I go ashore by dinghy. The two I have seen on the beach are Brother Francis Tofi and Brother Ini Paratabatu. Some of the children in the village have seen us landing and come racing towards me excitedly.

Ini Kopuria, founder of the Melanesian Brotherhood.

The Brothers are sent out 'two by two into every town and place'. Brother Stephen and Brother Richard on mission.

Admission of new Brothers.

Pentecost Mountain, the view towards Tabalia from the beach.

Procession around the Melanesian Brotherhood's Headquarters at Tabalia.

Lunch at an English parish church hall in Weaverham.

The members of the religious communities from the Church of the Province of Melanesia bring the story of the Prodigal Son to life in the Guard Room at Lambeth Palace.

'Blessed are the peacemakers, for they shall be called the sons and daughters of God', Ulawa, 2004.

The Melanesian Brotherhood Community, Easter, 2005.

They are hoping all the Brothers and Novices are coming to stay. I wish we were. I know one of these kids, and he is so disappointed when he realizes we are not staying. I would love to give some support to this brave Anglican village, which has faced so much over the last few years but still managed to stand strong and so prevent its own young men joining either side. This, I am told, is because of the former Brothers who live here and have kept the village united. The people believe the prayers the Brothers have made around the village have defended it from attack.

I ask Brother Francis how things are going. He says they have been able to encourage the village. Brother Ini is annoyed that the forces of the Combined Operation have frightened people by firing bullets at night to warn off Keke's men. Ini believes there is no need for this. He also warns against any of the Melanesian Brotherhood travelling by the police patrol boat. It has been misread in the past and people are still suspicious and uneasy about this police presence, even though it is there, supposedly, to contain Keke and his operation rather than attack his position. Ini says that some of the villagers have said they have seen Brothers wearing army uniforms, although the Brothers concerned vigorously deny this. Ini, who is from this area, is adamant that the Brotherhood must not be seen to be involved with the police force. Francis asks me if we have any spare petrol for their boat. They have arranged a meeting between Bishop Charles Koete and Harold Keke; they will go with Bishop Charles. It is an attempt at least to enter into dialogue for peace, and part of the Archbishop's plan to offer help in this process of mediation. We do not have much petrol ourselves, but it is the least I can do to help these Brothers in their difficult work.

Later Bishop Charles Koete travels back with us on the boat to Honiara but tells us that although he had been able to meet with some of Keke's men who had contacted Keke, there had been no meeting with Keke himself. It had, however, been reported to him that Keke welcomed the Church's offer of help in mediation.

16

Rejoice in hope, be patient in suffering, persevere in prayer.

Romans 12.12

From the diary of January and February 2003

I arrived back at Tabalia on 7 January. We had been on mission since 1 December and I felt tired, much thinner and in need of space. I have been appointed chaplain again for another term. As chaplain I have the luxury of a small house. It has no toilet or kitchen or even lights for the first month. But it is cool and it does provide me with a place to put my books and read and meet people and prepare lessons. I paint the whole house blue mist with a lot of Novice helpers, and reclaim two wooden chairs which were mine when I was chaplain before. My next-door neighbours are my old friends Peter and Emily Orudiana. Peter was ordained with me at St Mark's, Tabalia ten years ago. He is our new tutor. What's more, they both think I'm looking a bit thin so they always include me as part of their family when I'm hungry. Peter will prove to be the most wonder-fully supportive friend over the next two years.

A new Police Commissioner called William Morrell has been appointed from the UK. Both he and his wife Mary have a quality of openness and integrity that is like a breath of fresh air. They are Catholics but have also been attending the Anglican church. Bill wants to build relationships of trust with Solomon Islanders. I do not envy his position at all. Everything is so new to him and he is going to have to learn fast. He takes over a deeply divided police force, which has been so compromised that no one trusts anyone else. Many of those he must now work with are resentful of his appointment, and everyone will try to bend his ear. He has pledged to make human rights a top priority and to tackle abuses, beginning with the police force itself. This will mean decommissioning many of the former militants who were taken on as 'Special Constables'. This move has not proved successful and many have abused their power, but trying to weed them out now will be difficult and potentially dangerous. Bill and Mary invite me round for supper with the Assistant Head Brother and two Novices who are struggling to cope with a knife and fork for the first time. Mary is a brilliant cook and I cannot remember English food tasting so delicious. They have already got to know Brother Francis Tofi and the Brothers responsible for peace and reconciliation. They have been so helpful, helping Bill understand the culture into which he is thrown. He has asked Brother Francis if he and another Brother will accompany him on his tour of familiarization; he believes it will help build trust with the local community and disassociate his leadership from the suspicion which surrounds his own police force. I can also see how much he simply wants to be with men of God who will support him in prayer and in kind. He is very much a man of faith who has taken this position in Christian faith. He will need a lot of faith to get through the next months.

Today a Novice came to my house complaining of a very painful hard swelling in his lower stomach. The nurse suspected an acute appendicitis and so we raced the twenty miles along the very bumpy road to Honiara Central Hospital arriving at midnight. The Novice, Fordroy, wanted me to stay; you need an advocate at the hospital these days. They told us the operation would be at 3.00 a.m. and we were shown into a kind of operating overspill room with overflowing garbage containers full of used rubber gloves, syringes, bloody swabs and empty saline bottles. Fordroy lay on his trolley for several hours while I tried to remind nurses that we were still waiting, as they dealt heroically with an overflowing casualty department with its assortment of malaria patients, feverish children and bloodied drunks, with a limited supply of bandages, chloroquine and Panodol. Eventually we were told Fordroy's operation would now be later in the morning as there was no surgeon. In the medical ward Fordroy dozed as I watched a large rat wandering around the ward, probably living on the overspill of garbage containers. The worrying thing was that no one seemed particularly worried to see it, and the rat certainly didn't feel any need to run; it was as if it was enjoying the privilege of a well-fed ward pussycat. Several times in the night I supported Fordroy as we paddled into a flooded toilet with no doors or toilet paper or toilet seat, and then back to his bed washing his hands – with no soap – in a kitchen sink and drying his feet from the journey by rubbing one foot against the other. The hospital is only five years old but the floor tiles have broken loose, the door handles come off in your hand and every surface feels sticky and a bacterial nightmare. The hospital is still so short of medical supplies. The nurse tried to shave Novice Fordroy for the operation with a rusty Bic razor still clogged with someone else's hair. I rushed to get a new one but there was no time. If we delayed any longer he would miss this chance for his operation. We said a prayer on the trolley and Fordroy gave a radiant smile. I was there when he came round from the operation and he gave the same smile. These times feel special, holy, as though you have just witnessed someone's battle with death, and life won, and it was more than a privilege to be there. There is somehow an overwhelming feeling of love; you've seen the meaning of things, and you have seen that life is really astonishingly fragile, beautiful and miraculous, despite seeping toilets and sticky door-handles and filthy pillows. An old man with a horrible looking sore on his leg woke everyone in the ward with a fifteen-minute sermon praising God for the blessing of being in that hospital. He had a point; without it, and the skilled surgeon, our Novice Fordroy would not have made it. Fordroy told me he had a dream in which he heard heaven's angels singing for him. I told him I was glad he'd decided not to join them because he was very much needed on earth.

I have just heard that our tutor, Father Dixon Nakisi, who was diagnosed with cancer, is dead. He had done all he could to fight the cancer. When I visited him in his village in Malaita shortly before his death, we had to wade across the river to reach the place where he was living, and I found him sitting with his wife on the porch of his simple house, so thin and wasted that I knew he was near to death. We talked of things at Tabalia and then I asked him if Christ and his faith had helped him. I asked the question gently for I feared his answer. He had prayed so long and hard for healing – we all had – and he was such a young and good man to be dying in this terrible way, with two young children needing him so much, and his wife having only just given birth. It all seemed very unfair. But his answer showed no doubt whatsoever: 'Christ is the one thing I do have. Christ is everything to me now.'

While in Malaita I travel north with Brother Noel to visit James Ilufanoa's family. I have not seen them since James's funeral in 1999, but they welcome me as if I am a returning son. James's mother who speaks no pidgin communicates in laughter and language and by holding and stroking my hand. James's brother, John Samani, whom I helped get into secondary school, is now the young headmaster of Takwa Community High School with a wife and two children of his own. Within four hours they have killed and cleaned a pig and baked it in a custom oven under banana leaves and hot stones, for a feast to welcome us. They are as warm and generous as ever, and we sit up late at night telling stories with his brothers and his wonderful red-haired sister. Members of the gang of youngsters who used to follow James around emerge with their own wives and children to shake hands. Many of the kids are named James. I have brought a plaque for James's grave.

After two days Noel and I set off back for Auki. It is a long and uncomfortable journey in the open back of a small four-wheel drive Hilux, crammed with other passengers and produce for the market. Brother Noel has become a good friend to me and I feel somehow as though James has had a hand in this and is still looking after his old friend. It feels like a great blessing that we have come. The balance in the back of the truck is precarious. The road is in a terrible and dangerous state of disrepair. The conflict has brought an end to any road projects. In places the road crumbles away to almost nothing and there are huge craters and drops into the river below. I would prefer to get out and walk, especially as we go across high bridges, and at times we have to because the car's wheels are spinning in the mud. But I enjoy sharing this journey with Noel, and we swap places and hand-holds periodically to try to relieve each other's discomfort despite sacrificing our own comfort to do so.

I read *Hope Beyond Despair*.

It contains a charter of hope which seems to me to make a lot of sense and I make notes in my diary with some alterations and additions:

1. Be open to the world both inner and outer. Look and see.
2. Tell it the way it is. Reject deceit and double-talk. Be open about relationships.
3. Be distrustful of endless consumerism, current science and technology that often creates endlessly more choice but little time of quality.
4. Do not live in a compartmentalized world or seek to label yourself or others. Strive for wholeness of life which is an acceptance also of uniqueness.
5. Seek to grow in friendship and new forms of closeness, intimacy and shared purpose.
6. Welcome risk-taking which offers you the opportunity to grow, so that you can be vitally alive as you face change.
7. Care for others with a gentle, subtle, non-moralistic, non-judgemental, non-possessive, compassion and love, trusting in reciprocity and in generous sharing.
8. Feel close and responsive to elemental nature, respecting its power and caring for it.
9. Distrust highly structured, inflexible, bureaucratic institutions where processes have become divorced from purpose or meaning.

10. Trust your own experience and intuition and be receptive to the experiences and intuitions of those you respect and love, while staying free from domination.

11. Be indifferent to material comforts and rewards. Do not set your mind on money or status symbols or ownership.

12. Be a spirited beginner and seeker and find meaning and purpose that is greater than the individual. Experience the unity and harmony of the world.

13. Be present.

14. Seek space and silence within, even when you are with others. Do not feel compelled to speak when you have nothing to say.

15. Seek God in all things and in all people. Follow blessing, not curse. Remember it is life in all its fullness which is what God offers.[36]

Alleluia! Brother Francis and the Peace and Reconciliation team have destroyed all the weapons that the Brotherhood has collected. They went out to sea with the new British Police Commissioner William Morrell and scattered them all overboard far from land in deep water. It seems like a huge liberation from the destructiveness of those weapons. They will never be able to be used again to harm or threaten anybody.

---

36 Brian Thorne, *The Mystical Power of Person Centred Therapy: Hope Beyond Despair*, London, Whurr, 2002.

17

They will betray one another and hate one
another . . . Because of the increase of
lawlessness, the love of many will grow cold.

Matthew 24.10, 12

From the diary of March 2003

Sir Fred Soaki, the retired Police Commissioner has been assassinated in
a hotel in Auki, Malaita. He has been shot by a policeman. Sir Fred was
highly respected, of great integrity and a devout Christian. He has been
helping with the decommissioning of 'Special Constables'. There is
much anger about this decommissioning and perhaps the opposition are
sending a warning to William Morrell. Morrell is continuing with the
decommissioning unperturbed. He seems so exposed. I think of his
house; there is not even a security fence. I have lived in this country for
fifteen years. I have seen how in their e-mails other expatriates can exag-
gerate their fears and the dangers they face, and condemn islanders from
behind their three-metre-high fences, but now I am really concerned for
the Morrells' safety. Both of them have grown very attached to Brother
Francis and the other Brothers who seem to give them confidence. Bill
said 'if only I had police officers I could trust like your Brothers.'

The news of the war against Iraq bombards my senses and its horror
enters into my guts. I can tune into the BBC World Service from 10.00
p.m. to 6.00 a.m. I keep a lonely vigil with the radio, sleeping and waking

in snatches to hear the endless spiral of reports on a war that cannot bring peace. As analysts and experts emerge from every corner seeking carrion like vultures, I feel lonely, bereft and in grief for the things we believe in and have abandoned. How much more those who are directly involved. 'Skin burnt by phosphorous . . . the explosion turned the inside of the house white hot . . . we can only give dressings and antibiotics . . . if they live they will be disfigured for life.' There is a denial of civilian casualties and Iraqi army casualties are considered a sign of success or, still worse, treated as nothing, but each one has a family, perhaps sons and daughters anxiously waiting for them to return, a past, a present, hopes and dreams for the future.

In the Novices' classroom I have written on the blackboard the accepted Christian criteria for a just war based on the teaching of the Roman Catholic Church:

The Just War

The just war is based on the following grave considerations:

1 The damage inflicted by the aggressor on the nation or community of nations must be lasting, grave and certain.
2 All other methods of putting an end to it must have been shown to be impractical and ineffective.
3 There must be serious prospects of success.
4 The arms and weapons used must not produce evils and disorders worse than those to be defended against.
5 Moral law must be maintained during conflict and all civilians, wounded, prisoners, surrendering soldiers and those killed must be treated with dignity and respect and be provided with proper human rights.
6 Human rights abuses such as torture, physical cruelty, rape, murder, genocide and ethnic cleansing are crimes against humanity.
7 The degrading abuse of another human being by violence, fear, or threat is also a sin against God.
8 The use of chemical, biological and atomic weapons, and those

weapons deliberately created to increase pain and suffering (cluster bombs, incendiary devices, landmines used to debilitate and maim) and which target innocent civilians are also crimes against humanity.

9 The production, sale, and use of arms in a nation need to be tightly controlled and regulated. Those who make money from the sale of weapons without proper regulations are guilty of great evil. The wastage of public money on weapons prevents nations working to relieve the problems of the poor.

This list stays on the blackboard as an indictment, for as I wrote it, I realized how my own nation has failed on every count. I wait for the question to come.

'What about the United States of America and the United Kingdom?' asks Novice Kevin.

'What about them?'

'Is their war on Iraq a just war?'

'What do you think?'

I feel so much in support of my eldest brother in England, Tim, and his wife Jenny. On their door is a poster 'Don't Attack Iraq'. Tim knew this was disaster from the very beginning. He has a deep instinct and wisdom to detect what is false. He left the Labour Party because of it. He loved the Labour Party, campaigned right back in the days of Harold Wilson, sat up all through the election night in 1997, celebrating when Labour won again, and filled me with so much hope for the nation that I almost wanted to return from Solomons just to celebrate the end of Thatcherism. All that has changed with this unsanctioned war. It is about so much more than the Labour Party. It is about God and humanity. The Labour leadership have betrayed not only the Labour Party but our national integrity. A country that prided itself on justice and respect for human rights shamefully abandons all. We have become the terrorists. We, the unwilling, are pulled into this spiral. Is it any better that our insurgency is fired from a distance, that these perpetrators do not see the limbs and bodies they dismember? They say there are 100,000 dead and this is only the beginning.

18

I am sending you like sheep into the midst of wolves.

Matthew 10.16

From the diary of March and April 2003

We have just heard that one of our Brothers, Nathaniel Sado, seems to have been taken hostage by Harold Keke and his men. Why? Brother Alfred Tabo and Father Francis, the present priest at Kolina, went with him to deliver a letter to Keke from the Archbishop, Ellison Pogo. It was apparently a follow-up offer for the Church to work at mediation and dialogue in this conflict. They were unable to meet Keke but when Brother Alfred Tabo and Father Francis returned, Brother Nathaniel insisted on staying behind to meet with Keke personally. A week later when he had still not returned, Brother Ini went in search of him. He was told that Brother Nathaniel had been 'arrested' by Keke. Brother Ini saw Brother Nathaniel and was shocked to see that he was tied and looked as though he had been beaten. They would not let Ini go near him.

The Assistant Head Brother Robin Lindsay immediately called a meeting at Bishopsdale to discuss with the Archbishop what should be done. The Archbishop said that somehow Keke's attitude towards the Church seemed to have radically changed, and that he had just received a letter from the group full of false accusations. He said that he would make contact again and request Brother Nathaniel's immediate release.

25 April 2003

On Easter Day we heard news over the radio of Brother Nathaniel Sado's death. This morning I was awoken very early by Brother Alfred Tabo knocking on my door. Alfred had come from our household at Mbambanakira to confirm the radio story. He had made the six-hour journey by canoe with outboard engine to report the news. Apparently one of Keke's men had deserted and fled to Mbambanakira after witnessing Brother Sado's death. Brother Sado had been held in a cage and had been so speared and wounded that he had even asked to die.

A line has been crossed. A Brother, one of those whom people have always believed to be 'workmen blong God' and therefore protected by God, has been murdered. No one believed that anyone would turn against the *Tasiu*. They have always been considered holy men and that to attack them would be taboo, bringing down the wrath of God. These Brothers are seen to have lived a charmed life. They have weaved their way through bullets unscathed. They have been the hope of so many that God and goodness will prevail, and now it is as though the myth has been challenged. Keke has confronted their spiritual *mana*. Brothers are as mortal as anyone else. Yet because of the power of this belief, the temptation is to blame Brother Nathaniel himself or the Community, rather than Keke and his men. In other words, Brother Nathaniel has somehow forfeited divine protection, and this is therefore God's punishment rather than the work of evil. I have always had a deep aversion to such a theology. What kind of God would call us and then abandon us to torture and death if we fail? No, this is pure evil.

I have never wanted to belong to a magic Brotherhood buoyed up by superstition but to one that celebrates that the Word became flesh, real flesh. And yet the reality of that is that there is no miraculous divine protection, there is a young man bleeding to death in the misery and rain of the Weather Coast seemingly abandoned by everyone. This young man has died not only far from home but far from his Brothers. Not only have they taken his life, they have also tried to destroy his memory and calling. His only failing was his innocence. The witness told us that even when he was dying he sang a hymn 'Jesus you holdim hand blong me'.

The witness reports that they had forced a confession from Brother Nathaniel, accusing him of being a spy for the Prime Minister, Sir Alan Kemakeza, who is from Savo, the same island that Brother Nathaniel came from. They say he was carrying a passbook proving he had received money from Kemakeza, and that he admitted his guilt. All this, our witness said, was invented by Keke. Keke has a secretary who keeps a meticulous record of facts dictated by Keke, and Keke invents the plot as though he is writing his own history. The secretary is an ex-student from a Church school, a frequent visitor to Tabalia. I know him and had always thought him a thoughtful young man, so earnest I had thought he would join the Brotherhood. This is how life choices are made: he could have been a Brother working for peace or the apprentice of a psychopath. Somehow he was sucked into becoming the latter, and now he is indoc-trinated by fear. Keke's supporters believe that the record he is making is proof that this is a war of liberation. And yet they are making up the facts and the rules as they go along. In this cause everything, including the cold-blooded murder of prisoners and any suspect, is justified. The story is that Keke holds confession meetings. Anyone who is not for him is against him. Any follower expressing doubt must die, and he orders each of his men to carry out the executions as a sign of their loyalty, so that they are all bloodied and implicated.

Keke and his followers are challenging spiritual authority, claiming that they stand over others as judge and executioner. There was a trust that Brother Nathaniel would not be harmed. When Keke was sick he called members of our Community to pray for him. He had seemed to honour and respect the impartiality of the *Tasiu* and even requested that Brother Nathaniel Sado visit him. Only last year Brother Nathaniel helped Keke's brother, Joseph Sangu, with the disarmament of Gela and Savo. But there is no trust, no loyalty; they say Keke has killed his own relations; fear, paranoia and evil are growing on this Weather Coast. Keke no longer trusts his own brother. In the darkness of his cult he is suspicious of everyone, and everyone is his potential betrayer.

The Community has failed to help Nathaniel in the way we have helped others. Because no one was quite sure of why Nathaniel was there, or why he wanted to stay, because Nathaniel was one of those people who always seemed to be doing his own thing, and no one ever really knew quite where he was going or what he was doing, we simply did not do enough for him – at least that is how we all feel now. Our Assistant Head Brother Robin must feel this more than anyone, for as the leader in this region he was responsible for Brother Nathaniel, and was planning to visit the Weather Coast to try to secure his release. It is now too late for that.

30 April 2003

My last vivid recollection of Brother Robin Lindsay is at the Maundy Thursday Eucharist at Tabalia. The Governor General, the Revd Sir John Ini Lapli, was celebrating, and washed his feet. Brother Robin took the water and together with me we washed the feet of the Brothers and Novices. On Easter Day we heard the rumours of Nathaniel Sado's death. On the following Wednesday Brother Robin left Honiara with the other five Brothers for the Weather Coast. On the Saturday night I woke in the middle of the night with a vivid nightmare in which I heard Brother Robin crying. It was not an ordinary cry but a terrible sobbing that shook everything, and so strange because Robin was the last person in the world you would ever expect to cry. If you asked me now what the cry meant, I would say that it was the cry of someone who had come face to face with evil. It was the cry of someone confronting sin and being shaken by it. It was a cry for the loss of innocence. It was a cry that seemed to expose the sins of the world including my own.

On Monday I am called urgently to the church warehouse as there is a message on the radio for the Brotherhood. The radio message requests that the Head Brother go immediately to the central police station. We go together. The news is from the police position nearest to Keke's camp on the Weather Coast. The police there wish to report that they saw our Brothers arrive at Mbiti village the previous Thursday, 24 April. They left their belongings in the canoe and walked along the beach towards Keke's camp. The police had watched them through binoculars and had seen Keke's men, carrying guns, surround them. They had not been seen again since Thursday. They believed they were now being held hostage against their wishes.

Everything stops. Everything is changed. I cannot believe they have gone directly to Keke's camp. It had not even entered my head that they would do this except in that dream. Brother Robin Lindsay had been expected back for the celebration of the Feast of St Mark. I had thought they intended to visit our Weather Coast households, Kolina and Mbambanakira, where our Brothers are stationed. Surely they have not gone directly to the killer himself in search of their Brother? History will date from this point. 'Has anyone been back for their bags or their clothes?' I ask.

Silence. I keep on hoping that somehow they have got it wrong.

'How many Brothers?'

'Six . . . It is hard for anything to happen to the *Tasiu*.' We all believe this. Surely they would not do anything to harm these Brothers. But I am filled with dread. They went in trust, unarmed, with no other motive than the desire to find what had happened to their Brother and for peace. Has Keke turned on the Brotherhood now? I think of the twelve Novices who are doing three months of practical training and ministry on the Weather Coast of Guadalcanal. They will be in potential danger too. I make arrangements with the police that the Novices must be immediately pulled out of Kolina and transported round the coast to Father Lionel Longarata at Marasa. The next day they contact me to say they have done this. Brother Alfred Tabo, who is in charge of the household there, says the area is safe and that the Brothers at the Household, together with Father Lionel Longarata, will take care of them. I am much relieved.

But back at Tabalia the Head Brother Harry Gereniu has announced the news we heard on the radio that our Brothers have been taken hostage. This is later confirmed by a letter Keke has written to the Police Commissioner, William Morrell. Keke calls the Brothers 'prisoners of war' and warns that they will be killed if anyone tries to advance upon his position. At Tabalia all the Brothers meet in the chapel. Many want to go to the Weather Coast straight away and search for these six Brothers. Painful accusations are made by one of the Brothers that this is the fault of the Brotherhood leaders, but I do not think anyone knew they were going to Keke's camp. This was a decision that they seem to have made for themselves with the Assistant Head Brother Robin Lindsay, who went with them. The Head Brother Harry Gereniu seems more shocked than anybody. I myself had seen Brother Francis Tofi after I had heard news of the suspected murder of Brother Nathaniel. I had said to him 'Francis, do not go anywhere near Keke at this time. If he has killed Nathaniel Sado he will be more paranoid than ever and he will see you as the enemy.' But now it suddenly begins to dawn on me like a revelation. Of course they would go. That is the kind of men they are; they would go right to the heart of the darkness if that is where they believed they must bring light. They had gone to look for Keke in the very same way that Joseph Atkin had gone to look for Bishop Patteson 150 years before . . . 'Joseph Atkin reaching the *Southern Cross* immediately requested "I am going back for the Bishop, who will come with me?" Then Joe Wate stepped up and said "Inau" (I).' It was the same choice to face danger, the same faith, and the reality leaves you speechless. Brother Alfred Hill had used those same words; he was not even part of the peacemaking team but based at Chester Resthouse, looking after guests, and checking blood slides for malaria. Hearing that they needed one more to join them, he had said, 'I'll go.' Alfred looks so young. I remember seeing him smoking, and not wanting to see a young Brother with a cigarette in his mouth, I had said, 'I'll give up if you do.' I had prayed for him and he for me, blessed him with holy oil. These memories come back to you after they are gone, go round and round in your mind: Alfred sitting there on the floor, blessing his forehead with oil, the sign of the cross, like a sign of parting. The group of six had apparently met together at Bishopsdale and prayed together before they left. Brother Francis had spoken with the Archbishop.

Many of our Brothers want to go in search of them, they are talking of twenty-four more Brothers going, but there must be some restraint. It would be madness to send anyone else before we know what has happened. If Keke, in his paranoid fear of betrayal and suspicion, had turned on the Brotherhood, as he had turned on some of his own family and supporters, then our unarmed Brothers would be going like lambs to the wolves. I voice this concern, but in this context it seems almost like a failure of faith and courage and I keep thinking that Brother Francis, Robin, all of them may be suffering. We decide to consult the Archbishop. I speak to the Archbishop first and tell him my fear that many more Brothers will be prepared to go and risk their lives in search of these six, and I fear we will be putting more lives in danger. The Archbishop says he will listen to the voice of the Community. I say that they are young, faithful, and idealistic and they do not fear death, but that I believe we have the responsibility to protect their lives even from their own self-offering. 'We know that they can bleed and be tortured and die just like anybody else, and I do not believe we should risk the life of even one more Brother.' Again he says he will listen to the voice of the whole Community. He does this because I know he trusts their faith and God working through them. He has seen all their work throughout the conflict and he respects their Community decisions. As for me, I long that we may bring our Brothers home but I know *reason* is also of God and must balance and inform all faith. Do I feel I should go and search for them myself? Yes, of course it is in my mind. But I do not go, perhaps through fear, which is very real, perhaps also because I do not think it will achieve anything. God does not ask at this moment for another martyr or another hero, or anyone more to arrive unannounced to inflame Keke's fears. What I believe is asked of me is that I should be present with the Community. Not the hero I would like to be but what God knows I am.

Many months later we were to learn that at this time our Brothers were already dead, and that if we had sent more Brothers at this stage they would undoubtedly have been killed too. Nevertheless, these thoughts still haunt me and are deeply painful to remember, for we longed that we might save them.

When the Archbishop meets with the Brotherhood he calls upon us all, before making any further decisions, to spend time in vigil and prayer seeking the guidance of God. All the time we pray. The rain falls constantly. And in our hearts and minds we have the fear that our Brothers may be suffering.

19

Stay awake and pray that you will not come into the time of trial.

Matthew 26.41

From the diary of May and June 2003

'What happens if we just go on praying and praying that they are alive and will return only to find that our prayers are not answered?' I ask our senior Brother Caulton Weris. 'Won't this destroy the faith of the Community?' 'That is part of our faith too', says Brother Caulton. And so I organize a constant vigil in St Mark's Chapel. Night after night I put out a list, and for over three months members of the Community volunteer their names, wake up, and join the vigil through the night. When I spoke to Brother Caulton, it felt as if we were putting God to the test, but in practice it is not like that at all. It feels as if we are watching and waiting with them through the darkness. I know it is right that we must be present with them and never for a moment forget what they may be going through and suffering. And I sense that not only are we with them but they are also with us. It is like being at the hospital bedside of someone you love. You cannot change what will be, but you can be with them night and day. It is Eastertide and each night we are there held together by our prayer.

10 May 2.00 a.m.

Grounded by tragedy. But Easter is here and underneath our altar the Easter candle shines on the white pebbles of the empty tomb and the clover hill laced with white frangipanis in the Easter garden we have built. It is here, kneeling in the dark, watching the fragile flickering candle, that I wait out the tragedy of Brother Nathaniel's death and long for our six Brothers to return. Self-sacrifice in history seems clearer and untangled, but here in my subconscious it is painful, confusing and filled with fear. And the blame starts, and the regret and the constant re-run of events, the goodness of these Brothers and the sickening powerlessness of knowing they may be suffering and there is no one to help. All pride and confidence have burst and we are on our knees, touching the earth again, humbled and in the hands of God alone. And mingled with all the sorrow and longing, there is the knowledge that here truth is to be found. The pace slows, the tiredness of this wait comes, and each small daily duty becomes more difficult to perform. I see the Brothers and Novices faithfully praying through the darkness, silent and still, and I take courage from this presence. Somehow in the midst of this confusion we are centred again; we have one heart and one mind, the heart and mind of longing and hoping for our Brothers, and none of our lives makes sense unless we hold to Christ. And so it is like living the Passion of Christ. There is only God now and I thirst for him, longing for the time when I can sit in the mouth of this tomb, where my six Brothers have led me, and know the resurrection. The whole of our Community is waiting here outside the tomb, pivoting between fear and hope, warring mosquitoes soaring round my ears, joints aching, desiring to go, desiring to stay, longing to pray deeper, harder, more powerfully, and the desire in all of me for these prayers to be answered: that the whine of the outboard motor in the night will be their homecoming, that the engine in the distance is a truck bringing news, that they have been there into the world of the dead and converted that world too. I imagine them singing the offices into the darkness of the night. If anything can awaken the hearts of Keke and his men it is the love and faith of these Brothers. But can the lamb really lead the wolf home?

Tuesday 10 June 2003

We have prayed for their safety but evil is escalating. I return from a few days at our household in Gela with my youngest brother Daniel, who has come to visit from England, and the station of Tabalia is ominously quiet. I am told that the police checkpoint has retreated and Keke's men have advanced to Mbambanakira and beyond to Marasa. Two more of our Brothers and five Novices have been taken hostage. I am gutted. I don't want to hear this. Let me wake up and hear it is not true. Have all our prayers and intimations of hope been simply mocking us? Why was God silent? Why in my prayers did there seem to be no warning of this? The fear and the dread attack deep in the pit of the stomach. If anything happens to those Novices I will never be able to forgive myself. But everybody had said the Household at Mbambanakira and Marasa district were safe. Why listen to God when we seem to have been deceiving ourselves? This evil is hard, cold and brutal. Its weapons are real guns which really kill, and our God is a mirage. I want others to realize there is absolutely no one who can help us. The police force are worse than useless, any contact with them will be at the risk of being accused of complicity. No one is venturing out of Honiara. Not one priest or bishop has visited Tabalia since the news of the Brothers being taken hostage was received. The whole community is completely vulnerable.

I tell Daniel what has happened, and for the rest of the day I cannot speak. I find him praying in my room, kneeling beside the bed. And now I am irrationally terrified something will happen to him. Or is this fear so irrational? Every day the news is worse. Keke's men are now in Marasa. Twenty-two members of our Community are now believed to be held by Keke. We have no idea if some of them are alive or dead. I watch my young brother like a hawk when he goes outside the house in the night, and follow him to the outside toilet just to see he is safe. Foolish, for I am equally unarmed, but how could I ever explain if he were taken hostage without me? Now it seems our Community is being directly targeted. So what is to stop anyone of us out here at Tabalia being taken? Keke's gunmen have been seen at the school less than a mile from us. Of course I can't mention this; it would be seen as a failure of faith and courage. But what have our prayers achieved except a certain peaceful passivity? And when do you take the decision to say 'Look, this is turning into a children's crusade, let's abandon all that we believe and get the rest of the Community to safety'? But the Brotherhood will never countenance that, and their faith is what for the last five years has given hope to this nation and me.

At 2.00 a.m. I wake up. It is dark, and I don't want to turn on any lights in case that will disturb all that I fear. I am going over to the chapel, as I do every night. Daniel wakes. He wants to come too. Silently we slip out of the house through the hedge and across the deserted grass, past the Community graveyard, then down the footpath by the side of the square. Bare feet on wet grass and then sharp coral, I know this way even in the pitch black. I have followed this same way at least five times a day for more than ten years. And yet still, as I approach the chapel, there is an anticipation, each sense heightened, as though a meeting is about to take place which is more than anything else in my life. Fear, but it is not like the fear of darkness: holy fear, an awe of something greater and beyond anything. It cannot be seen or quantified but it is longed for. At times it seems like nothing, a yawning emptiness, and yet it is everything. It is our hope. It is everything we are waiting for. Often I will leave this chapel feeling I have just missed what I came for, or the futility of my faith is mocking me, and yet I will long to come again and be, be more deeply. It is all we have to defeat the darkness. There is a candle burning at the front; Novice Jack Alec and Novice Ishmael are there praying, solid, silent and so still, as they always are, as they have been since the beginning, for they share this hour of vigil when everyone else is sleeping.

> I feel your presence in the night
> The fragrance of God and man
> I breathe in the stillness
> And in the middle of night
> Both flesh and spirit live
> Live deeply
> Live to the brim
> Reach across time and space
> And touch eternity

And I long for all to be drawn and held together by this invisible God
Whose love burns in the darkness with the life of the Son
And whose blessing touches us as softly as the rustle of the night wind
and rain in the trees.
How strange that when we are most abandoned we are drawn into this
passion
How miraculously you wait for us just beyond our fear

Lord Jesus Christ, Son of God, have mercy on us.

20

Even when I cry out 'Violence!' I am not answered; I call aloud but there is no justice.

Job 19.7

From the diary of June 2003

It is the Queen's birthday and I have been invited to the Governor General's Residence with the Head Brother Harry Gereniu and my brother Daniel for drinks. Everyone is there: the Prime Minister and members of Cabinet, the High Commissioners and important Honiara expatriates and the leaders of the different churches. They all know about our Brothers being held hostage and talk to me with a look of detached sympathy. I feel like a man on a mission, and that I must advocate for my Brothers at every opportunity; that is why I have decided to go. Yet, as long as Honiara is not threatened, it appears to me that the suffering of our Community seems peripheral to their concerns and drinks. And of what good is telling these Brothers' story? Their courage? It makes them all uncomfortable. For these are the Brothers who have risked their lives to bring peace, who have offered hope even when all other protection, police and security could no longer be trusted. These politicians were the ones who begged them to come to keep watch over their houses and families at night during the conflict. I have this dreadful realization that now they are no longer useful, they have become more of a liability, exposing rather than redeeming the failure of this government. The good-luck charm has become unlucky. And, as for the expatriates, I have the intuition that the Brothers' years of courage appears like reck-lessness, a religious dementia of which they now believe they had good

137

reason to be suspicious. The Prime Minister seems uneasy when he meets me and asks me about what has happened to the Brothers, but it strikes me he must already know far more than I do. The Governor General himself is different: Fr Ini Lapli is a man of genuine humility and Christian concern. He is a real priest and looks more at home at Tabalia in a white alb with the Brothers than he does when surrounded by these Honiara big men. At the end of the garden party he invites the Head Brother, Daniel and me to stay behind after the important people have gone. He has always feared that the government that called upon the Brotherhood to help in the peacemaking would be seen to compromise the Community's integrity. He said he had tried to warn Brother Robin Lindsay. But it was perhaps impossible to warn someone about deception in whom there was no deceit or no guile and who always trusted and went straight, too straight for his own safety.

Our Church of Melanesia is holding a Mission Conference in the Quality Motel, Honiara. I cannot believe that, in the light of events which are unfolding, life continues seemingly oblivious. It's as though reality is too painful to mention, so they talk about methods of evangelism and church growth and enlivening public worship, while the wider Church seems only concerned with the condemnation of the loving relationships of gay bishops, as if that is the world's major evil. Meanwhile, news is filtering through that Marasa has been attacked and burnt to the ground, and two young people publicly executed by the militants, government money forced down their throats with a stick. One of our priests, Lionel Longarata, is being held and the militants are threatening to execute him, and our Brothers and Novices who are also held captive. The news breaking is told in hushed whispers in the conference, as though to articulate it is somehow to be involved and to acquiesce, better to feign ignorance. Today it was not even mentioned in the prayers, as if somehow a prayer would compound the failure of our faith, the failure of God, the failure of any of us at this Church conference even to face these events. To me it is like playing the violin as the Titanic sinks.

Frank, a Christian carpenter from Australia, seems to nail the truth of things. 'People like Keke can only be stopped by a greater and superior force and power. What is needed here is an outside military intervention, nothing else can stop brutal bullies like him.' I, who have always been against military intervention, now long for it. It is all right to criticize Western 'imperialist' armed forces from the comfort of a sitting room, but not when your own Brothers are being threatened by a psychopath. I wander about in total distraction unable to focus on anything else. I seem to be walking in powerless circles sucking at cigarettes for comfort, while everyone else at the conference seems to be carrying on as normal, queuing around the buffet table, laughing together in groups while eating beef in oyster sauce and crunching on chicken wings.

I phone Bill Morrell, the Police Commissioner. I tell him that news is filtering through that Keke's men have murdered two boys and that Father Lionel Longarata, the priest at Marasa, is being held hostage and that they are demanding a payment of financial compensation or ransom for his release. Has he heard any more news? Bill says he is not feeling good about the situation himself. He tells me that his attempts to send Royal Solomon Island Police Force reinforcements have failed. Keke's men had been waiting on the beach and fired on the boat while it was attempting to land in the rough surf of the Weather Coast beach near Marasa. They must have intercepted the news. They were waiting to attack them. The police apparently abandoned the boat, jumping into the water as they were shot at and Bill fears that all may be dead.

'What about outside help? What about Australia? Can't you ask for special forces?'

'I am trying for that, of course.'

I feel totally powerless. *Me*, the one who thought I could fix things and help and cook and get medicines and persuade and teach and create chances and opportunity and advocate for the Community – but now I just don't know what to do apart from somehow wait this out and be there and hope and pray. Daniel my brother is leaving Solomon Islands for

England. I sit with him in silence at the airport, unable even to tell this latest development of news just before he leaves. The Governor General's wife, Lady Lapli, sees us and waves and comes over and sits on the grass. She has bare feet, and I realize she has come to the airport not on an official duty but specially for us. Daniel has been such a support. At least he is returning safe. I have agonized over something happening to him. Being here is my choice, but he is here because of me. I should be protecting him. Yet he has been so present for me and delighted in every-thing good, despite all that is happening. He does not try to advise me or say anything meaningless like 'Be careful' and I admire him so much, for he knows how bad things are and I know how much he cares. At my most desolate he said to me 'No one could ever doubt how much you love this Community and care for your Brothers.'

'How did they kill Nathaniel Sado?' Father Thomas Rowland asks. He has just arrived for the conference from Vanuatu. 'They put him in a cage and speared, tortured and beat him to death. He died from his wounds over three days.' Thomas starts to cry uncontrollably. I do not think he fully understood before. Last week Thomas came to Tabalia to visit me. He talked non-stop, as always, while reclining on the mat on my floor, his toes pointing at the sky. I thought his constant amusing chatter and endlessly good nature and supply of cigarettes would push back the darkness. It did for a while, but this is too big. I cannot concentrate on what he is saying. I did not tell him much, I couldn't. I just need him to rattle on, to talk about other things, keep up all our spirits with his betel nut and eccentricities and endless and amusing knowledge of church gossip and ecclesiastical haberdashery, but then when he went to buy his betel nut I could hear him talking loudly and innocently in the market about the militants and the hostages. I want to tell him to stop. We never do that now. It's dangerous. I trust no one outside our Community. They call the spies 'spears' and news of anything people say travels back to Keke fast. See the same paranoia is infecting me! It's infecting us all. I have no idea what Keke hears or how many of these villagers and men hanging around the small market outside my house support his cause, perhaps none of them. Some of these men I haven't seen before. One of them is carrying a bundle that could be a gun. I call Thomas back to the house tell him it's better not to talk about Keke. Are they enemies of our Community or supporters? I no longer have any idea. Thomas asked me why I locked the door at night; he said he never did this in Vanuatu. I never did it either, but now I am sleeping with a cross in my hand, waking at every moment, thinking of those Brothers and Novices on the Weather Coast, rewinding memories, listening.

Back at the Mission Conference unable to contain the story any more, I arrange to meet the Mission Conference facilitator, Fuzz Kitto, in his hotel room. He seems to be the only person with an objective ear who will listen. I tell him the story and it sounds like pure fiction, the stuff of a horror movie, not a reality from which we cannot escape. Are our prayers and our religion pacifying us into a pathetic acquiescence to any kind of horror? Why, I ask Fuzz, have our prayers deceived us? It is one thing to accept that God has not made a magical, miraculous intervention, but surely in all our prayers he could have at least awakened me to the danger of what was coming. Or why bother to pray at all, night after night? For two months our prayers have flown through the night. Have our feelings of well-being and peace been simply self-delusion? Has my reason deserted me? I really had believed our Novices would be all right there. I had arranged for them to be transported to Mbambanakira for their safety and I, the cautious one, had felt at peace when I knew they were there with Father Lionel. Only a few months before, I had been at Marasa myself with a whole mission team. Now every one who assured me of their safety has vanished, and I am endlessly condemning myself for my failure to protect them from these horrors. Fuzz listens to my story and holds out a thin lifeline for me. 'Have you ever thought that God did not warn you because he wants them there?' This had never entered my head. What God could knowingly subject his sons to this? Are our prayers simply excusing our failure to confront? And yet I cling to this hope.

21

My soul is full of troubles; my life draws near to the land of death.

Psalm 88.3 (Common Worship Psalter)

From the diary of June and July 2003

Friday 20 June

We heard today that Father Lionel Longarata has been released after being held captive on the beach for two days. Some of the Novices and Brothers who were held with him were also released, but Keke is still holding seven of them in addition to the original six. Brother David Gano went back by canoe and outboard for them. What guts this humble Brother from Ysabel has. He volunteered to go to Marasa to pick up the Novices and Brothers by canoe, fully aware of the danger. He was taken captive when Marasa was attacked. He witnessed the horrific murders there. For three days he was threatened with death while tied up on the beach, huddling together with the other hostages through the night to keep warm. They told him they had not seen him before and that he must be a spy and that he would be killed in the same way as he had seen the other two young men die. And when he is released, he comes all the way home to Tabalia, which takes six hours in rough seas, takes another canoe and heads straight back once again to the Weather Coast to pick up Father Lionel and the other Novices and Brothers who have been left behind. His courage goes unnoticed. He's so traumatized by what he has seen that he disappears back to his home village for several weeks. Months later he will tell of how deeply he was affected by what he witnessed, of his sleep constantly disturbed by fear and the nightmare that they are coming to get him. Yet he still went back! A year later this same young man who has served the Brotherhood for ten years in every remote place in the same selflessly sacrificial way, applies to train as a priest and is turned down by Bishop Patteson Theological College Board of Governors despite all my letters of recommendation. They have turned down a saint.

We make our way to a village north of Honiara where Father Lionel is now staying with his daughter. It is like arriving for a funeral. He looks broken, ten years older than six months ago when I stayed with him and in the rain we acted our now prophetic drama, of how guns and violence will destroy all that is good. He hugs us awkwardly. Lionel's eyes contain all the trauma, and his terrible experience at the hands of the militants cannot be held back. His whole body is telling it. And as he tells it we live it too and are infected by it. He was tied up and led down to the sea. The whole village was assembled, mothers, children, everyone. Then the militants began their brutal humiliation of two men they said were collaborators. They forced them to dance in front of their captive audience, while they beat them with pieces of timber, smashed their teeth with stones. Covered in blood, in terror and panic, pleading for mercy, they danced for their lives, while their torturers forced the village to applaud. One of the victims was only sixteen years old, still at Mbambanakira Community High School. After six hours of humiliation their backs were slashed open with bush knives. For three days Father Lionel was tied up next to their two dead bodies by the sea. Each day he and the Brothers and Novices were threatened that they too would die in a similar way. Keke, they were told, would decide their fate. Father Lionel said he was prepared for death, but on the third day news reached them that Keke had sent word that 'God says you will live'. Keke was God. Those who witnessed these events will never forget them. Months later they will still be reliving these scenes which will haunt them for ever. It is a great enough horror to kill in an outburst of anger and aggression, but to make the fear, pain and torture of a human being into a spectacle of entertainment, a sadistic ritual, defies all understanding. And some of the same boys involved three months before had perhaps received Holy Communion from my hands and helped carry my bags as we toured from village to village with a message of Christ's peace. Similar acts of barbarity are happening throughout the world, and are not video screens full of them, perhaps copied from them? And what about Srebrenica, Abu Ghraib, Al-Amarah in Basra, Guantanamo Bay? Here too prisoners are beaten, die under torture, and are even photographed as entertainment.

We leave Father Lionel in silence, shaken and sickened by all that he has related. We return to Tabalia where, unable to sleep, I crouch in the dark, my senses alive and amplifying every movement outside, every gust of wind, creak of timber, sound of distant voices, and I rewind and rewind the story I have heard. I am paralysed with dread. If any of those Novices die, as my friend John Hovell wrote in one of his many letters, 'It will be a sin against the Holy Spirit.' There can never be forgiveness.

I know some members of the Community are blaming me that five of our Novices are held hostage. They should never have gone there. It is easier to be wise after the event. I do not care any more about the blame, but I want them back more than anything I have ever wanted in my life. Novice Benjamin, who led with such spirit and faithfulness – if anything should happen to him . . . if anything should happen to any of them . . . The fear is a relentless spiral.

Our Canadian Brother John Blyth is back from the Philippines. He has attended our Brotherhood Council chaired by the Archbishop. We go through the motions of the meeting but all our thoughts are elsewhere. The Archbishop says that he believes the Brothers will be released by October. No one responds. I sit in the meditation chapel at Tabalia. The wind is playing gentle tunes on the black Japanese chimes. It is good to have Brother John Blyth here. I know he understands. He's just come in, and I know he wants to encourage us all and give us faith. I know he wants to support me, but I know him well and beneath his gentle holy words of prayer and consolation I can sense he shares the desolation. He sits erect and praying against the post of the chapel, his long white legs stretched out before him. We talk a little. He too is very close to Brother Francis, and yet we skirt the issues because the pain of this wait has become too much even to talk about. Silence is easier, just the chimes and the gentle wind and our prayers floating over the surface of our fears . . .

Please do not put out the light
For having walked in it I dread the darkness
Do not block the spring of water for having drunk deeply
I am racked by thirst
Do not take away your spirit which held me
Or the house you filled with your peace is empty forever.
It was you who made me
You who have shown me eternity.
Do not abandon me to despair.

I believe that Christ is incarnate
His love made manifest
I see Christ in my brother
In action, in presence.
In the interplay of love
Not in an imaginary never never land
But here and now
In this world not the next.

And fear kills the incarnate one
And we run from our wounded God knowing nowhere else to go.

I have loved deeply
Given my life for it
Valued little else
But if you tear this away too
What else is left?
Apart from this silent shouting pain
Which I must bury too.

22

Blessed are you when people revile you and persecute you and utter all kinds of evil against you falsely . . .

Matthew 5.11

From the diary of August 2003

2 August

It is the second time I have waited on the beach by the Yacht Club in Honiara. I received news earlier in the afternoon that Keke is freeing the hostages and that the Japanese businessman Y Sato, who has negotiated their release, will bring them today in his motor boat. Three weeks ago we waited, and the first four Novices were returned. I had taken them back to our Resthouse and cooked for them. Brother John Blyth couldn't understand why I was cooking, but to me it seemed the best way of trying to re-establish normality and a sense of care. The Novices were paranoid, fearing to say anything lest they endanger the lives of the other hostages. Keke and his men had indoctrinated them with fear, so that they no longer knew to whom they owed allegiance or what was right or wrong. But Brother Andrew was different; he had refused to be intimidated, refused to beat up his fellow Novices when ordered to by Keke's men, refused to dance on demand or take part in their own humiliation. He had therefore suffered most and his body was covered in bruises from the beatings and rifle buttings. On arrival he talked non-stop through the night, pouring everything out in the adrenalin rush of his freedom. Again and again he told me how he had refused to believe the lies of his captors when they told him his Brothers were spies. What courage! When you live in fear for your life day after day, it's so easy to let them twist your thinking. Yet somehow Andrew had moved to a place beyond fear where he could express the truth without fear of its consequences.

Two Brothers and one Novice from their group were still being held by Keke. 'But what about the original six who went in search of Brother Nathaniel?' I ask him. 'Have you seen or heard from them?' Silence. 'Did you hear anything about them?' Andrew was reserved on the subject. He said that he thought they were being held in another camp and that sometimes Keke's men would come and say things like, '"Francis passes his good night to you" . . . but we never saw them.' Andrew never sounded convinced. After his initial euphoria he too plummeted into troubled silence and a deep anger towards those who had beaten him. I took him to the doctor to have his body checked for any internal damage or bleeding. We made the doctor promise to say nothing, for fear it would get into the media and endanger the lives of the other hostages. Keke had warned them if any bad report was leaked those still held would die. Andrew and the others who had been released wanted to get out of Guadalcanal. I arranged for them to go to Gela and bought towels and new clothes and Bibles for them and a soccer ball, anything to take their minds away from the horror they were still living.

And now we wait again. The expatriates are drinking at the club and some of the world's media, who are gathering in Honiara for the Australian-led intervention, come across to the beach to see what is happening. The white Yacht Club Commodore comes across too to complain that he has not been informed of any event taking place on this bit of beach, and to demand we end this disturbance. He has no idea. We totally ignore him. Ever since I received the phone call I have been hoping, praying. Let it be all of them. Let *all* the hostages be released. Let the six led by Brother Robin and Brother Francis, let them be in the boat too. Y Sato's daughter-in-law is on the beach, and his wife sitting in their four-wheel drive. I thank her on the Brotherhood's behalf for her husband's courage. A two-way radio crackles into life. The boat has now come into radio contact and Y Sato's son is speaking to him. I am unable to keep silent now. 'Ask them . . . ask them how many hostages have been released, how many Brothers and Novices are in the boat?' A dialogue takes place. It is not clear what is being said but I hear the number three, and wish I had not heard and that somehow the number will multiply before the boat reaches shore. Y Sato's son tells me he does not know how many hostages are on board but I know the truth now. The original six have not returned.

The boat arrives and instantly the two Brothers and one Novice are surrounded by photographers. They look bewildered. The boat is towed out of the sea on its trailer. Still the Brothers and Novice sit there unsure of what is happening, as the media frenzy engulfs them and they are barraged by reporters demanding interviews. They stand in line for the photos looking sheepish and disorientated. I want them to know how much we have longed for this moment, how thankful we are that they have returned, and yet if only, if only the others had been with them. I try to disguise the disappointment that more have not been released. I manage to get close to them and protect them from this media intimidation, and I tell them we want to get them back to Chester Resthouse away from all of this. Back at Chester I cook for them while Brother Alfred Tabo, his eyes as bright as stars, wants to tell me everything. He tells me of how at one point he had decided he had had enough. 'Kill me now!' he had told them, 'but remember God will judge your soul and mine.' He does not want to be alone. We try to sleep on the floor of the office. Alfred is unable to sleep.

Novice Benjamin, who had led the group of Novices, is similarly restless and unable to settle. Who would not be euphoric and speeding after weeks of believing that at any moment he may die? Benjamin talks disconnectedly, mumbling away at speed. I cannot follow what he is saying. He has always been close to me and now I am feeling as though he may blame me for all he has suffered. I feel as though he trusted me, as all those Novices did, and yet I was unable to save them from Keke and his men. This is my own projection. Later, as we cross the sea together on the church ship to Gela, to join the rest of the group and to get away from Guadalcanal and all those crowding and pressing him for his story, I apologize once more for not seeing the danger and getting them out. We are sitting on the top bunk of the cabin. Benjamin suddenly says to me, 'Chaplain, I don't want you to feel guilty. It was not your will that we were there, it was God's will.' And his words are healing, and I remember Fuzz Kitto's words in the hotel two months before. And I thank God that Benjamin is back. What a man!

Benjamin tells me how, in the latter weeks of their captivity, Keke called them down from the bush to the seaside. There he came to stay in the same house as them. He seemed anxious to prove that he could be friendly. By this stage he did not trust many of his own men, and the Brothers must have appeared a safer option. But who could stay with the likes of Brother Alfred Tabo and Novice Benjamin and not be touched by their goodness and their prayers? Keke got them to preach to his men. He constantly justified his actions to them. It was as though he was searching for redemption. Benjamin had not been taken in by any of Keke's self-justification. Keke's brother had taken him aside and warned him 'Never believe he is your friend, he can kill you at any time. You must escape.' All this time they preached to his men. Keke seemed intensely religious, and claimed that his actions were commanded by God. 'This is unbelievable,' says Novice Benjamin, 'how could God ever use anyone to kill his *own* Solomon Island brother? It was not God's will, it was human disorder, but God has used this time of disorder to counter-attack. God will always win in the end.' After all those weeks in captivity, Benjamin seems to have emerged with even greater faith. I wish I could share it. And I wish I could help him to come back from the precipice of life and death where these memories are still holding him and help him to rest a while from all he has so bravely endured.

On one subject he too is silent. None of those released have seen our first six Brothers and I fear they may suspect a tragedy which is too great for any of us to bear. Why, I ask myself, if they are alive has Keke not released them too? It would be so much to his advantage with the Regional Intervention Force on the brink of arrival. And why had Keke continued to denigrate the character of those seven Brothers to those Novices and Brothers he had now released? And why was Y Sato also silent when asked, as if he had not heard the question? I too fear the truth, but perhaps there is a time for everything and the intervention force needs to be in place before what has really happened to our Brothers can be revealed.

How we bargain with God! Like Abraham, how I had longed for Novice Andrew, Novice Gabriel from Malaita, Novices Wilfred and Robert, and then, when they returned, even more agonizingly waited for Novice Benjamin and Brother Alfred and Brother Peter to return. And now my prayers have been answered. Every Novice has returned, and yet, despite all my relief, it is *not* enough. How can it be enough, when seven are still missing? We want all of them back.

In Gela I feel suddenly exhausted. I do not want to have to talk or explain what has happened, and for a few days I just sleep and watch DVDs. They are peopled by heroes who fight evil with every weapon and technique imaginable. Mel Gibson is the star of one, and he appears to be so courageously defending his men and killing the Vietnamese with conscience-free abandon. It seems a travesty of reality. For if there is glory in violent conflict, it is the reverse of most fictional presentations, fictional fearlessness. We all believe in courage but don't see the reality of violence or the fear. They don't show us the corpses of the soldiers killed in Iraq. The reality is about mess and confusion and loss, and trying somehow to get to the other side of the chaos and regain the bank. The reality is about victims who are people you know and care about and who are human like you. It feels far more like a terrible tragedy which has stripped all those involved of defence, and left them exposed and in pain – like a crucifixion. And strangely the courage is here, in frightening vulnerability, like a hostage held in the lens of a terrorist video, pleading for life. And the glory is here, in this exposed humanity; here is where our loyalty and our hearts belong. We belong to those we love and not to the oppressor. And that love must be greater than all the fear.

> Blessed are the poor in spirit;
> the kingdom of heaven is theirs.
> Blessed are the sorrowful;
> they shall find consolation.
> Blessed are the gentle;

they shall have the earth for their possession.
Blessed are those who hunger and thirst to see right prevail;
for they shall be satisfied.
Blessed are the peacemakers;
they shall be called God's children.
Blessed are those who are persecuted in the cause of right;
the kingdom of heaven is theirs.

(Matthew 5.3–6, 9–10 Revised English Bible)

These are the real heroes to whom I wish to belong.

How suddenly things change. Out of Guadalcanal and in the village on the island of Gela, those Novices taken hostage are coming to life again. With a change of place the darkness of all they have been through lifts a little. They play football and wash in the river and sit together on the sago palm verandas, as the old men cut tobacco with bush knives to roll in sheets of exercise book paper for smoking. The young kids sit next to the Novices swinging their legs and leaning their heads against the Novices' shoulders, wiping their noses on their forearms and grinning. The young girls sidle over and giggle in the half-light playing with their hair and twisting their fringes into curls. They want to hear stories of what it was like to be a hostage. But Andrew is not letting on. He wants to leave those memories behind. 'It was not me, a different Novice', he tells them. At night the Novices act out a simple parable and Novice Benjamin Kunu's voice is booming out through the night, 'Change! Change! Receive the water of new life!'

Back at Tabalia, fear is in the air. In my neighbour's house Mummy Emily is worrying about rumours she has heard in the market. Peter her husband tries to quieten her. This man of endlessly good spirits, songs and laughter smokes his pipe dejectedly. His son is ill, a reflection of the woundedness of this whole community.

The last shall be first

After the attack of epilepsy
Alfred calls for his father Peter
Who holds him
Awkwardly but tenderly
Wanting to take away all that is past
And defending him from the future
Now a gentle sleep comes
A gentleness too in his eyes as they close and then open
For we have seen him shake
And there is nothing to hide
Yes there is a sadness in this woundedness
For who wants to be so exposed
Or to witness another suffer
But we love him more after the storm
A deeper truth
A deeper life
Nothing to hide
The face of Christ.

The Regional Assistance Mission to the Solomon Islands (RAMSI) led by the Australians has arrived: 2,000 troops and support staff and back-up. The first contingent of soldiers arrived at Honiara airport and came running out of the plane in battle formation fully armed. It took the rather tatty looking Royal Solomon Island Police Force by surprise. They had lined up as an official welcome party and guard of honour. I think they must have felt somewhat threatened. Images come back to me of the US Forces arriving in Somalia where they practically beat up the ground staff at the airport. Here in Solomon Islands, the spectators found the display rather amusing. But every one is impressed by the weapons. This is not like the International Peace Monitoring force, this is a full-scale army operation, and everyone is already feeling safer. The Prime Minister has been in hiding for the last few days after threats from Malaitan militants; he can come out now, he has full RAMSI protection. The RAMSI police are already on duty in Honiara, and truck loads of soldiers have started making patrols out of Honiara up towards where we are based at Tabalia. The militants have quickly vanished from sight. In Honiara you can hear the constant whirl of military helicopters overhead as RAMSI set up their base near the airport. It's a much bigger operation than anyone here was expecting. There is talk in terms of a ten-year presence, not just to establish law and order but tackling the whole corrupt fabric of what the Australian media have been calling 'a failed state'. They have even set up a military hospital and they have had spy planes out over the Weather Coast of Guadalcanal. None of us cares much about the long-term implications, if only they can help get our Brothers back from Keke.

23

So have no fear of them; for nothing is
covered up that will not be uncovered, and
nothing secret that will not be known.
What I say to you in the dark, tell in the light;
and what you hear whispered, proclaim from
the housetops. Do not fear those who kill the
body but cannot kill the soul.

Matthew 10.26

From the diary of August 2003

5 August 2003

The rumours are not good. Today a villager at Maravovo asked one of
the Brothers when we are going to stop praying for our six missing
Brothers and hold a requiem for them. The Brothers believe bad news is
being kept from us, news too bad for anyone to want to be the messenger.
Now RAMSI is here people are braver and speak. Brother Caulton Weris
and Matthias go to Marovovo to search for news. When they return they
say very little. I receive a telephone call from one of the advisers working
for the Australian-led intervention force. He tells me that Nick Warner,
the special Coordinator of RAMSI and Ben McDevitt, the Deputy Police
Commissioner, are meeting with Harold Keke on the Weather Coast
tomorrow. There will be a show of Australian military strength, soldiers,
helicopters, a frigate offshore. They will try to convince him to surrender. 'Will you find out news about our missing Brothers?' I ask. 'We need

to know now, it's been so long.' 'Yes, that is a priority.' We both know things do not look good.

8 August 2003

The phone rings with the news I have been dreading. The Police Commissioner says he will come to Chester Resthouse to tell the Brothers in person. We are all sitting downstairs, some on chairs, some on the floor; the room is packed and tense. We all know the news already but we wait just the same, hopelessly. Everyone is looking down. No one is speaking. Brother Matthias has just arrived from PNG and is trying to tell me how terrible this news will be in PNG where the family of Brother Robin Lindsay are still waiting in hope. I know it already. The Police Commissioner's car is arriving. He shakes hands. I cover my face with my hands.

9 August 2003

I sent this message to Companions, family and friends, it was forwarded to Christians around the world:

> Yesterday our worst fears were confirmed. The Melanesian Brotherhood was officially told by the Police Commissioner William Morrell that they had been informed by Keke that all six of our Brothers were dead. They had been murdered over three months ago when they arrived on the Weather Coast on the 24 April in search of Brother Nathaniel Sado who is also confirmed dead. Our months of waiting have been in vain. It is hard for such news to sink in. These were six young innocent Brothers who went out in faith and in love in search of their Brother. It seems too much to bear that they should have been murdered in cold blood. I would like to tell you a little about each one of them for each one will be so missed.

Brother Robin Lindsay is our Assistant Head Brother and has been in the Community for many years. He was four years Assistant Head

Brother in Solomon Islands and four years Regional Head Brother in PNG. I call him 'the encourager', because he has time for everyone and helps build on their strengths. He is known and popular wherever he goes in PNG and Solomon Islands and even in Norfolk in the UK. With his strong handshake and absolute dedication to his work, the Community feels in safe and caring hands whenever he is around. He is always there for his Brothers, there when you leave, there in the truck to pick you up when you get back. There is no Brother more committed to the Community or to his fellow Brothers. He is so greatly loved; how much he will be missed. My last memory of him is on Maundy Thursday when together we washed the feet of the Novices in the Community, he washing and I drying.

Brother Francis Tofi from the time he was a Novice was so bright and attentive in all his studies. When you met him you knew straight away that here is someone with a deep spiritual life and gentle wisdom. He asked constant questions and understood intuitively what it meant to be a Brother. First in Malaita and then on the Weather Coast of Guadalcanal at the time of tension and its aftermath he showed incredible courage. Here was a Brother who was prepared to speak out, to condemn violence and the use of weapons, and protect the lives of others even at great personal danger. There are stories of how he was able to resolve conflicts and rescue those who were being beaten or in danger from the rebels. Early this year the World Council of Churches offered him a place at the Bossey Institute in Geneva to study and contribute to a course on conflict resolution. I was aware of the possible danger he was in working for disarmament, and particularly because he had not been afraid to speak out against Keke. But his courage was very great. He told me he would be frightened if he died doing something that was evil 'but I am not frightened to die in God's service doing something which is good'. I reminded him that God wants LIVING sacrifices and he had his whole life ahead of him. We laughed, for death never really seems a possibility in one so brave and full of life. I told him I wanted to visit him in Geneva. Today we packed his only possessions in a small, grubby, black rucksack. A few shirts, a couple of pairs of shorts, his uniform and some books to return to his family. I cannot believe he is dead.

Brother Alfred Hill. He is a young and humble Brother. For two years he has been looking after Chester Resthouse in Honiara. Sometimes the guests find him a bit quiet and vague but he has great kindness, always giving up his bed and mattress to provide extra room for guests. He takes particular care of the kids who love coming to the house. He makes sure they get fed at lunchtime and has been helping young Selwyn, whose parents have deserted him, learn to read. This year he trained in malaria research and qualified to read blood slides at the local clinic. This has been so helpful to all the religious communities who bring their blood slides to him for the fast diagnosis of malaria. And now dead. They shot him in the arm and then they beat him to death, this gentle man. How can I write in the past tense about one so young?

Brother Ini Paratabatu, free-spirited and outspoken, brave and full of energy. He is a brilliant actor and became a key member of my dramas and joined me on the Brothers' mission and tour to New Zealand in 2000. Before joining the Community he was a member of a drama group from the Weather Coast, performing dramas about development and health issues. We got on well for he knew I recognized his potential and the fire within him. Ini as a Brother has been brave to speak out against all injustice. He even confronted the SI Police Force when he believed their methods were unjust, brutal or failing to respect the rights of the people.

Brother Patteson Gatu. He is full of joy and so motivated as a new Brother. He was only admitted last October and always smiles from ear to ear whenever you meet him. The last time I saw him just before Easter he was telling me about when he was fired at while trying to land on the beach, as well as enthusing about a sermon I had just preached. I was never quite sure whether he was not teasing! He had such youth and warmth and confidence of faith. Not some narrow religiosity, but natural and real and strong. Indeed he made Christ's beatitude a reality: 'Happy are the peacemakers, for they shall be called the children of God' (Matt. 5.9).

And **Brother Tony Sirihi**, who lost his father when he was young, and found in the Brotherhood a real family and home. He developed from a shy, thin and humble Novice into a stocky and bold Brother. But he never lost his simplicity. So many memories. I remember so clearly the night before he was admitted as a Brother how we climbed Pentecost Mountain together and celebrated the Eucharist on top with all those about to make their vows. All night Tony had been lighting fires to keep us warm. I remember taking a retreat with him on a desert island in Lord Howe atoll, in which we fended off clouds of mosquitoes all night. He was easy company and a natural and unassuming friend to me and to many of the Brothers who loved having him around. He showed his courage throughout the tension and continued to help the disarmament process.

And **Brother Nathaniel Sado**, the lost Brother, for whom they had gone in search. As a Novice he was in charge of the piggery and cared for those pigs with great dedication. He made a sweet potato garden for them and cooked for them. They often seemed better fed than the rest of the Novices. The dogs followed him round too and he was one of the few Novices who got on well with our donkey. He loved to welcome guests to the Community and made friends with many of the expatriates, arranging trips for them to his home volcanic island of Savo where he took them up the mountain to see the hot springs and sulphur smoke and to dig for megapode eggs in the warm sand. He delighted in these expeditions. He had little formal education and had a somewhat childlike nature, always on the move, and as a Brother a bit hard to pin down. During the tension and the disarmament he had made friends with the militant group and was rather proud of the fact that he knew Harold Keke and believed Keke to be his friend. The trust was misplaced and he was the first Brother to die. Stories say that he was beaten to death after being accused by Keke of being a spy for the government. They say he sang hymns as he died. *Jesus iu holdem hand blong mi.* There was no darkness in this young man: not wise perhaps, proud of his status as a Brother and the kudos of mixing with the militants, but entirely well-meaning even if naive in his trust – innocent as a child is innocent when caught up in events out of his depth.

Of one thing I am certain: these seven men will live on in the hearts and minds of our Community. Their sacrifice seems too great and hard to believe. The Community sat up through the night telling the stories of these Brothers and trying to come to terms with the enormity of their loss. And yet beneath the trauma there is a peace too – the knowledge that each of these young men believed in peace and in goodness. They knew that there was a better way. They were prepared to oppose violence and to risk much. At the end of the day they stand against all acts of brutality which are at present disfiguring our world, and bravely, boldly, and with love, lived what most of us proclaim only from the safety of a church. Oh how much the worldwide Anglican Church at the moment could learn from their witness! And when such real-life issues are so much at stake in our world, is not this what the gospel should be?

The six Brothers came ashore on 24 April. They were surrounded by a group of Keke's men led by Ronnie Cawa, Keke's henchman, who had ordered the deaths of the two men killed in front of the villagers at Marasa. They shot Brother Robin Lindsay and Brother Francis Tofi dead. They shot young Brother Alfred in the arm and then beat him to death. They took the other three Brothers back to their camp where during that night they forced them to make confessions on a tape recorder saying that they were enemies of Harold Keke. You can hear Ronnie Cawa shouting at them what to say. Then they lined them up in front of a single grave and shot them in the chest and buried them. One of the killers was only fifteen years old.

While I am walking through Honiara a man I know comes up to me and asks me about the Brothers who have died. It has been in the newspaper. Everyone is asking us. I keep silent. And then he asks me:

> 'What's wrong with the Brotherhood? How can the Brothers die? Why didn't God protect them?'

And I read the subtext of this question as 'What did they do wrong?' For this is the cargo cult theology where goodness gets a reward from the sky and those who suffer and die must have done something wrong or been cursed. And I have had enough of this kind of religion. It is not just in the Solomon Islands; this kind of religion is everywhere. They have stolen the Christian faith and made it into a prosperity cult which has nothing to do with self-giving love. It has nothing to do with the gospel that Christ proclaims. In fact it is the polar opposite.

'Why did the Brothers die?' I answer 'Why did Jesus Christ die? Why did St Stephen, St Peter, St James die? Why did all the Christian martyrs die? Why did Bishop John Coleridge Patteson die? They died because all humans die if people beat them and torture them and kill them. Christ died on the cross 2,000 years ago to save us from this but we have not learnt this lesson yet.'

At Tabalia many people are gathering. In the chapel there are those who have come to support the Community in their grief. There are others who have not once been to see us over these months of waiting but now are offering their analysis of events. Different people stand up to offer words. Head Brother Harry is not there but lying down in his room next door, broken-hearted. Brother Robin Lindsay was his greatest support. He admired him so much, came to stay with him when he was a schoolboy at Selwyn. Robin had encouraged and inspired his longing to join the Brotherhood. Ten years later Brother Harry had been so grateful when Brother Robin had willingly given up his studies to support him as Assistant Head Brother and provide the help in leadership and loyal moral support that young Brother Harry had so much needed. It had seemed like a sign of hope and blessing. 'Things feel really different now', Harry had told me. But it was not to be for long.

I have just got back from Honiara where I have been trying to get messages through to Brother Robin's relatives and the bishop in Port Moresby. There is one particular priest wearing big boots in our chapel even though there is a notice outside to take off all sandals and shoes as a sign of humility and respect. This priest is saying that the Brotherhood has become too involved in politics and needs to return to its true vocation of prayer. I can't believe this. Sister Doreen speaks out. She and her Sisters have visited us regularly to support us in prayer. 'Why are you trying to spear the Brotherhood? Haven't they suffered enough? Haven't we come to support and encourage them?'

Do you know what? Those six Brothers who have just died were not involved in politics at all, if by politics you mean intrigue and double-dealing and deception. Not at all! If this was true, they would not have gone, they would never have had the courage. They would have made someone else go and do their dirty work. No, they went not because of politics but because of their goodness and because of their faith, the faith that teaches us that we have nothing to fear in confronting all that is evil, even if we have no weapons to protect us – faith that says we have nothing to fear even in death. If their death is a failure it is not because of politics, it is because they had too much Christian faith. Francis Tofi, Robin Lindsay, Toni Sirihi, Alfred Hill, Patteson Gatu, Ini Paratabatu, they are the most innocent holy men I have ever known, and if you knew them you would know this too, and you would not be talking of *returning* to a life of prayer. Their whole life was a prayer . . . my prayer now. If only you could have known them. If you could have known any one of them you would not be talking of spies or politics, you would be on your knees before God begging for his forgiveness for this nation and for the death of these most holy simple men of God. Weep for your children!

Stories begin of how each one of these Brothers seemed to know the danger they were heading into before they set out. They had told people that they may not return. They knew before they said goodbye. I remember Francis speaking to me 'I am not frightened of dying doing something good.'

'Yes, but surely God wants *living* sacrifices, not your death.'

I leave the chapel without speaking and go home. We who loved them know the truth.

24

... in honour and dishonour, in ill repute and
good repute ... as dying, and see – we are alive;
as punished and yet not killed; as sorrowful,
yet always rejoicing.

2 Corinthians 6.9

From the diary of August 2003

12 August 2003

Head Brother Harry was in his room. He had carried so much for so long
and now his leg had swollen up with a huge seven-headed carbuncle.
'One for each of the Brothers who died' he told me. I went to Brother
Caulton Weris, our longest-serving Brother and told him that the
Community needed his help. He has the gift of discernment and real
spiritual wisdom although sometimes I have thought that he has hidden
these gifts. He had been Head Brother from 1996 to 1999 and that time
had been a time of great transparency, integrity and achievement in
leadership. His simplicity had kept him focused on the important things.
He had always delegated and entrusted responsibility to others. So as
chaplain I went to Caulton and laid before him the Community's need for
him now. Brother Robin Lindsay was dead. Brother Harry would be in
hospital because of his leg, his deep faith shaken to the core by these
deaths. Somehow we had to cope with the aftermath of this trauma
and we needed someone to support Harry. Caulton has always been
respected and loved for his integrity. I knew he would have the support

of the Community and the Archbishop too and I knew that together both he and I could help the Community through this tragedy.

I remember at this time meeting Brother Caulton in the vestry after I had celebrated Communion. I was full of grief myself. I told him that I felt broken by all that had happened and felt like giving up; I had failed as a Brother. He replied that he had noticed that I had lost my spirit. 'I am not criticizing you,' he said, 'but it as though you do not have the "power" you had before.' He said that I must let go of my feelings of 'guilt'. His words did not crush me as I thought they would. As I reflected upon what he had said, I realized how much I was needed at this time, but that I had been afraid, not so much of the enemy without, but afraid that I had somehow failed to save those Brothers I loved. Yes 'guilt' was the right word, guilt that I was alive and they were dead. Yet with this admission there was the knowledge that I would not fail them or their families now. Those Brothers knew me, and they would give me courage, some of their own courage to die to self and to live.

Bold Humility

And now I find myself
No longer the messianic figure of my dreams
Capable of redeeming others
And redeeming myself
I find myself lost
Without pride
Stripped to the bone.

And yet I find that I am free
Free from the image that has constrained the Truth within me
And perhaps it is here that the true self can grow
I gentle man
Who loves imperfectly
But loves

And longs for love
With empathy and compassion
With creative gifts
And skills of speech
Who can see and dramatize
But is less sure of life
Who loves God
Who loves Christ
But is not
And fears sin and fears rejection
And longs in the simple actions of his day
To be who he is
A Christian.

And in the warmth of darkness
God gives me the gift of life
It is truly a gift
Not deserved or fully understood
And not earned in the eyes of an audience
The audience has gone home
We wait for the Word to begin again.

It will always be a miracle of faith that, at the very bottom, at the point when I really did not know how we could go on, God took over. When I look back I am so thankful at the way there were those who were present like aspects of Christ, making those following weeks possible. I did not realize at the time, but this tragedy was to become the saving event, a place I would revisit again and again in my memory, not to relive the pain but to discover that it had become a place of hope and of courage. The mystery of these events will never go away and three years later I am still unravelling everything that happened and discovering a little more of the truth of our gospel. Suddenly I find I am touched by a memory so strong, and I find myself grieving for these seven Brothers again, or being blessed by them, or given courage by them. I remember a dream I had: I was drowning and each time I tried to reach the surface I was pushed back under the water, and then I saw Christ swimming towards me, brave and free, and he breathed into me and he said 'Do not be afraid, you can breathe underwater.'

> Goodness is stronger than evil
> Love is stronger than hate
> Light is stronger than darkness
> Life is stronger than death
> Victory is ours through him who loves us.
> (Desmond Tutu)

How do you tell seven different families that their sons have been murdered? How do you find healing for a Community that had been so badly beaten up? And how do you do this when you yourself are hurting so deeply? I can only say that we were led forward by God. Somehow the grief of their seven families and the grief of our Community would be transfigured. Somehow the whole nation needed to come to its senses and return to the Father they had forsaken. If we believe in Christ's death, we are also called to believe in his resurrection.

What I am trying to describe was not a moment but a new movement, and it was not of my making: like a piece of Bach for piano,[37] which has spiralled down to nothing, and then seemingly from nowhere, when you least expect it, a new note has arrived as a pure gift, to begin a new pattern, a new sequence and dynamic, from beyond but now within, and all of a sudden a beautifully tender tune is growing like a new shoot; new life begins to weave ahead of you like a mysterious path, opening up a vista of possibilities that you could not have imagined before they were revealed. Listen. You do not know where the breath of the Spirit comes from or where it will lead, but it leads you. And you know it is real.

On the day after the deaths were confirmed, Brother Noel arrived from Malaita. I met him off the boat and I was so pleased to see him. We sat at

---

37 Bach's Concerto for piano and orchestra No. 3 *Adagio e piano sempre.*

Rosie's cafeteria and I told him what had happened. I have told him since that over the next few months his friendship was like grace; it was an undeserved gift of God to help me and, through me, the whole Community. It was unconditional friendship that helped me live through that time. Noel is a true Christian and a friend to whom I will always be thankful. Over the next months he was there for me, calm, steady and supportive. Staying at my house Noel, Novice Jack Alick and Novice Fordroy (who I had been with in his hour of need at the hospital) now provided a kind of trinity of unspoken loyalty and care and my next-door neighbour Father Peter and his wonderful family were brilliant too, offering twenty-four-hour food and hospitality to me or anyone I brought to their home. Brother Jude was also a constant visitor. The tragedy we faced has bound me to these my Brothers and to this Community forever.

Resurrection

Resurrection begins in darkness
There is distraction
There is confusion
And uncertainty
In the mind and stomach
The yawn of despair
And I look round
And I cannot find whom I am looking for
And there is fear so caustic that I will never find him again
And then Christ comes
Comes so simply
As though to dispel all fear
He comes like joy comes without introduction
Like healing which has dissolved the pain
He comes
Like rain on a dry brittle land
He is simply there
Like light which ends darkness with no struggle

For then it was dark
But now it is light
He comes with his balance and his beauty
And order returns
Like a bird returning home from another land
Spring comes
He comes with no explanation or reason
And there is song
And a hope
And a future
We are surprised by his love
But he is not
For though he kept us waiting and doubting and trusting
He always knew he would never leave us.

14 August 2003

I am in Honiara when someone tells me the news that Harold Keke has surrendered to the Australian-led Regional Assistance Mission (RAMSI). Chris Elstoff, an adviser to Nick Warner, RAMSI's Special Coordinator, had already told me by telephone that they would be meeting with Keke on the Weather Coast. He had told me that they did not intend to bargain with Keke, or make deals; they would simply guarantee his safety if he willingly submitted to justice. I wished that they had arrested him the last time they met, when he had told them that all seven Brothers were dead. I feared Keke would never be caught. Chris said that RAMSI wanted a non-confrontational approach and this would hopefully lead to a full surrender of all Keke's followers and the recovery of their weapons.

Their strategy has paid off. Ben McDevitt, the Assistant Police Commissioner from Australia, has the reputation of being tough but fair. It was a display of strength. The Australians had the HMAS Manoora waiting offshore. The helicopter with RAMSI troops landed at Mbiti village, very near the place where five months before our six Brothers had landed and met their death. Three hundred villagers watched as Harold Keke and his henchman Ronnie Cawa surrendered along with Keke's wife and members of his family. All ten of them were flown by helicopter to the Manoora. Later on the same day at Mbiti Village, fifty-nine of Keke's men handed over forty-eight weapons including twenty-eight high-powered guns, which were then publicly destroyed. The militants lifted their hands in the air and the chant went up 'The war is over!'

There is a palpable sense of relief. Everyone is repeating the news. Keke and Cawa are now being held in captivity on the Manoora. Cawa has made a full confession. Not a bullet has been fired. I ask Chris Elstoff on the phone if Keke shows any regret at the murder of our Brothers. He says that Keke says he was not there when they were killed but insists they were 'spies'.

'I know these Brothers', I tell Chris. 'They were not spies.'

'Richard,' says Chris, 'this is his language, the language of his cult. This is not a war, and the word "spies" is meaningless as a defence for what he did. This is the murder of seven defenceless men, and the murder of many others as well. Justice will be done.' They said that Keke seemed excited about travelling by helicopter. He is not educated or sophisticated and obviously deranged, yet he is a ruthlessly skilled commander and keeps his word to the 'white men'. RAMSI has reported that his camp and defences are pretty impregnable. If he had chosen to fight it would not have been an easy position to attack. The peaceful surrender comes therefore with a deep sense of thanksgiving and relief. I think of him sharing a house with Brother Alfred Tabo and Novice Benjamin during the time he held them hostage, and all the prayers that have been said around the world, and I realize that all this has not been in vain.

21 August 2003

I see the opposites most clearly now: cruelty, death and fear, side by side with love and life. Both have traces of the other. Love undermines cruelty, opposes and threatens it; it lets the light in upon the atrocity and longs to heal. But love too is tainted by fear, the dread of losing and hurting and being separated from the beloved. Love opposed by fear and hatred. There is a simple choice here, and again and again I know which I choose, setting the fibres in me free to live again. That's what John Coleridge Patteson, the first bishop of these islands and one who was also martyred, wanted. He wanted 'an apostolate of love'.

John in his Epistle expresses it so perfectly:

Beloved let us love one another, because love is from God.
Everyone who loves is born of God and knows God.
Whoever does not love does not know God,
for God is love.

(1 John 4.7–8)

The Brothers' brutal death has a gentleness in its aftermath. As though the struggle for them is over and they have made their choice and made that last terrible journey and have reached the other side: 'Good and faithful servants, come and enjoy my kingdom.' We, who have been left behind, still have a long way to go. We have received so many letters and messages of support. This support from around the world in prayer is palpable. It is holding up the whole Community. Christ's gift of peace silencing the storm.

25

No one has greater love than this, to lay down one's life for one's friends.

John 15.13

From the diary of September 2003

While for these three months my entire being has rebelled against the whole notion of martyrdom, for it seems such a terrible price to pay for such lives, yet there is a real sense in which these Brothers will live for ever, and who would not rather be with them than the perpetrators of such brutality?

Of course there have been plenty of recriminations and blame in the press, largely generated by Keke's followers trying to justify their atrocity, for some still think Keke will be vindicated and return to the Weather Coast with untold wealth. Why did the Brothers go? Who sent them? Last Sunday God seemed to answer loud and clear. We held a memorial and thanksgiving service at St Barnabas Cathedral in Honiara. It was overflowing with thousands of people. The Brothers and Novices were there in force: rows of them in their white uniforms. The beautiful harmony of their combined voices was the sound of faith, faith in the midst of all adversity. And then one after the other there were testimonies and messages witnessing to the lives of these seven Brothers: the Archbishop, the Companions, the families of the seven, the Governor General, the Peace Council, the other churches, the Police Commissioner, and messages read out from around the world. We have had letters from the UK, Australia, New Zealand, Canada, the USA, Vanuatu, Switzerland, Germany, Ireland, South Africa, India, Brazil, and even Iraq. Each message of sympathy was also one of thanksgiving for the courage of these men who had gone without weapons or defence in search of their lost Brother. 'Greater love has no one than this . . . ' Seven candles were lit as different Brothers interceded for each of the seven, giving thanks for their lives. This was followed by a Eucharist in which the lines of communicants went on and on for so long that it seemed it would last for ever. The service lasted for almost four hours but we were not aware of time passing. The service in its entirety was broadcast to the nation.

How strange that in the finality of these young deaths we glimpse something life-giving. As one of those who wrote to us said: 'I think it is your testimony that six good, humble and faithful men died because they were so devoted to one another and to Christ, that simultaneously causes me so much pain but also affords such hope.' They offer hope to the whole nation. You see, they were not from one island or one tribe but from Melanesia: they have extended the Christian family in this nation and far beyond.

Among the many tributes we have received was one from a Canadian writer, Charles Montgomery, who had spent time with our Community last year writing a book which explores his own journey to discover the meaning of the myths and faith he encountered in Melanesia. His words have captured the spirit of these Brothers:

Only yesterday I was writing about Brother Francis Tofi. I remember our trip to CDC1, how he was the one who huddled in the back of the truck, he was the one who whispered and chuckled and remained very small, so small that I decided he was not central to the day's events, until the moment came, during a tense negotiation for the release of a kidnapped boy, when Francis stepped forward and brought the two enemy groups together in a prayer. He radiated something so good and true and bigger than the moment and the tension was washed from the afternoon, and the men with anger and guns were made humble. And of course a boy's life was saved and a gun was retrieved. I hope you do not think I am throwing platitudes at you when I say I am certain the Brothers will become larger in their deaths, and their cause must certainly ripple outwards. I know this cannot ease the pain of losing such friends and brothers in your journey. But even as a man with little faith, I am certain of it. It is happening for me already.

And now we return to our lives. There is a long way to go and somehow the Community seems older and wiser, hushed by the events that have overtaken us but not without hope. It is as if the paschal mystery has been lived out among us, not a re-creation but the reality of our faith, and though I pray that none of us have to go through an event like this ever again. It is as though we have been given a glimpse into the mystery of things; we have seen the brutal face of evil and known the fear and darkness it brings, but we have also witnessed goodness and love and glimpsed the promise of that which is eternal, and all of us know which side we want to belong to. The seven Brothers are a constant, aching reminder of the integrity, values, and love which alone can bring hope to our world.

The angels of God

There are memories of breaking, curses and brutality
But I will let them go now
Not these memories
But of those who were there with me
And sought to repair the damage done
To save and protect from harm all that is good
These are your disciples, Lord
They have pushed back the darkness
For they have hovered like faithful angels over the invasion and
  lessened it
No, Lord, more than that, they have transformed it by their costly
  loyalty
It is as though they feel the hurt more deeply than if it were their own
And now they sit down and stay without judgement or fear for
  themselves

And the broken house is full of the warmth of their goodness
Lord, as I begin again, it is your angels I will remember
And I will be forever thankful for the blessing which they brought.

26

But if we have died with Christ, we believe that we will also live with him.

Romans 6.8

From the diary of September 2003

I went to PNG in September and attended and preached at Brother Robin Lindsay's requiem in Popondetta Cathedral. There were hundreds present. It was not as finely choreographed as the thanksgiving service at St Barnabas Cathedral in Honiara, yet sincere, moving and deeply felt. A huge procession went into the Cathedral of the Resurrection with great dignity, only to find that the seats had all been taken, forcing the priests to stand or squat in the wings and the Novices, Brothers and invited guests to sit on the floor with the primary school. The sermon went well. It was the story of our Brothers and when I finished the whole congregation rose to its feet and spontaneously applauded them. Bishop Roger Jupp celebrated with a deep reverence and preparedness and our tragedy seemed to be taken up in Christ's own life and death, the only story capable of containing it and giving our grief a shape, and a meaning – like Christ, our Brothers' lives had been taken, blessed, broken and given. The paschal mystery we see offered on the altar is the mystery these seven Brothers have lived: total self-giving, total vulnerability in love, and yet this is our strength. The Eucharist was cathartic. After the service relatives hugged me and cried. Pauline transitions from sorrow to hope are easier when you are preaching but when face to face with close relatives no words are capable of touching the enormity of the loss.

From Popondetta I moved on to Aiome, miles from the sea. I travelled by four-seater aeroplane after being told that the airline's two other planes had both crashed within the previous year. I was shown the mangled wreckage of one of them in the hangar by one of the air stewards. It was not a well-designed advertising strategy for 'Island Air', but I seem to be getting used to near-death experiences. We flew through clouds, took a sharp right around a steeply rising mountain and landed on a very bumpy grass and stone airstrip cut in the side of the mountain. This was our first stop, Simbai, and we were only in transit long enough for a small Companion to stow away unseen in the luggage before we set off again. I was met off the plane by warriors with spears and bows and arrows and drums, and led back to the Melanesian Brothers' Headquarters where, in the trees, Brothers were waiting with buckets of water and floating flowers to pour down on my head, which in the heat of this place made the steam rise. In this island in the middle of the bush, in sweltering heat and dust, in this amphitheatre at the base of the mountains, I felt at first in limbo-land. I had longed to get away for a few weeks from the shadow of Guadalcanal but now I was away, I found myself like an exile wondering what was happening and counting the days until my return. The Brothers here in PNG reminded me of what the Brotherhood must have been like in Solomon Islands before. Many of the Novices here have never been as far as even the nearest town. Their usual diet is basic – sweet potato and more sweet potato – and mostly, it seems, only once a day. They have none of the resources or slick presentation skills or confidence of many of the Solomon Island Brothers, but a dusty humility, a patient acceptance of the poverty and simplicity of their lives and lack of stimulation, and such a sensory awareness of the needs of others. They come and sit on my veranda with me at all times, offering water and coconuts and waiting on me with such hospitality and asking me for stories of our departed Brothers and of Solomon Islands, or they sit patiently while I read. A Novice seeing my kerosene lamp smoking comes and cleans the carbon away on the front of the shirt he is wearing. God has brought me here, I realize, finally to rest a little from the tragedy we have all been living.

Three days after my arrival there is an all-night *sing sing*. Groups of young dancers descend from their villages in the mountains carrying with them their extraordinary two-metre-high headdresses made from feathers, flowers and the plumes of birds of paradise. All night they sing: an otherworldly sound like a repeating mantra in semitones. Their dance is like the mating rituals of birds of paradise. They stand as still as statues in the half-light and then set off in short runs to the beat of the kundu drums they carry, head-feathers nodding, the leaves of their bustles waggling like the tails of ruffled cockerels. Side by side with this a generator-powered video screen shows karate and vigilante DVDs to an audience most of whom have never seen a two-storey building or a town, and the kids roar with laughter each time the American hero sprays the baddies with machine-gun fire.

These Brothers seem to have a wonderful relationship with the community; children gravitate towards them as does a mentally handicapped young villager, Bartholomew, whose skin is covered with wheals of a fungal infection called bakwa. He shares their mats, cooking pots, clothes and food, and finds acceptance. Yesterday I saw a Novice washing Bartholomew's clothes, which were stiff with grime, as he stood naked under a tap rubbing away at his peeling skin. They met him on mission in one of the mountain villages and he followed them and has been with them ever since. I give him some antifungal cream and a pair of shorts, because he is wearing two pairs both so shredded that they need to be double to cover the holes. Later I watch our Brother Joshua patiently squeezing out the last squirt of cream from the tube to rub on to the skin of Bartholomew's flaking back. I am reminded of the great tenderness I have found in Melanesia, which counterpoints and outweighs all the brutality. Later, when I depart from Aiome, Bartholomew washes in the rain of the overflowing gutter of the shelter where we are waiting, takes off the trousers and runs naked to the aeroplane window to try and hand them dripping back to me. I manage to communicate that they are for him to keep. It has been healing to be here, Bartholomew and his Melanesian Brothers have shown me such love and attention.

Back in Port Moresby, I go to visit Brother Robin's sister, brother and close relatives. I feel anxious about the visit, for it is so hard to be the bearer of tragedy. They have, of course, known for a long time, but I am their first visitor from Solomon Islands. When I arrive at their village, I realize straightaway I have nothing to fear, for the compound is decorated with flowers and as I enter they put *leis* around my neck. I tell them the story from beginning to end. They weep, and Nancy, Robin's sister, puts her arms round me and sobs. They want Brother Robin's remains to be buried with the brothers he died with, at Tabalia in Solomon Islands. It is a sign of their generous spirit and their faith and their love for their brother who they know belongs to God. We then eat together. I come away realizing that I, who wanted so much to bring comfort, have been comforted by them. Nancy tells me repeatedly that I have become her real brother.

27

Blessed are the peacemakers, for they will be called children of God.

Matthew 5.9

From the diary of October and November 2003

5 November 2003

All seven martyred Brothers lie together at the Mother House of the Melanesian Brothers at Tabalia. The day of the funerals of the six Solomon Island Brothers, 24 October, was declared a national day of mourning. Thousands lined the roads and gathered at Tabalia to witness their coffins go past, and their burial and their funeral service was broadcast live to the nation.

On Wednesday 5 November, our Assistant Head Brother Robin Lindsay from Papua New Guinea was laid to rest beside the six Solomon Island Brothers with whom he had died, and who had been buried twelve days earlier. On Wednesday night we lit candles and sang around the seven new graves.

Before the funeral I had waited at the airport for Brother Francis Tofi's father and mother to arrive from Makira. I had not seen his father, the tall, strong Tikopian and former Brother, since his son's admission as a Brother in 1999, when he had worn traditional *tapa* cloth (bark) dress and had such pride in his son who would take on a ministry he had left off twenty years before. Now arriving at the airport he looked so frail, and bent with grief. He put his arms round me and sobbed, and his cry entered into me and I was crying too for this wonderful son of his, and because of the senseless brutality that had led to the death of someone so good. Francis's father had been fasting since he heard of his son's kidnapping in April. Around his neck he had hung Francis's faded black Brother's shirt into which he cried continuously. This was the grief of just one of seven families. What I still find impossible to understand is the failure of imagination, or compassion, or heart with which people can commit atrocities without perceiving the suffering caused. Perhaps they do perceive, and that is the horror of human cruelty, where pain is mocked, torture is sport and the inhuman takes on a diabolic logic of its own. I have believed so much in the forgiveness of Christ. But it is so hard to learn how Christ forgives those who do not seem to repent.

Yet the funeral somehow contained this pain and transcended it. The full Community of Brothers and Novices in white stood at the bottom of the hill that leads to our mother house in Tabalia. Behind them a huge crowd, ranging from the Governor General to village children, was waiting for the final homecoming of their beloved Brothers. As one by one the coffins were unloaded from three trucks the wailing of the crowd grew louder and the people broke ranks and pushed towards the coffins. Yet the Brothers, with dignity and inner strength, took the coffins from the RAMSI combined police force, and a long procession made its way up the hill to the chapel. In front of each coffin there was a banner: 'Blessed are the peacemakers for they shall be called the sons of God', and the name of the Brother who had given his life in the cause of peace. In the chapel the crying was silenced by the singing of the Community. Brothers placed the Brotherhood medals and sashes on the coffins with such respect, and then the families came forward with wreaths and flowers. As we moved towards the Brotherhood graveyard, there was a great surge of grief among the huge crowd and yet again this Brotherhood, like bulwarks against this ocean of loss, held the chaos of grief together, gave it a form and a structure and a dignity. And I was struck, as many of us were, not by a morbid darkness but by faith and light.

That night the late Francis Tofi's father called me to the house in which he was staying. He told me he had buried his grief in the grave with his son and now he would eat again. He bent low over my hands and breathed on them. And I knew that the miracle of God's life was beginning again. It gave me joy to eat fish with him. He is such a dignified, beautiful man, just like his son. And it is the love for his son which so shines in him, and I remind him this can never die, for it is of God and eternal.

Yet, still our Community could not fully rest because no decision had been made concerning the burial place for Brother Robin Lindsay. On 26 October we celebrated the admission of forty-eight new Brothers who took their promises in the Square where seventy-eight years ago the founder of the Melanesian Brotherhood took his promises. Our first Filipino Brother, Alejandro Junior, led the cheers that followed the celebration of their admission and gave such an effervescent and bubbling speech about his gratitude at being a Brother.

Meanwhile the Community continued to wait patiently for the family of the late Robin Lindsay to agree that he too could be buried alongside his Brothers at Tabalia. Robin's grave remained dug and open and there could be no closure for any of us until he too was laid to rest. By Monday 3 November eight of Brother Robin's closest relatives had arrived from PNG. They met at Tabalia and late in the evening called the leaders of the Community to tell them that the final decision had already been made. Brother Robin's bones would be 'planted' at Tabalia. It had been a hard and costly decision for the family, for we all felt Brother Robin belonged to us. Some of his relatives back in PNG wanted his remains returned to his native land. Yet his sister Nancy knew the truth: he was first and foremost a Brother, and he belonged to God and so should rest with those he led at the heart of the Community he served.

The delay had seemed painful and yet it allowed for a funeral that gave special respect for Robin as our leader, and for his family from PNG to be fully involved. Although we had only twenty-four hours to arrange the seventh and final funeral, everything came into place as though it was always meant to be. The Governor General, the Prime Minister, Ministers, the Police Commissioner and Members of RAMSI, the PNG High Commissioner and hundreds of others were there as the Archbishop, the Father of the Brotherhood, officiated. The whole of Brother Robin's life was reflected. His Auntie Prisca told the story of his life, his Uncle declared bravely that he forgave his nephew's murderers but called upon them to repent and lift the curse of violence from these Islands, the Prime Minister praised Brother Robin and the Brotherhood for their work for peace. The Archbishop told Brother Robin's family that they had given the Church the very best, the most precious offering they had, their own beloved son and brother. But perhaps the most powerful sign of all was when all the Brothers and Novices gathered to kneel around the coffin to show their last respects, linked to the coffin and to one another by outstretched hands, their grief, their faith and the song they sang. And then together as one Community they slowly lifted the coffin on to the shoulders of six of their Brothers to be led to its final resting place where Brother Robin's relatives sang in his mother tongue.

A month before he was murdered Brother Robin came to me to ask me about a dream that he had had three times. He told me he dreamt he was on a beach, and that he looked up and saw the most terrible storm clouds and cyclone approaching and huge waves mounting. He was full of fear and dreamt that the storm engulfed him. He said he drowned, and that everything was swept away by the waves. He dreamt that the wave carried him to the top of a mountain and that as the water receded he was in warm sunshine and that he could see for miles, the world flooded with light. He said that he believed that God was saying to him that he must not be afraid and that all, all would be well, all would be made good. I told him he had a lot on his plate an the moment with a coming conference, and not to worry . . .

How could I know all he was about to face? I did not know the tragedy that awaited him on a beach that fateful 24 April. It is only when you stand back from the pain of the loss that you begin to see another story emerging. Who could have imagined the following months – the arrival of RAMSI, the unconditional laying down of guns and surrender of militants, the arrest of leading instigators on both sides and, for the first time a public no longer frightened to speak out in support of justice? No, no one could ever have imagined the aftermath of these Brothers' deaths, nor that the funeral of these simple, humble men of faith would stop the nation and line the streets with thousands of those longing for peace, nor that churches throughout the world would hold requiems in thanksgiving and prayer for these unknown, ordinary, men of God. And for our Community, stripped of all pride and pretensions, a melting down too, and, we pray, a new understanding, a greater compassion, and a still deeper heart for the gospel.

A prayer at night

He is here
At the bottom of the fall
A peace below the waves and the currents
An easy stillness
A stillness where birds land
Where rain falls
And where the ground drinks
Listen, the wind is moving through the trees
A stillness within too
Where we can move freely
Possessing nothing
And connected with all
Come, Lord
Take us home to the centre of the pattern
So that we may belong
And yet be free
An easy love
To walk with no hands tied
But with you forever.

Why did they go? They knew the danger. It seems too great a sacrifice for anyone to make. They went because they believed the gospel, not just in word but also in the action of their lives. They believed that the Good Shepherd must go in search of the one who is lost. They believed that the Good Shepherd must be willing even to give up his life for the sheep. We profess a gospel which, at its heart, proclaims a love, so great that God is prepared to send his only Son who will die for that love. That is how costly that love is. The action of these Brothers challenges us deeply. Yet others of us stayed behind and God's resurrection must be ours too. For redemption is not simply in death, but in this world. A longer struggle perhaps, one requiring love, courage and faithfulness and a deep commitment to peace and justice, which I pray will be our martyred Brothers' lasting gift for us.

It is easy to criticize RAMSI for its affluence and failings, but for us, who have experienced the fear, the criticisms are simply a manifestation of the luxury of peace. We are especially thankful to the Police Commissioner William Morrell, Rob Walker, Tony Stafford, Ben McDevitt, Darren Folau, Grant Spooner, Tom Abraham, and Paul Green. They have worked so closely with us to find and identify the bodies of our Brothers who died on the Weather Coast and made it possible for us to bring our departed Brothers back to Tabalia, where they could be buried with respect and dignity. We are grateful too for the lengths to which RAMSI personnel have gone to ensure that a full and professional investigation of the crimes takes place. They have been truly supportive, and, I believe, deeply moved personally by the work they have done.

28

Believe in God, believe also in me.

John 14.1

From Correspondence December 2003

Charles Montgomery from Canada writes to me again. He is writing a
book called *The Last Heathen: Encounters with Ghosts and Ancestors in
Melanesia.*[38] He came as the sceptical dilettante searching for their
myths, exposing their underbelly and becoming disillusioned by many of
them, but I know how moved he has been by the story of these Brothers.
You see, ultimately I believe he came in search of faith. That was what
Brother Francis wrote in Charles's notebook the last time they met:
'Believe.' Charles writes to me with so many questions. Perhaps it is
Brother Francis who will provide the answer to his search: 'Believe.'

Charles writes: *'You said that at the end of the day one can only tell stories
about that which is life-giving and eternal. What did you mean? Can you
give an example?'*
I reply to him: A story can tell a larger truth than a factual statement,
because a story grows in the experience and response of both the teller
and the hearer. A story has a life of its own; it lives on and is enfleshed by
our own lives. Thus it is story that can help us approach spiritual truths,
because all spiritual truth must be a response of individual faith. It is not
dry fact. It is a deeper knowledge incarnated in our own lives. You want
an example? Your own example of Brother Francis is a perfect illustration of a spiritual truth told in a story. You could have said he was a
humble man, you could have said he used prayers in the process of

---

38 Charles Montgomery, *The Last Heathen*, Canada, Douglas and McIntyre, 2004.

disarmament. Your story conveyed a deeper truth about the nature of this man and the transformation that meeting him has wrought in your life.

When preaching at the requiem of Brother Robin Lindsay in PNG I too told a story about the dream Brother Robin had of how a cyclone engulfed him and a wave had transported him to the top of a mountain and that he was left standing in light, a light so bright he could see for miles. He said he heard the voice of God speaking to him and saying 'All will be well, all things will be well.' The dream is true. He did come to me. It has a factual basis. This is the real dream he told me. I tried to explain the dream in terms of troubles he was perhaps facing at that time. I had no idea of his approaching death, and neither had he. Yet now, in the light of all that has taken place, the dream has taken on a new meaning. My own memory of the dream is now coloured by the shock of his death. As I witness to what he told me, I find that the words I remember him saying are perhaps not his words but that I have in my own memory drawn on the words of a spiritual writer, Julian of Norwich, who at the end of her vision of the cross writes 'All things will be well, all manner of things will be well.' And yet as I describe Robin's dream I am not fabricating. This is the truth he imparted to me, a truth that only now makes sense. I could have tried to explain that Robin believed in eternal life and now he is in heaven, but his own story of this dream imparts this truth far more vividly and miraculously, for in my memory it was a revelation of immortality and God's love being greater than his coming death, a spiritual truth he left with me.

'I asked you about the literalness of the Bible. Was Jesus just the greatest of teachers or did he walk on the water?'
Did Jesus actually walk on water? My answer would be yes he did in their memory of him; he did in their faith experience. The walk on water could not be captured on video or analysed by a scientist, and yet it was profoundly true for those who witnessed it. The event in their minds became a drama of an even greater truth that Christ, a flesh and blood Christ, not a spirit, was there with them, crossing the water (water the symbol of chaos, the home of Leviathan the devilish monster of the deep), reaching

out to them in their fear and calling them to trust him and come to him, even when fear and doubt were undermining that call. They too could do what was impossible if they truly believed in him. And they did do what was impossible: this group of fishermen have profoundly changed the world with their lives and proclamation, until this very day. And their story lives on in the waves and fears we too face, with Christ bringing life out of chaos. Do such things really happen? I believe they do if we are receptive to them.

I am on a beach in Java in 1985, lost and alone, profoundly disturbed by events in my life, and I remember on this beach praying for help and seeing three crosses shining in front of me, literally burning with light in the dark. I remember those crosses years later. As I direct a passion play in Solomon Islands we move towards the Calvary scene where three crosses have been erected on a hill. It is dark and we move toward that hill with flaming torches, and there in front of me are the same three crosses. And in my memory something speaks so profoundly. This is the cross I have been following which has led me from Java and has somehow provided the meaning and the shape to my life, the underlying thread which has pulled me and led me here through apparent confusion. It has made sense of things. You may ask was the cross real when I saw it in Java? And I can only answer yes, it was for me profoundly real, for in the following years it became the sign of Christ's love, which gave meaning to my journey.

'I asked you about some of the miracles which people relate about the Tasiu. You told me that we must decide which stories we will believe, which we will see as metaphors and which we will reject. You said you did believe in miracles of love. What did you mean?'

We all have our own faith stories. Some speak more profoundly to us than to others. A faith experience for one may seem dubious to another. And all faith stories must be tested against reason and all the other sources of our knowledge of God. For just as these faith stories can inspire faith, they can also mislead us. For me personally the story of a gun turning into a snake does not sound believable, neither does it help me personally. Nevertheless, it was genuinely believed by many who recounted it, and did help the process of disarmament. The danger was that it could also lead to a false concept of invulnerability and to a spiritual pride. As events have progressed, the recent deaths of our Brothers have purged many of such pride. I believe a true revelation of God's love must ultimately lead us the same way that it led Christ: to a greater humility, to a sense that we are part of his mystery and not creating our own. All true signs of God, I believe, must, for the individual, be redemptive. This means they must set people free to love rather than imprisoning people in fear and superstition. Brother Francis and Brother Robin showed people what it means to be of God: they pointed beyond themselves to a better way, to God's way. At other times the Brothers' practices have not always done this. I believe a practice becomes cultish when it points to its own power, when the symbol itself becomes the idol, and no longer do we look beyond the sign to God's redeeming love. This is imprisoning. People love to create such idols for they become ways of controlling our own destiny, creating our own controllable gods. Thus I believe a Brother's walking stick has no innate power. It only conveys power when it is used as a sign of God's power to release a person from fear. In the temptations of Jesus, he too is tempted to turn stones into bread, but he refuses to become a magician or to create idols which can never satisfy our longing for the eternal. Perhaps the story about a snake served a purpose, but what happens when there is no snake? I look for a story that will change us so profoundly that again and again deep within us we will recognize the gun for what it is, and no longer want to be contaminated by its destructive power. For me, our seven Brothers have done just that: now to look at the brutality which surrounded their death is to be repulsed by such evil and to long to stand in solidarity with them.

'Where do you stand?'

My own beliefs have been formed by, and yet differ in some ways from those I have experienced in Solomon Islands. I do not share, for example, a belief in bullets which bend or in *vele*, the Guadalcanal magic men, who are said to move faster than a motorbike and kill by swinging a *vele* bag with crooked finger and blowing lime. Perhaps by believing in these things we give them power to influence us, and they can influence us for good or evil. My scepticism with bending bullets is because again the implication is that the miraculous defies nature, rather than restores it and heals it. I believe that a bullet will kill and is profoundly dangerous. At the same time I share and long to share more of the Melanesian faith in God's providence and care. Like St Paul, I believe that neither life nor death separates us from God's love. Thus through God's providential care he spared the life of all the Novices and Brothers who were in the second group taken captive by Keke. But also through his providential care he gave life to the seven who were brutally murdered and life to others through their tragedy. Perhaps you think I am just arguing that whatever happens it is the working out of God's providential care, thus giving God the benefit of the doubt in all circumstances. Yes, I do think that that is true: if we have faith, even a crucifixion can become the means to life. Melanesian theology has influenced me and taught me much. It has made me more receptive to mysteries of faith that cannot simply be explained. How was it, for example, that a few days after announcing the death of our Brothers Keke agreed to a complete and unconditional surrender? How is it that these seven young men were willing to sacrifice their lives in an action that has precipitated both the intervention and the surrender of nearly all the weapons still held in these islands? When Bishop Patteson died his friend wrote 'God's ways are not our ways.' His own seemingly futile death also is said to have precipitated the end to the 'blackbirding' trade of Melanesians kidnapped to work in Queensland and Fijian plantations. I am prepared to stand with Melanesians in trusting in God's providential care even when it seems, for a time, nowhere in evidence.

Neither do I believe that because my belief is different it negates the reality of what many of my Brothers believe. God uses the language of his people, and while a picture by Duccio can hold me transfixed and be a revelation for me, I know that for a Solomon Islander God speaks through different signs. The test is whether the revelation is leading us to life in all its fullness. Is it exploding prejudice and leading us to a deeper humanity or is it creating new prejudices and fears?

'Bishop Terry Brown (the Bishop of Malaita) was concerned that Solomon

Islanders were concerning themselves too much with mana. *He talked of the essential Christian sign not being power but brokenness. What do you think?'*

Yes I share the concern about *mana* and it is one of the transformations of a maturing Community that we move deeper than simply believing in a God who gives us what we want, to a God who loves and longs for us to love as he does. As C. S. Lewis said, prayer should not be about how we change God, but letting God change us. The humbling effect of our seven Brothers' deaths has been very profound. It allows for a true Christology to emerge, a Christology that has always been there but is not always what people either want to hear or want for themselves. The incarnation was about healing and forgiveness and life in all its fullness, but it was never about the manipulation of people and events for personal power. Christ never offered an escape or divine immunity. In fact quite the opposite he said they must carry the cross and pass through pain and suffering; Paul says that God's power is made perfect in human *weakness* and that is hard for anyone to understand and embrace.

'You teased me about my search for proof of supernatural power. Why?'
You cannot stand detached from faith and analyse it as a scientist tests for the purity of water. Ultimately you have to swim in it and then try to make sense of this experience. I feel you are already swimming but are constantly tempted by the society you live in to get back on the bank and abandon the discovery they have perhaps never had. The world has always looked for proof and yet we tell a story, a story of someone who has changed our lives and continues to work the mystery of his love by incarnating his truths in the lives of our brothers and sisters and in his creation. That is the gift that Brother Francis has left with me: his courage to live the incarnation and thus for me to witness the miracle of the incarnation of Christ's love in the life of my brother, and I pray, in my own life too. It would be hard to prove this, but it is, nevertheless, a reality for me.

'Have you always believed that good and evil were palpable things?'
Yes, I think I have, but now I believe this more than ever. Earlier this year I lay awake at night listening to the BBC news of the war against Iraq and

felt the most profound experience of darkness. The belief that my own nation in this war has become, albeit for the most part unwillingly, the perpetrator of evil, has never left me. You can sense good and evil in the air, you can discern them in movements of your own heart from consolation to desolation. Evil has a power and a momentum of its own which sucks others, often the innocent, into its whirlpool. But God's love has an even greater power for it cannot be defeated. Even the cyclone can take us to the top of the mountain where we stand in the brilliance of the light. St Paul says that sin flows but that grace overflows.

When Charles sends me a copy of his book he has revisited the story of Brother Francis. He writes so beautifully that he has been able to capture a truth with words that are beyond words, like a painter or a musician, and each time I read what he has written I am moved again by that truth, and feel somehow that I can be at peace because someone else has understood and somehow caught that mystery. He writes on hearing of their deaths: 'What can you do when you learn something like this? What can you do but look out your window and watch the buses and bank towers disappear behind a haze of tears, and wonder whether you are crying for the dead, for yourself, or for something shining and good that once called to you, dared you to believe and then was gone again?' He continues:

They journeyed alone to the darkest edge of their world. And there, far from home and light and love, under the unceasing rain, amid the mud and the squalor they had offered themselves up as martyrs . . .

Their deaths would mirror those of their heroes, of Bishop Patteson, Stephen Taroaniara, Edwin Nobbs, Fisher Young and all the other fallen martyrs of Melanesia – and of Jesus. In one audacious leap, the Brothers had moved from *mana*, the hoarding up of political power advocated by the old cosmology, to self-sacrifice, the transcendental love and martyrdom of the new. They had abandoned the God of Power for the God of Love. And in their sacrifice, surely they would become more powerful, more illuminated than they had been in their lives . . . I would like to trade the shark boss and his circling shadow, for a clearer image of Brother Francis. Return with me now to Tetere police post and the shade of the oak tree and the tension that showed in the twitching muscles of the young militants. Return with me to the very moment when Brother Francis stepped forward, removed his wrap around sunglasses and began to pray, would it be wrong of me to paint a faint saintly glow around his head? It would be like the halo that surrounds the moon on a humid night, so faint it would be easy to believe I had imagined it. And the militants, did they not remove their sunglasses too, and did they not wipe tears of shame from their eyes? And the cicadas, did they not cease their incessant whirring for the first time in many months? And the wind, did it not rise? Did the wind not tear at the grass and lift the dust so it swirled in a circle around Brother Francis, never quite touching him, and did the wind not wail and whistle, not to obscure but to strangely amplify his whispered prayer? And were we not all lifted? Did we not all hover there, for a moment, just above the rustling grasses, at once humbled, helpless and yet buoyed by holiness? Would it be wrong for me to tell the story that way? Because that would be closer to the truth of things. That is a story I could claim as my own.[39]

I would like to claim it as my own story too. It is Brother Francis's gift to us.

And the miracles did not end on that day . . .

---

39 Charles Montgomery, *The Shark God*, London, Fourth Estate, 2006, pp. 352-3 (originally published as *The Last Heathen*, Canada, Douglas and McIntyre, 2004).

29

Peace I leave with you; my peace I give to you . . . Do not let your hearts be troubled and do not let them be afraid.

John 14.27

From the diary of March and April 2004

The Melanesian Brotherhood has been awarded the United Nations Pacific Human Rights Award for 'its sacrifice above the call of duty to protect the vulnerable and build peace and security in the Solomon Islands during civil conflict and post-conflict reconstruction'. At the presentation of the awards Archbishop Ellison Pogo said: 'Much of the work done by some of the Brothers was the sort of work that no person should ever have to do. Many of the things witnessed were things no person should ever have to see. Many of the stories told to them first hand were stories no person should ever have to hear. Yet the brothers continued without ceasing to commit their own lives to the cause of peace and justice.' Brother Jude Alfred who himself has shown so much courage and goodness accepted the award on behalf of the Brotherhood with these words:

Our Community is made up of Brothers from every province of the Solomon Islands: Guadalcanal, Malaita, Ysabel, Temotu, Makira and the Western Province. As a community we have always tried to live together as one . . . Today as I accept this award, I accept it on behalf of all those who have worked and longed for peace but most especially on behalf of seven of our Brothers who are no longer with us, but who died wanting so much for peace and happiness to return to the Solomon Islands. May their deaths and the deaths and suffering of many people in the Solomon Islands during the last four years, not be an end but a beginning of a new justice and integrity for our nation. Jesus Christ said 'Blessed are all peacemakers for they shall be called the sons and daughters of God.'

Before the ceremony Brother Jude had been so typically humble about receiving any such award and somewhat embarrassed that the Community should be thus singled out. For our Christian friends and supporters around the world it is an acknowledgement of all the Community has been through and done in the last years, and there are many messages of congratulation. And yet for the Brothers themselves there is no interest in awards or recognition. The ceremony passes the Community by with little mention, and I am reminded of those words at the heart of our Brotherhood's calling: 'if I honour myself my honour is nothing.' While publicly we were being honoured there were many who within, were still not at peace.

I had realized that some of the suffering and the trauma of the events specific members of the Community had been through was still not understood and remained unresolved. I had noticed that some of the Brothers were still distant, detached or unable to settle; others had come to me expressing how hard it was for them to let go of feelings, memories and the painful events that they had been through. The funeral and the public expression both of loss and hope, and the continuing community life and structure of prayer, had helped members of our Community involved in the peacemaking to come to terms with the events they have faced. But for some there was evidence of longer-term repercussions which I began to see needed professional psychological and spiritual help to deal with. This was, of course, not just true within our Community but even more so in the wider community, particularly on the Weather Coast of Guadalcanal and among former militants and those who had become witnesses and victims of the conflict.

With the agreement and support of the Brotherhood, I set about trying to find help. During February I had met with two people in Melbourne who had been recommended to me. Father Peter Hosking is a Jesuit priest and a clinical psychologist. He had much experience working with the victims of trauma and torture in Vietnam, Cambodia and, most recently, in East Timor, where he had worked with victim support during the Truth and Reconciliation Commission. With his background of Ignatian spirituality, I believed he could be helpful in bridging the gulf between the more culturally unfamiliar concept of psychological counselling and the Community's understanding of prayer and Christian ministry.

Through his own and others' recommendations I was also guided into meeting Felicity Rousseaux, who had worked in the field of trauma counselling for more than fourteen years and recently for the Victorian Foundation for Survivors of Torture as a counsellor and advocate. She was to prove a great gift to our Community, working indefatigably in individual counselling sessions and in group work to bring help and healing and to train Brothers to help others. She also developed a great love for the Community and even after she left continued to offer generous help, support and concern.

I managed to find funding from AngliCORD, a Melbourne-based overseas aid body, and organized the workshop for peace at Tabalia in April 2004. For a period of three weeks Felicity and Peter worked with those in our Community and Father Lionel Longarata and others, who had been most affected by the conflict.

We began with a time of retreat and prayer. Peter Hosking led the retreat and I include here just a little of what he shared:

Love and healing

'Some of us here carry deep within us wounds from the past that still unsettle our spirits and rankle in our hearts. And unfortunately, when we are wounded, and those wounds remain unhealed, we tend to wound others. So if we haven't been healed of the wounds of our past life, there is a strong possibility that we'll pass those wounds on to others – our community, family members, friends and so on. Some people even suggest that these deep hurts or traces of trauma can pass from generation to generation in a society. Some suggest we see this sometimes in the patterns of problem drinking, addictions of various kinds and domestic violence and abuse in some families that travel on down generations.

When we are freed to love, we will be healed. God is love. And when we love, we know God. An unwillingness to forgive others for the real or imaginary wrongs they have done us is a poison that can affect our health – physical, emotional and spiritual – sometimes very deeply. That is *not* to say that every illness in our bodies is caused because we need to forgive someone in our lives or be forgiven. But the need for reconciliation and healing are often interconnected. It is also important to know that many hurts require truth and justice for reconciliation and healing to occur. Forgiveness is not the same as forgetting. Forgetting is amnesia and that never helps true reconciliation.

We may need to ask God to break the cycle of our woundedness.'

God is the healer

'We must remember that *God* is the One who will heal us. In healing the most important relationship is you and God. When we are close to that relationship, then we become closer to each other.

How can I be sure that God will heal us? Jesus promised that wherever two or more are gathered in his name, that he would be there. And we are gathered here in Jesus' name. There is a Presence here that is not of this world, a Presence that pervades and invades us, a Presence that breaks through our smallness and our sinfulness, makes us better than we are, a Presence that is awfully real because it is a Person, a living, risen Person. Again and again we see in his life that Christ is the liberator, the one whose presence sets people free.

Because Jesus resides in us, we all belong to one another. We are the Body of Christ and his healing power is in our gathering, our Community here. We all need affirmation and emotional intimacy to affirm the core of a person's identity. And when we minister to one another, we are ministering to Christ. By our regard, our affirmation, our listening, by being present to each other we can take part with Christ in this liberation from fear.'

God's call out of suffering

'Often our call in life – our vocation – grows out of the compassion that we have built up because of our own woundedness. What does my suffering show me about how I could spend my life in the service of others? This is an exercise of honesty and transparency before God. When we have allowed God to uncover and heal our woundedness, then our woundedness can become a gift for the Community. Our pain is sometimes the key to our vocation because it shows us where we can best help to heal others. In that sense we can begin to see our woundedness as a gift rather than a failure. It is out of our woundedness and our personal limitations that our healing gifts will come. It is in the place where we feel most separated and most abandoned, as Jesus felt at Golgotha, that we can be most in need, most dependent, and most connected to God.

Healing, praying and loving all go hand in hand. Healing is loving. When we heal, we love; when we love, we heal; when we love another, we affirm, we nurture and we cherish that person. Sometimes in our lives we can try and try to solve a problem and there is a time for that. But sometimes just letting ourselves love again and be loved can solve so many problems. When we let go and just soak up love from the Lord and others, we have a whole new power to go on again. When we get burned out, it isn't usually because we're doing too many things but often because we're not letting ourselves be loved.'

Release from resentment

'Forgiveness is not a simple matter. If our lives have been violated in some way, this hurts us and it is natural to feel deep anger and hurt. In order to forgive it is necessary to experience helpfully and then express appropriately difficult and challenging emotions like anger. Anger is a natural and healthy psychophysical response to a transgression of our boundaries. We should not speak too easily or too quickly of healing and forgiving. An important step in the healing process may be to give ourselves permission to express our anger and find means to a truthful expression rather than repression of the pain and bitterness we feel. Truth is essential to reconciliation.'

Accepting our weakness

'The power to change comes when we hate the sin and love the sinner. If we do not notice and abhor our sinful actions, then we become insensitive to our imperfect behaviours rather than conscientious to change them for the better. If we do not love the sinner, we become depressed and scrupulous with no power to correct our destructiveness. The discovery of our sin, perhaps is a healthy discovery because it means we see our destructiveness, take responsibility for it, and with God loving and empowering us, we begin to take steps to change the evil that can be changed. It is healthy but often difficult to discover and admit our sin. Our capacity for self-defensiveness in this area is strong. We readily regress to self-justifications or self-pity. One way to get in touch with our sinfulness (perhaps that which we cannot forgive in ourselves) is to note where we react excessively to others.

Sin is also corporate

We discussed the way sin is often not the fault of the individual but part of the injustice of the society we belong to or the circumstances we are in, over which we seem to have no power. In such situations it is easy to lose our confidence and self-esteem or even to believe we are punished or deserve the suffering we face. We may feel abandoned by God. We learn from Jesus Christ that God is our loving Father. Our God does not desire or require that we suffer or put up patiently with situations of injustice and abuse. We are told that Christ comes to set the captive free. We have to ask ourselves how are we being imprisoned and work for liberation both of ourselves and others. Sometimes this will involve great courage but that courage is easier when we realize that God is with us and desires that we have life in all its fullness. Perfect love drives away all fear, just as light drives away the darkness. Corporate sin requires solidarity in our response to it.

Vicarious trauma

Peter talked about the way Christians are often called into positions of extreme empathy and caring. Yet there is also the danger of becoming over-involved and taking the responsibility for too much of the pain and thus becoming weighed down by it, and over a sustained period the victim of the trauma oneself. The danger of vicarious trauma is that it can lead to an avoidance of the issues involved: a dread of the pain of the situation and a failure to be able to face the victim because of our own inner fears and hurt. The truth is blocked out and the victim believes he or she is not being heard and the suffering is never addressed. Vicarious suffering can also lead to an over identification with the victim, in turn leading to over dependence, or the violation of boundaries or to burn-out. Vicarious suffering finds expression in anger or projection or the obsessive need for affirmation. The Christian carer needs to recognize these symptoms and realize that they too can become honourably wounded and those wounds too need attention and time and space for God's healing.

Inner healing and strength

'Healing does not usually take place instantly but is a process. Deep pain and resentment, which have developed over some time, will usually take time and love and patient prayer to heal. Often there are layers of hurt, resentment and un-freedom that need to be uncovered in prayer. Once one layer of hurt, resentment and un-freedom has been healed, others may present themselves for healing. We know we are healed when we can recall the hurting experience without trauma.'

In the time together, Felicity helped the Brothers to identify the symptoms of pain and trauma which they had experienced.

Felicity and Peter asked the question 'How do you feel after traumatic, violent, and painful events?'[40]

'I have thoughts which are not good and full of sorrow.'

'My senses too, smell, someone touching me, the taste in my mouth can make me think of terrible things.'

'I feel violent things are going to happen again.'

'My body and mind do not stay together, as if my mind has left my body.'

'I cannot think of anything new.'

'I cannot sleep and yet I feel so tired.'

'I dream horrible dreams and keep waking up from my sleep.'

'I am frightened of things which make me think back and I do not want to think about those things again.'

'I get angry quickly and can't control the anger.'

'I don't look after myself, I am not interested to eat, to swim, to wash or wash my clothes or shave my beard and I do not look after my life and my ways of behaving.'

'I can't stay with other people or feel close to others or feel part of anything.'

'I feel restless. I always want to be on the move because when I stop moving I remember.'

'I shake too much and jump when I hear a loud noise.'

'All the time I am waiting for something to happen and my body can't stay still or at peace and I am always looking around.'

'I have headaches which won't go away.'

'I have stomach ache.'

'I keep thinking I have a sickness and that I am dying.'

'I think I am going to be killed.'

'My heart beats hard and works faster.'

'I am frightened of people I don't know and I am frightened to be by myself.'

---

40 These ideas were originally expressed in *pidgin* which is the language used among mixed island groups throughout the Solomon Islands. I have translated it as closely as possible to their own words.

'My body and my interest in everything feels weak and I feel I can't cope with everything.'

'I can't pray, God does not help me.'

'I want to die so I don't have to face this fear anymore.'

The participants began to realize that many of these symptoms were shared and that they were not alone or going mad. Many of the symptoms of trauma had cut them off but now they were able to identify and share. They began as a group to discuss and develop strategies which helped them to cope. I include the list the Brothers made. As I re-read it I see how much wisdom each of the seemingly simple ideas contains. Their strategies range from immediate steps for coping or finding daily habits that help them, right through to discovering a new outgoing sense of mission. In this list one can discern not only the pain they have been through but, just as Peter had spoken about, the way woundedness can become a gift to the community and the foundation of a renewed vocation. Whether self-focused, God-focused or other-focused what is evident is that their faith is playing a vital role in this healing process. Felicity Rousseux was to observe frequently how she had never been able to work so effectively because the prerequisites for healing were already present: faith, hope and love. The miracle is in that word which Brother Francis Tofi had written: 'believe'.

Coping strategies

'Thankfulness that I am still alive.'

'Prayer helps, praying for others, and being prayed for by others.'

'The feelings attached to a place gradually get less intense over time.'

'The incident has stopped. The pain has ended. It is over.'

'Being with children I feel happy and alive. We see there can be a bright future and all that is possible.'

'Being with others who understand us.'

'Food and drink, eating together and good nutrition.'

'The encouragement of family and friends outside the Brotherhood.'

'Doing things to process the experience, for example retreats and workshops, study and reading.'

'Talking with others who have had and overcome similar difficult experiences and offer us hope.'

'Perpetrators saying they are sorry for what they have done and knowing their wrong.'

'Friendship, feeling connected with others and also yourself.'

'Sharing feelings with those you trust and who understand.'

'Fun, for example: soccer, exercise, music, choir, custom dancing, pan-pipes and entertainment.'

'Working hard to release the tension in manual work, cutting timber, clearing the land, farming.'

'Feeling safe and being secure.'

'Following familiar patterns and ways of doing things.'

'Following a daily routine and disciplining yourself to do things.'

'Doing mission work.'

'Sharing the story and being listened to and understood but having a choice, when to talk about the experience and with whom and how much to tell.'

'Having control of our own lives.'

'Creative activities, making things, carving, writing.'

'Making dramas which express the meaning of our struggles.'

'Going to another safe place, a new environment.'

'Learning to understand that God's ways are not our ways.'

'The constant love of God.'

'The faithfulness of God.'

'Scripture, Offices and prayer, giving strength and encouragement.'

'Asking God to help the militants to change their minds.'

'The forgiveness of God.'

'The Holy Communion, knowing God is with us and in us and gives himself to us.'

'People who love and care for me without condition.'

'People who understand without judging us.'

'Friends who know our weaknesses but still trust us and are loyal to us.'

'The support of the Brotherhood and knowing we belong.'

'Rest, sleep, and time to recover.'

'Advice and encouragement of friends and Brothers.'

'Finding the problems we face are reflected in the life of Christ.'

'Unexpected blessings.'

'Memories which encourage us.'

'Discovering some good in the midst of evil.'

'Seeing the problem from a distance and seeing how some good has come out of it.'

'Time brings healing.'

'Using our life to help others who have faced difficulties, transforming the pain into something for good.'

'We never forget, but the memory of those we loved is no longer a wound but a blessing we carry with us.'

Forgiveness is most difficult when the perpetrators of some of the most brutal acts do not even admit they are wrong or any responsibility for the pain they have caused. There is no answer to this. But as I meet these Brothers who suffered and read again their list of strategies I realize that forgiveness is a mystery and a miracle of grace. It is not the settling of an account or based on a balance of logic; it is freely offered and undeserved. This gift is not always received, but it is a hand held out against all the odds in the hope of final restoration. I think of the father in the parable of the Lost Son watching and waiting. There is profound pain in that waiting, which is the result of the sin which has violated the relationship, but there is an even greater love in the waiting, for it is also an inner realization that the love of God is still more powerful than the worst wrong.

If you ask us how this Community can forgive Keke or Cawa I do not know, and yet when I see Christ in my Brothers I realize they are holding no hatred or bitterness, but are free in a way Keke and Cawa are not. Thus strangely even hatred can be transformed into compassion and mercy for those who are still prisoners.

We have decorated the room for Felicity's counselling sessions. The walls are light blue and there is new blue and grey lino on the floor. It is next to the Head Brother's room and a quiet and peaceful place. She has a great skill in counselling; she is attentive to every detail and responds perceptively. She has seen many of the Brothers who have needed help.

And now, in this blue room, she talks to me and she asks me to imagine a place of happiness and peace in my mind, and to describe it. The kind of place I could return to, which will bring joy and comfort. And I imagine that I am standing at a cooking stove cooking a huge pot of rice and a pot of what my Brothers here call 'white man's stew'. And this is my home in Solomon Islands, and into that room a lot of people are coming in and out. And I am feeding them plates of food and they are grateful and I am grateful for them. And there is an easy closeness, and although the house is full, there is a peacefulness and holiness: a receptivity to each others' needs, a to and fro, a giving and a taking, a taking and a giving, a stable door swinging backwards and forwards, a breathing in and a breathing out – and it is the movement of trust and friendship and regard and real brotherhood. And I look round and realize that my own family from England are here: Tim and Matthew and Andrew and Daniel, and their families too. And of course my mother and father are there, who created a home not so different from this, where everyone was welcomed. And the house is no longer in Solomon Islands but beyond culture or specific place, but where I am my true self and able to give and receive and be who I truly am. And then I realize that this picture is not a dream and that I have been truly blessed by this place and these people, and I will carry them with me. The human family has widened.

Joy

The less longing
The more presence
The less we bang on the door, the more it opens for us
The less we demand, the more we can open our eyes to the beauty
    of gift
The less we expect, the greater the joy and surprise
The more selfless, the more self
Clamorous need shuts us off from the needed
It is our clinging which is our death
The less we cling, the more we embrace
The less we fear, the more we love

Peace I leave with you

All joy reminds us
It is never a possession, it is always behind us and before us
And our love a taste of things to come
Go lightly
Go simply
A breathing out
A breathing in
A shared breath
A letting go
That we may be held forever.

30

And now faith, hope and love abide, these three; and the greatest of these is love.

1 Corinthians 13.13

From the diary of Thursday 22 July 2004

Today the Archbishop of Canterbury, Rowan Williams, visited Tabalia. There were tremendous preparations. Suddenly it seemed to get into everyone's head that an Archbishop would not be able to cope with a bump or a curve in any road. They had steamrollers and graders at work all the way from Honiara right up the hill to Tabalia. Every green verge and stripy shrub was stripped away leaving these huge brown dust tracks like logging roads. And then, throughout the night, truck loads of stones were brought from the beach and river bed and levelled out to cover the dust. I stood at the entrance to Tabalia banning any steamroller from entering, with the Brothers laughing, and then when my back was turned for a moment a huge steamroller thundered towards the guest-house crumbling those pebbles of our road into grey dust. I managed to stop the steamroller driver and explain to him that this was holy ground on which the Brothers were not even allowed to wear shoes, and that it had taken God thousands of years to shape and smooth the pebbles, which he was in the process of destroying simply because he was sitting in a very big machine. There has been enough wanton destruction, now we want God's creation to speak!

To be honest, Tabalia looked more beautiful than it had ever done. The Brothers and Novices had gone into overdrive and decorated the place with those fresh young green strips of palm and flowers; the grass was cut, the hedges pruned, the graves of our seven Brothers natural beds of seashore stones and colour, with hanging fronds tipped with bougainvillaea and frangipani. We wanted the Eucharist to be simple, the way we worship each day. After all the ritual and dancing of his cathedral welcome, we cut the ceremony back, and it was a beautiful spacious and reverent service, the Brothers singing their quieter meditational hymns, the Archbishop celebrating with a small golden chalice inscribed with the names of our departed Brothers, and preaching with his deep Welsh voice resonating around the chapel. He spoke with authority and simplicity, without small-talk or decoration or notes. He spoke about what he saw that mattered in our Community. He said that Christ was in God and in humanity, and that's where our Brotherhood is called to remain: close to the Father and close to the people. A highlight for us all was his request, which we had received the day before, for him to be admitted as a Companion of the Melanesian Brotherhood. I ask him if it's all right for me to bless an Archbishop of Canterbury as it's part of the admission service I conduct and he replies, 'Of course it is!' At the end of the service we processed to the graves of our Brothers, which he sprinkled with holy water, and then he planted a kauri tree with a beautiful brass plaque in memory of his visit and of our departed Brothers, bearing the inscription that their faith should be the seed that yields a harvest of peace.

A Blessing

I saw this place again today
Through his eyes
The dancing and the song
And watching from the side, saw again what I have loved
And stumbling through the darkness
We have arrived at the place of pan-pipes
And joined the song of the birds as they whistle, pump
    and weave their tunes in a sound which is one of joy
There is harmony here
Let it be
Lest it slip away

This warm dance
This grace of brotherhood.

Solomon Islands is a place where it is much easier in many ways to confront life's mysteries because one is in touch with them constantly. There are no defences or modern conveniences to separate you from the elements: when it rains you get wet, and when the floods come you get hungry because there is less food and, like today, we are skidding about and sliding through mud with bare feet and rushing around picking and squeezing bush limes with 4kg of sugar for sixty-four Novices who have flu – and that's how the morning is spent. And when friends die, you are very much part of that too: no undertakers, no crematoria, just the bare earth and a hole you have watched your Brothers dig, and this fragile life of ours being lowered down and taken up into something greater and beyond our understanding.

This whole event was like entering into the greatest drama one has ever witnessed or conceived, and the drama was real and I kept hoping it wasn't, and it went on day after day, so that you were inside it and outside it and longing for it to find a reconciliation. And then like a tragedy, I suddenly realized that all was changed unalterably and nothing would ever be the same, and there was no possible way of ever going back or bringing back, but that in the place you expected to find bitterness and dread, instead there was, alongside the loss, a deeper humanity. And in this situation you know where you belong and what things you believe in and all the appendages and props and façades and nonsenses are seen for what they are. You are face to face with what you are – naked as it were, without pride or delusions, but human, and present – and you are not alone but there are others there with you, and strangely you are no longer afraid. I love being here with my Community. It is much harder in many ways being back in the UK, where everything seems distant and removed and death seems like a terribly bleak alien and anonymous thief which has no relationship with the modern world, rather than something we knew intimately. The death of these Brothers was more like a painful birth than a death.

PART 3

Acts

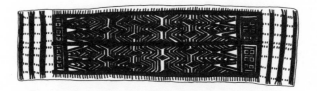

31

As the Father has sent me, so I send you.

John 20.21

From the diary of April to August 2005

What a joy it was to see this mission team arriving at London Heathrow airport on 25 April. Three hours before departure from Solomon Islands they still had no money to buy shoes or long trousers let alone to buy food for their sixteen-hour stop-over in Singapore, until a generous Australian Companion came to the rescue and lent them some. Some of the black nylon Chinese trousers were at least six inches too short and the soles of all their shoes broke in half after little more than a week of wear. At Singapore airport they had slept on the chairs and had been woken by the police with machine guns pointing at them. A cold grey English spring afternoon was filled with infectious warmth as they hugged their UK welcome party. They carried two huge crates, one the shape of a coffin, stuffed with grass skirts, rattles, costumes, tapa (bark) cloth and pan-pipes.

'Did you pack these yourselves?'

'No.'

'Are you carrying anything in your luggage for others?'

'Yes, everything!' How they got through immigration and customs I do not know. There were twenty-five in this mission team: two Sisters of the Church, two Sisters of Melanesia, two Franciscan Friars from the Society of St Francis, fifteen Melanesian Brothers and three of their Novices, and myself as chaplain.

Over the next three and a half months this group would make presentations in more than a hundred primary and secondary schools, in parish centres, in prisons, in centres for the handicapped, in civic halls, in town centres, in theatres, in churches and cathedrals, covering the dioceses of both Chester and Exeter and also visiting Bristol and London, performing at St Martin-in-the-Fields in Trafalgar Square, and for the Archbishop of Canterbury at Lambeth Palace, ending our mission at St Michael's Convent in Ham.

The first accommodation was an empty vicarage at Weaverham near Chester. Barefoot they stood on the cold grass of the back garden sharing cigarettes, as they marvelled that they had made it to the UK for the first time. They slept on pump-up lilos or sleeping mats, fully clothed in sleeping bags, amazed by the climate, even though the central heating had been turned on specially and was in overdrive. The bathroom was soon awash with water from the shower. In Solomon pidjin to have a bath is called 'swim', because it is done in the river and it was not long before the river was dripping through the kitchen ceiling. During the night a gift of six roast chickens was consumed and by 5.00 a.m. everyone had prayed morning prayer and was out barefoot in the garden, amazed that the sun should change its time for rising.

I wonder what the people of this small town thought. They stared as if there had been an invasion of asylum seekers. There was often a slight awkwardness at first. People were unsure of what this group was or what they could do. Even church people seemed a little wary and wondered what was happening to their familiar traditions and routines, and yet it only took a song or a burst of pan-pipes to break down the barriers. But what a burst of song. It is like nothing they had heard before and so far I have never met anyone, however grumpy or judgemental or uptight who was not in some way freed by this music.

It was the same on that first morning. The parish helpers who had come in to cook lunch were soon peering through the hatchway and then gathering in the kitchen doorway to watch as the Brothers and Sisters practised their drama, sang and danced. Again and again I witnessed a similar transformation: rather damp and drab Anglican church halls, with their little stages and curtains drawn to hide cardboard boxes and twenty years of accumulated junk, halls built in the days when people had time for parish pantomimes and music halls and youth clubs, hobbies and handicraft exhibitions, harvest suppers, barn dancing and nowhere else affordable for wedding receptions, now superseded by fair trade coffee in glass-panelled church narthexes – but now with this mission team community and life was flooding back in! There was suddenly a reason for cakes and quiche and generosity. In the kitchen the women whispered to me 'Aren't they wonderful?' and a chore had become a renewed vocation to care and to serve:

'I've got warm clothes at home. I'll bring them in for them.'

'Do they like a cooked breakfast?'

'When are they going to sing again? They take the roof off. I must get my husband along to hear this!'

Teams of cooks, men and women, materialized; even a chef, on his day off from feeding the staff at a large supermarket, came in to cook breakfast. In one parish after another people began to love them, and the church hall kitchens began to fill with gifts of bananas and cakes and bread and bags of rice and tins of tuna which disappeared at night. For the Brothers it was like the end of rationing. They began to make friends in a way that all of us long to do, but often do not have the opportunity and cannot, because in the West we are busy and need to seem independent rather than interfering or needy, and therefore we put up defences and pretend we are managing 'fine'.

The primary schools are fantastic. We divide into three groups so as not to overwhelm the kids. The headteachers welcome us and seem a bit unsure of whether we will be able to hold the kids' attention:

'You'll have the whole school in the hall. Do you think you can manage about twenty minutes?'

I want to tell them not to worry. These Melanesians work their magic like the Pied Piper. They are so laid back when they arrive, so unassertive. The West is not used to humility in public, for we are taught at an early age to push our own talents. In contrast, the Brothers have no desire to sell themselves. They wander about setting up bamboo pipes on stands next to the wall frames and the basketball hoops of the school hall.

They look crumpled and un-ironed after the nights spent in Church halls. There is no rush and no pretence. Now they are setting up. In a minute they will perform. So why perform while you are setting up? Yet I am rushing about nervously, straddling these two cultures. I want to pre-empt the experience: 'They'll really enjoy this, you'll see.' But for my Brothers there is no need for this. All we have to do is to wait, listen and see. And then they begin to play and the pan-pipes fill the hall and the Brothers and Sisters dance and jump and sway and the bass bamboos pound, and Brother Francis and Brother Moses weave their tunes in and out of the underlying melody and rhythm, soaring and swooping like tropical songbirds, with sudden rushing whistling scales up and down the pan-pipes which the children adore. And after the pan-pipes we ask them what it sounds like and they say:

'Joyful . . . and exciting . . . and like it makes you want to dance and . . . bouncy.'

And one kid in the Wirral says 'It sounds like sunshine.' It does. It sounds like creation celebrating. Another boy in Devon says 'It sounds like we don't have to go to school any more.' The music is freeing. We give the kids permission to loosen up a bit and sway to the music and they do. At the front the juniors look on in wide-eyed innocence. In the middle the kids are completely involved and in the back row the older ones are knocking into one another and the teachers are not sure whether they should wade in to quell them. There is no need. The music wins them over. Soon they are joining in all the songs and every hand is in the air hoping to be chosen for the Malaitan fishing dance or the Ysabel Devon duck dance which is an apocryphal story of how the first missionaries brought ducks to Solomon Islands from Devon, told in a dance because that is how Melanesian memories are often recorded.

Now they imagine they are in the South Pacific with all the fish they have seen in the film *Finding Nemo*. The Melanesian Brothers and Sisters sing a song of meditation, soft and peaceful and ending in a hum which everyone joins in. And then the questions start and they want to know everything:

'What do you eat?'

'What kind of houses do you have?'

'What do you do if you see a shark?'

And the Brothers and Sisters tell the stories of hunting and fishing and house building and life without televisions and computer games or even many shops. And then we can turn the question back to them. 'Do you need a television to make you happy?' 'So what makes happiness?' And primary school kids deep down know these truths and start to share them.

'Friends make you happy . . . and sharing stuff . . .'

'And I think we ought to do more to help people who haven't got things they need.'

'And what about the fighting we see on the news between people of different countries, what do you think of that?'

And they can even talk of God without fear because it doesn't sound like indoctrination; it sounds like part of life and good and life-giving and inclusive.

Dialogue is taking place and it is special because it is not just theories, but those theories are being realized here and now in these assemblies. And people from the developing world are not simply beggars on the television requiring pity and donations but here in the classroom making a relationship: they are magnets whom everyone in the class wants to know more about. Before they can grow tired of the talking, the talking becomes the words and the actions of a song and dance: *'We are one big happy family, God's family.'* And by the end in school after school there is total participation and the headteacher is thrilled and saying it is the best assembly they have ever had. Education is taking place on all levels, barriers are being broken down, and the rich diversity of difference is being experienced and celebrated.

I remember going out into a playground and watching after one of those assemblies. The headteacher had been so delighted with the programme that she announced an extra playtime would follow. As I looked round every one of the Melanesian Brothers and Sisters was surrounded by young children. Some were playing football with them, some a playground game of chase, some were just sitting down in a circle talking, some were looking at their school work and exchanging addresses in Solomon Islands and autographs. But every single kid in the whole school had chosen to interact with a Solomon Island Brother or Sister. And it was a picture of how things should be in the world, and could be. And one day, we are at an assembly in a small school and there is this same sense of harmony, and then the parish priest comes in and whispers to me something about bombs going off on the London Underground and on a double-decker bus. And the reality of our divided world kicks in. I find myself like everyone else desperate to hear news that members of my family living in Central London are safe. But the mobile phone frequencies are blocked and there is a feeling of panic, and all you can get on the mobile is answer messages, after which you leave messages of love, imagining as you do so some person's mobile ringing away in the darkness of an underground tunnel among the tangled wreckage with no one to answer. And our mission and the struggle we have faced on the other side of the world no longer seems so far away, but here and now and deadly relevant.

In the secondary schools, among teenagers, the barriers and defences are up, and to begin with there seems so little connection and so little response. The Solomon Islanders read the postures and the students' eyes staring into space, they notice the flicks of the head and the slight turns away and the initial failure to engage in dialogue, and believe them to be bored or not interested. But they have read them incorrectly. For behind their poses these students are watching and listening, faking that everything is 'boring' until they suss out what they are being subjected to. You can tell that in some schools the staff are nervous, worried that their students will sneer and wanting to keep a tight rein. When the Brothers appear in *kabilatos* (bark loincloths) and grass skirts for the opening scene of *The Lost Son*, there are cat calls from the back, quickly followed by stern staff voices:

'We have had quite enough of that, thank you! I don't want to hear anymore of that . . . do you understand?'

But it is usually not long before Cheka, who is the lost son, begins to win them over. They start laughing at his jokes and are with him on his journey from Solomon Islands to Manchester. Novice Joseph who plays this part has a warmth and cheeky charm that is disarming and infectious, and they are attracted to him. They enjoy his riotous living and by the time things sour for him everyone is on the side of this black migrant. And then the knife turns; they see the hero they have empathized with being plied with alcohol, ecstasy, cocaine and prostitutes and then losing everything and getting beaten up by a racist drug dealer calling him 'an asylum seeker'. Where are their loyalties now? And at the conclusion of this drama they are given an insight into the meaning of unconditional love and forgiveness. I have taught London secondary students in Hackney, and I know the instant you lose kids and enter into a conflict situation, and that to talk openly about things like God is often a no-go area. But this drama has bypassed their defences, and in their chairs the postures have relaxed and opened up and, as the drama ends, the applause is loud and spontaneous, and the whistles are now those of approval and appreciation and no longer derision. A number of the students hang around afterwards to shake hands, ask questions and say things like:

'That was really good that.'

In the dining hall they make way for the Melanesians in the queue, sit down with them and share bits of their packed lunches and talk.

On the streets a car-load of youths drives past with horn blaring. They lean out of the window sticking their fingers up at the Brothers who, unaware of the racist insult, wave back in greeting. 'What does that sign they made mean?' one of the Brothers asks. I am silent. I do not have the heart even to try to explain that 'he is telling you to fuck off', the vile lunacy that makes someone hate another simply because of tribe or colour or creed or nation or sexuality. Perhaps it is better simply to wave back rather than let their poison poison us.

There was one moment playing *The Lost Son* which I will never forget.

In Chester Cathedral we made this drama into a workshop which the school students joined. They became the crowd in the town scene and at one point they were instructed to walk past the lost son who had been beaten up and left homeless in the street. 'Imagine he is one of those people you walk past quickly, like someone who is selling *The Big Issue*,'

I tell them. Everyone follows the instructions except one small ten-year-old who comes up to me and asks:

'I don't want to walk past him, can I help him?'

'That's not part of the story, it's not in the script.'

'But I want to help him.'

'Well then, I suppose you'd better help him.'

He knelt down by the side of Cheka, put his arm round his shoulder and said:

'Look, if you are hungry, I can get you something to eat. You can come to my mum's – she'll cook for us.'

It was then that some of the others started gathering round Cheka too. Cheka had crossed the barriers in a drama. A man from the other side of the world had become their neighbour. A ten-year-old had stood out against group conformity and had the courage of his compassion, which influenced the others. The parable had begun its work. It was very moving to watch. I do not think I am overstating the case when I say there is a beauty about these pieces that is holy. It is strange how these Christian parables can cross time and culture and be as relevant in London as in the Pacific Islands.

In the parishes the people ask the Melanesians 'How do you find the Church of England?' Novice Kevin answers with kindness:

It is very special. We have seen such beautiful buildings. We have been welcomed with great kindness by many people and it is wonderful. We have much to learn from you, especially the elderly. It was your ancestors who brought us the gospel of peace and now we have returned to thank you. But one thing is lacking: a family consists of the grandparents, the parents, young people and children, but we have not found many young ones of our age in your Church. God is their God too and we must bring them back.

Novice Kevin tells of his own life: 'It is not always easy to live the life of poverty, chastity and obedience but I have found joy in sharing this life of simplicity. It is the life of Christ in us which is like a small seed which will grow into the strongest tree of all.'

32

Just as you did it to one of the least of these who are members of my family, you did it to me.

Matthew 25.40

Where do you find God in our twenty-first century? You find him in the same place he was during his life on earth among those most open to his presence. We arrived half an hour late at Woodlands School near Plymouth. We were tired and running out of steam in a programme that seemed to rush us from one place to another with no time to recharge. It is a school for those with severe physical needs and as I entered I wondered how our programme of dancing and participation could ever work because many of our audience were in wheelchairs with very little control of movement in any part of their bodies. They had been waiting for us but it was a hot afternoon and I was aware it had not been an easy wait. Some were growing uncomfortable and restless. Once the music began, however, there was connection: huge smiles and all manner of sounds of happiness. Then spontaneously the Brothers came forward and offered to push the wheelchairs and suddenly everyone wanted to participate; the wheelchairs were weaving in and out of each other in the most amazing spaghetti-junction maze of a dance. It was like a great kaleidoscope of movement and rhythm, music and dancing wheelchairs, and everyone joining in. The bass pan-pipes were pounding, the melody was soaring above the pandemonium of the shouting and singing and the more able-bodied were rattling rattles. The music dissolves the handicaps which keep us divided, and we who had come to the centre and those who were there reciprocally freed each other, so that all our former tiredness and the apathy of a hot frustrating afternoon was lost.

The prisons also felt like holy places. In Exeter prison, after showing our passports and being carefully counted through the gates with so many locks and massive keys, we were briefed by the chaplain. Many of those we would be meeting were category A prisoners. Over fifty-five prisoners had asked to attend our session but we were warned that some of these probably just wanted to have time out from their cell. 'Don't be put off if they get up and walk out, or if they are inattentive to what you are saying.' We began with pan-pipes and then sang the South African song '*Freedom*', which seemed relevant. We had decided to tell the story of the ethnic tension in Solomon Islands and the death of our seven Brothers. As we told the story you knew that every prisoner was listening because it was a story about how people can get sucked up into cycles of violence through lack of chance, frustration, bitterness and misdirected hatred. It was about the way brutality steals, kills and destroys not only the victims but the perpetrators of violence, and their death in life is even worse because there seems no way forward, let alone escape apart from further violence. It was about fear and the way fear insidiously infects us and reduces us and makes us prisoners of our memories and of our guilt. It was about the way we put God to death in ourselves and in our neighbour. And then Brother Benjamin Kunu spoke – the one who had been held hostage by Keke for all those months, the one I had waited for on the beach and for whose release I had constantly bargained with God. He was the one who had seemed to come back from the world of the dead at the time when seven of our brothers had been murdered, not with recrimination but with a message of hope, and a greater faith which had set me, his doubting chaplain, free. Brother Benjamin told of how he had been taken hostage, his suffering, and how he had struggled to eat with hands tied behind his back and to walk through rivers and along dangerous cliff paths with his hands still tied. He told of how Brother Alfred had been so badly beaten that he had asked his captors to kill him to end his suffering. But Brother Benjamin also told these prisoners about the unfailing love of God. How he had never been closer to Christ than he had been at this time. How Keke and his captors had changed in their treatment of them and asked them for their prayers, and how finally he had been released. He told these prisoners that God does not fail us even in death. He said 'I now no longer fear death. I know that death is nothing in God's eyes.' Benjamin told them in a shaking voice that he forgave those who had abducted and abused him, but that he wanted to stop these things from ever happening again and to use his life to speak out against brutality and violence and injustice. 'If only,' he said, 'we could see Christ in the face of one another.'

The hour and a half disappeared before we had realized it and a prison warder came in to escort the prisoners back to their cells. They were told it was time to leave us. And then one prisoner stood up and said that before he left the prison chapel he wanted to shake hands with Brother Benjamin Kunu who had just told his story. And he wanted to say thank you for everything he had heard. And then all the prisoners wanted to shake hands with Benjamin and with all of us and as they did they whispered messages about wives and children they wanted us to pray for and scribbled names on scraps of paper for us also to remember in our daily prayers.

None us will ever forget our visit to Lambeth Palace. Here we were welcomed with evident joy by the Archbishop of Canterbury, his wife and staff. After the performance of *The Lost Son* the Archbishop looked up at the gallery of rather severe-looking former archbishops looking down from the walls of the Palace Guard Room and said to us 'I don't think these archbishops have ever seen anything quite like the perform-ance that has just taken place.' 'These archbishops whose portraits hang on the walls,' he said, 'who were at the beginning of the life of the Anglican Communion, never in their wildest dreams imagined that what they had begun would come back to speak to us as you have today.'[41] He later wrote to us 'Lambeth was electrified by your visit.'

41 Bergner Robert, Anglican Communion News Service, ACNS 4011, Lambeth, 28 July 2005.

In the West the choices are so many and often confusing to a Brother or Sister who has learnt to accept whatever is given:

'Would you like red wine or white wine?'

'Both of them.'

'Would you like tea or coffee, or a cold drink? Do you take milk or sugar? How many spoonfuls?'

In Solomon Islands everyone gets everything as long as we have it, and when we don't everyone does without. But choice has become obsessive. It can even spread to the Eucharist. At an ecumenical service we attended when on mission in Australia there were wafers, or white bread, or wholemeal bread or gluten free bread, then there was red wine, or non-alcoholic wine and an array of choices for the children, grapes and biscuits and blackcurrant juice.

'And do you want fries with that?'

Endless choice can clutter us and fill all the spaces so that our lives are so full of distractions there is no longer any space or place for God. Too many alternatives can lose us in never-ending possibilities. How quickly God gets pushed out in our busy-ness, one of the least seemingly exciting choices in a busy schedule. Yet we are lost without that centre, and how quickly we become forgetful of the reality of our faith. Again and again I realize that more is less.

And when you have been away, you notice that endless desire so many Anglicans in Britain have to talk all the time before church and the moment the service has ended and even during it. There is an English art of conversation, which seems quite strange to the uninitiated. For a Solomon Islander it sometimes seems like a stream of endless questions, as though silence were a thing of which to be ashamed. And it feels like there is a weighing-up taking place in that small talk with the pressure to create a good impression and to be coherent or interesting or amusing. And yet how strangely empty all this talking often leaves me, as though we have been papering the cracks of our loneliness and failed really to connect:

'Oh that was lovely. I have a friend who lives in Singapore.'

'I loved that drama. How on earth do they remember all those lines?'

We talk at tangents and are so busy talking that we do not notice the real needs of the heart. It is like playing music so loudly that we become too distracted to notice the life in one another. Or language invades us and leaves us awkward and uncomfortable.

'Are they all right?'

'You are looking tired.'

'They look absolutely shattered.'

'I hope we haven't been overworking you.'

'You must be feeling the cold.'

'It should warm up a bit tomorrow.'

'What do you think of England?'

'Funny lot aren't we in England?'

'They must be finding it so difficult.'

'It must be such a terrible culture shock for you.'

These may well be kind comments and yet they can seem a bit like interrogation and to imply somehow that you are failing to relate. They are difficult statements to answer. Yes we are tired, but that is not a criticism or complaint. We are tired and happy. We are tired one moment and not another, for the tiredness often leaves you in song, with a prayer, a presentation, or a word of encouragement or affection. We are shattered before a drama and exhilarated after it. We are not used to putting on a disguise or a face. We are. We are used to being together. We can live together and still have space. There are times to be tired and times to communicate. Sometimes communication flows as sweet as honey, sometimes the mission team would like to retire to their sleeping bags and it is only 3 o'clock in the afternoon, and they do not feel guilty about that at all.

'Are they all right?'

'Yes, they are fine.'

'It's just they all seem to be sleeping in there.'

'Yes.'

'I was expecting them to be doing things . . .'

'Like what?'

'Like singing.'

'They have actually done a lot of singing, about five programmes a day, so now they are having a sleep and that hall is their bedroom.'

'It sounds like you're doing too much.'

'No, everything is fine, it's actually very exciting.'

'Well that's good, but they'll need to move out in a minute because we've got the Beavers coming in, and I was wondering if they could do some songs and dancing for them.'

Sometimes being on a mission is a bit like being in a zoo. The visitors expect some action and seem quite upset if we are looking a bit sluggish or searching for a bit of hidden shade.

In Solomon Islands time belongs to people, not people to time. It has taken me many years to realize it but you simply cannot hurry a Melanesian. It is not that they are rude or obstructive or meaning to make you late, it is quite simply that they do not understand the need to rush. They spent a lot of time even in the UK waiting for others and did not have any anxiety when they themselves were a bit late.

'Yes, but for a school you need to be on time.'

And yet many schools kept us waiting, and the Melanesians waited patiently. I think there is a bit of a hierarchy in patience based on who is prepared to wait for whom.

'Could you tell your Brothers to eat now, because they are due at another school at half past one and we can't be late.'

But there are others, often when you are least expecting it, who do understand, and who do connect. These are the many saints in hiding whom a mission like this also reveals. They are found at the back of churches and often outside them. They sometimes say a few words which lift you up and show you that they have understood, or been moved, or they hug you, or are simply just there for you when you need them. Attentiveness is one of the greatest of graces. It was often the retired and the elderly who were especially receptive and welcoming. But wherever we went, this mission team uncovered the most wonderful generosity and kindness among all age groups.

There was Richard who seemed silent at first and walked with a stick. He volunteered to drive for us and during this time he told me more and more about his life. To be honest he had been to hell and back, and had far more than his share of suffering. Yet the amazing thing was, he had not let it poison him or make him bitter. On the contrary, he seemed to have an even bigger heart as a result of it. He looked a big bloke and pretty tough from the outside, but he drove for us with such reliability, never bossing us or ever losing his patience with any lapses in time-keeping. There was no racism in this man at all, even though the cultures were so different, only friendship and respect. I was worried he would feel put upon because he did everything without pay from early morning until late at night, but the opposite was the case. Even after his time as a driver was over, he kept on turning up to watch and support. He even drove down from Chester to be with us for our final four days in London so he could say farewell at the airport. When we finally said goodbye to him, he looked away and there were tears on his cheeks.

There was Teresa who was the sacristan of a church, and was starting her own business sewing vestments. She told me she had tried many jobs and that some people felt she did too much for the church and should get a life, but all I can say is that to us she was a saint. Church halls were never designed for people to live in. They have no showers and nowhere to wash or dry clothes. Teresa arranged for us to wash at the public swimming pool, and each morning she had organized transport to take us there. She gave us all plastic bags with our names on for dirty washing, and while we were at the schools she went to the laundrette and did the washing for twenty-five. Then she took it home and ironed it all, and she returned it all on the same day, and offered to do this every day. She said it was a privilege to help missionaries. To a group who had so few clothes to wear, the clean and ironed clothes carried the fragrance of heaven!

Craig is a vegan. He appeared to me a bit like a hobbit because he was full of light and goodness, and aligned himself against the bigots of our Church and nation. His little four-year-old son was exactly like him. Whenever they were around they brought an aura of peacefulness, gentleness and practical wisdom. He drove for us and continued to drive for us even when he was no longer on the schedule simply because he wanted to help. He towed a horse box containing the set of our passion drama, and mended its tyres and lights and brought tools and timber to help us build the set, and seemed to know in an unobtrusive way just what was needed. His face was round and healthy but we seldom saw him eating anything apart from fruit and berries or stinging nettle leaves, which he gave me too as an antihistamine for my hay fever. Then Novice Joseph, who was playing Jesus in the Passion Play, got this huge carbuncle on his thigh. It had a lot of heads and would not fully burst, and it was depressing poor Joseph and causing a lot of pain and sapping his spirit. The doctor treated him with antibiotics and it did burst, but a few days later another even bigger one came up and the doctor said he would have to have it operated on. I couldn't do any of the dramas without him. Joseph didn't want any operation and said he would try to carry on but he was silent and in pain. Both as Jesus and as the Lost Son he had to take a terrible pounding, and physically and emotionally he had given everything. Then Craig stepped in and said he would try some herbal remedies. Novice Joseph trusted him, and Craig made pastes out of saffron which he activated in the sun, and oils, and also gave him herbal infusions to drink to improve his natural resistance. And quite quickly the swelling went down and the carbuncle started to dry up. I insisted Joseph still went to see the London surgeon for the final decision. Craig said he would come too because too many surgeons believed in unnecessary intervention. But when the surgeon took a close look at the leg he said 'Isn't it amazing how nature heals itself?' I wanted to shout for joy. Joseph looked as though he had been born again and even Craig looked a bit nonchalantly pleased with himself, and had to admit that this particular doctor was not part of the Western conspiracy theory after all. And Novice Joseph continued to give the best performance of Jesus I have ever seen.

Craig and his family booked into a hotel in Kingston so that he could be with us to help for the final performances. During the final performance his young son Michael sat with him and watched the whole thing with great attentiveness, even though I was worried it would be too brutal for such a small boy to see a crucifixion. And then both of them quietly disappeared back to Devon without even saying goodbye because they did not want to disturb us. And when I phoned him up to thank him I asked about Michael and the violence, and he said that

Michael had understood everything, and on the way home had asked his father 'Did they hurt Jesus like that because they wanted to teach us that we must never hurt anyone like that again?'

33

But we proclaim Christ crucified.

1 Corinthians 1.23

Throughout our mission both in the Pacific and in the United Kingdom we performed *The Passion of our Lord*. This drama came out of all the fifteen years I had been with the Melanesian Brotherhood and in particular out of the last five years of the Community's struggle and sacrifice. It was the only story that could contain the tragedy of our Brothers' death and give their deaths a means of expression, and a meaning. This, for me, was a drama without artifice. It was performed not by actors but witnesses.

We began with Christ being tempted to follow a different path, the path of the world: to use his power to give the people what they wanted, to answer their material needs and longings; to create a cargo-cult following, based on superstition and the manipulation of the miraculous; to gain power and wealth and authority, but to sell his soul to the devil in the process. And how often our religion has become just that: a source of greed and prejudice and power-mongering. In the name of God we have stolen and hated and victimized and made war and justified all manner of exploitation and cruelty. In the name of God we have crucified God.

But our Christ, simple and strong, rejects all these temptations. He chooses a different way, the way of offering, the way of gift. He who wants to be first must be last. He who wants to follow Christ must become the servant of all. At the centre of our passion is powerful vulnerability, gentle strength, the authority of love, the justice of forgiveness.

And yet this Christ has enemies. The chief priests and Pharisees of Christ's day become the political leaders of ours, secular or religious, seeking to gain power and manipulate the people. They are threatened by goodness because it exposes them and reveals their corruption. The religion they preach justifies their own position, and they fear that our Christ by his integrity and by his love will undermine their authority and expose them. He is winning the hearts and minds of the people and he is dangerous.

He becomes the scapegoat of the conspiracy theory, which keeps the people trapped in fear and suspicion.

> From a different tribe
> A different nation
> A different faith
> Influenced by the devil
> He is a suspicious Arab
> A communist
> A terrorist
> An asylum seeker
> He has weapons of mass destruction
> A Jew
> A Muslim
> A Christian
> He is the enemy.

And yet Christ fails to be drawn into that conspiracy. Instead he proclaims love for God and love for neighbour. He says that the kingdom of God is in us, as small as a mustard seed, but it will grow. He claims that God's rule is coming now. He calls the poor and the humble and the pure in heart 'blessed'. He proclaims not hatred but the reign of peace. 'Happy are the peacemakers, for they shall be called the sons and daughters of God.' He calls upon his disciples to pray, teaching that God is their Father, a father who loves them and provides for them and can guide them through temptation and forgive them, just as they must forgive others.

Yet division has begun even among Jesus' own family of disciples. As the tension mounts, Judas claims that Christ loves too much and that all this talk of love is weakness:

You can't feed empty bellies with love!
You can't stop a tsunami with love.
You can't defeat poverty with love.
You can't defeat terrorists with love.
You can't fight a war with love!

But once more Christ is there at the centre, calling them to a peace which is greater than human understanding. And now he offers them an example from the new kingdom, not of domination and fear, but of service. He washes their feet. This is how the new kingdom must be built, from the bottom up. He says 'I have given you an example, and you must follow what I have done.' He does not fear Judas, even though he knows he will betray him, but he realizes what suffering that will result both for himself and for his betrayer.

And now he shows his disciples a sign of his love. He gives them himself, all that he is: bread broken for them. It is a sign both of death, but also that his life will be within them. Of course they do not understand. How can they understand? But later they will know, and we will know, and we will share this Eucharist both in troubles and celebration.

The night is coming. The crowd has been stirred up with hatred. In our drama the fickle crowd becomes the militant youth. It begins almost like a game, but they get sucked into violence and, like a lynch mob, evil takes over. Christ is the scapegoat and his death will become a brutal spectacle.

The trial is a mockery of justice. Like dogs that have smelt blood, there seems to be a barbarity which no one believes possible. The drama becomes our own. It becomes so real that at times I think that the suffering is happening here and now, and I want to rush in and stop all of this and take Joseph down from the cross and bring back our seven Brothers from the Weather Coast. And the militants are beating him too hard. The blood flows.

As Christ is taken down from the cross, the red sheet in which he is wrapped flows after him. It is a sign of his blood, his costly love, but also his kingdom. The Beloved Disciple now directs the drama towards the audience.

Perhaps we did not beat him
or drive in the nails
or mock his pain
but by our fear
through our silence
in turning away from the pain of our world
and in finding excuse for inexcusable evil
we are all guilty of this

Is this what you wanted?
Is that what you wanted for your nation?

To crucify love?
To kill the innocent?
To beat and to torture all that is good?
Is this what we wanted for Solomon Islands?
Is this the victory of violence?
Is this what we wanted for Palestine?
Is this what we wanted for Iraq?
Is this what we wanted for London?
Weep for your children

But Jesus cannot die

Perhaps today it is we who have died
and Christ who lives.

And his enemies and those who perpetrate these crimes say:

'There was no other way.'
'He had to die.'
'We did it for the land.'
'We did it for the people.'
'For democracy.'
'We did it for freedom.'

'We warned him but he refused to listen.'
'No other way was possible.'

For those of us who witnessed
We know
He was the Prince of Peace
He was the Truth and the Life
He was the Son of God.

At the end of the crucifixion the Beloved Disciple comes to the front and asks:

What about the rest of us?
We know how to destroy, but it is God who alone can give life.
None of us really understood. How could we?
We were lost and frightened. We hid behind locked doors.
We thought that everything was over.
But it was not the end but the beginning. At the very bottom of the fall, when darkness covered the earth, it was then that God took over and the resurrection began.
It was on the third day!

This was our story too. For ultimately, in our own Passion, we found it was only God who could redeem. This *Passion* was our testimony to our seven Brothers who were murdered in 2003. For they became the innocent victims of the violence they had worked so hard to stop. They were honoured and disgraced, insulted and praised, treated as liars and yet they spoke the truth. They were beaten and tortured and recorded on tape recorders in the sickening mockery of a trial. They were put to death for the sins of the people. And they live on.

Our story of the Passion of Christ took place 2,000 years ago but it is still taking place throughout our world today. But we have been changed. We did not travel from the other side of the world to preach a death, but to preach a resurrection. For we know where we stand and we know who we belong to. And we believe there is a choice in all of this, a choice to belong to the life-giver, for God is love. The work of Christ is to make redemption. We believed in the goodness of Christ. Now we have become witnesses. I am no longer afraid to proclaim the life that Christ brings. We have only one life and that life is a gift. The foundation of so much that we hold as sacred in the world is not there by accident. It is there because others have fought for justice, for forgiveness, for hope, for peace, for freedom of speech, for the handicapped and vulnerable; they have fought for life. For Christians, that way, that truth, that love has a name and has a story, the name is Saviour, the name is Jesus.

What have I learnt?
I have learnt that God is real
He spans the void
His cross, from top to bottom
From side to side
From God to flesh
From flesh to flesh
He is there
He is not deceiving you but you will never know his truth
Unless you let go of the edges and trust

And so we dare to love
Dare to follow
Risking all
A vulnerable life
For the vulnerable life giver

But there is a greater beauty
a gentle strength
a tender discipline
a touched hope
an embraced unity
a bold humility
a courageous love

It is that which, as I stand back, has been revealed
There is, in truth, no other way
Unless we want to betray and destroy our inner nature
Our Christ nature
Again and again they have shown me the life of God in us
Radiant and good
From inside out
Out, out to all the world
That love is for us and for others.

The light shines in the darkness and the darkness has never put
it out, 'The passion of our Lord'. Exeter Cathedral, 2005

PART 4

An Epistle

34

I came that you may have life,
life in all its fullness.

John 10.10 (Good News Bible)

From an address given to celebrate the Feast of St Simon and
St Jude, 30 October 2005

In October 2005 more than 10,000 people gathered at Tabalia on Guadalcanal, the mother house of the Melanesian Brotherhood and the place where the seven peacemakers are buried. They had come to witness the laying of the head stones of those seven Brothers and to give thanks for their lives. They had come also to witness the admission of forty-four new Brothers.

I was given the great privilege to preach on that feast day and these are the words I shared:

'I want to preach today especially for those Novices who became Brothers, for those Brothers who renewed their vows, and for those who were released in order to become disciples in the world. I want to preach for all those former Brothers who have been formed by their training and ministry in the Brotherhood, and now continue to live out their vocation humbly within the local community. I want to preach for all those who have been called by this Community to come today: the beloved families of our departed Brothers, our Companions, relatives of the Brothers and friends – all those whose lives have been inspired, touched, healed or helped by this Community and all those who want to be connected. Today belongs to all of us.

It seems to me that at the centre of our celebration today is the idea of offering – offering our lives to God with open hands and open heart – not because we want something back but because we love. Not a shopping list for God but an offering of thanksgiving. For today we celebrate an offering: the offering of seven Brothers who met a brutal and terrifying death because they believed in love and peace; the offering of young men who desire to give their lives in God's service; the offering of Companions serving this Community; the offering of former Brothers often continuing unnoticed, and with little affirmation to live the gospel. These offerings are often small (much less than the supreme sacrifice of our martyred Brothers) but they are cumulative. They add and join together to form the miracle by which the 5,000 can be fed. Each offering, seemingly insignificant in itself, is capable of building community and bringing change.

In today's Gospel we were warned of coming struggle, struggle which all disciples of Jesus Christ face, for we walk in his footsteps:

'If people hate you remember they hated me first.'

'If people persecute you, they persecuted me first.'

In the last five years this Community has seen the reality of this, the pain and struggle of following Christ.

Yes, there has been hatred.

Yes, there has been persecution and abandonment.

And yes, there has been the horror even of the most brutal deaths.

But as we look back, strangely it is not the pain that is remembered but the hope born in that struggle, the light which shone in the darkness and which the power of darkness could never put out. In the midst of tragedy, right down at the very bottom – blessing – blessing as we opened ourselves up to God and put ourselves in God's hands, for there was no one else. In the midst of this conflict there was a deep sense of calling, that despite our own sinfulness we had been called to bear witness to the love of God. A calling which did not depend on self but upon God: 'You did not choose me, I chose you.'

Today as they became Brothers each Novice made the following prayer:

'I want to live the gospel. O Lord give me grace.'

What a wonderful calling. It still holds my heart. You are called to be the bringers of Good News. Not of horror, war and disaster which bombard us through the daily news, but messengers of hope. What is your ministry? It is to be the bringers of love, joy, peace and resurrection. You are called to live fully and to make others fully alive.

Do not take this calling for granted; it is precious and holy, as precious as water in the desert. Hold on to that calling. Do not let it slip through your fingers. It can be lost and gone even before you realize it, unless you are careful. It is a wonderful calling and privilege to do God's work, the work of his love. Yet at the same time you pray 'O Lord give me grace', which is an acknowledgement that this ministry is only possible as God's gift to you.

You are indeed blessed. You have been given the blessing of prayer and sacrament. When you leave this Community you will know how fortunate you have been, for so many find it so difficult to find any time in their crowded lives for God. There are children to look after and work to be done and money to be earned and one hundred and one other reasons why prayer becomes difficult. But here in the Melanesian Brotherhood seven times a day you have been given a place and a space for Christ and the time to grow in relationship with him. You have been called to become men of prayer: those who can intercede on our behalf. Never become forgetful of that. Love prayer, love being with Christ. You must be the bamboo pipes on which God will blow his tune. You are the swept surface of the sand in the chapel, waiting for Christ to leave his footprints. You cannot be forced to pray but you will find that prayer can become your privilege and joy.

You have been blessed with the freedom to live the gospel NOW. We spend a lot of time remembering the past. In our nostalgia we imagine that the past was so much better and things are no longer the same as before. We spend a lot of time planning our unknown futures in our minds. And we spend so much of time in the past and future that we forget the present. We can meet God now. God's kingdom can be brought closer today. Each day can count. As the Archbishop of Canterbury reminded us, even if the world were to end tomorrow we would still have time to do the work of God today. Each moment can be a chance to see God and to bring change and hope.

You are blessed with community. It is hard ministering alone. I see many priests in the Western world who face a lonely struggle, for they feel forced to be in so many ways all in all self-sufficient. But that is not your task, rather you are called to be an interdependent Community in which Christ is always present, for when two or three are gathered in his name, he is there in the midst. Christ is with you on your journey, and reveals himself to you in those who share with you in this ministry. You are called to share in the combined gifts of your Brothers. You are not called to become competitors but a family. The successes and achievements of any of your Brothers belong to all of you. What a wealth of talent you have when you can share one another's talents in music, drama, dance, communication, practical skills, knowledge and wisdom; there is such power in these combined gifts. But we must be on guard too against the dangers of division and jealousy, which, like the family of Jacob, can divide brother against brother. Jealousy is an ugly and mean-spirited sin which seeks to pull down rather than build up the body of Christ. We have been called to lift one another up. To become the St Barnabas, the Brother Robin Lindsay, the encouragers of our community. 'Community is total', as Brother Roger of Taizé claimed; it must allow no frontiers or barriers or prejudices, it celebrates the love and care of others just as much as the love of self.

You are blessed with joy. Nine times in the Beatitudes Christ proclaims the poor, the humble, the peacemaker, the pure in heart 'blessed'. Our Community has always been a place of joy and laughter very much as I imagine the first community of Christ's disciples would have been. Did not Christ call them to celebrate the wedding feast while the groom was still with them? It was the religious leaders who saw their work as that of condemnation and judgement, and in contrast Christ condemned this hardness of heart and invited all to his wedding feast. It is right then that the Community should be a place of pan-pipes, song, dance and laughter, even in the face of struggle. The gospel transforms mourning into dancing. It is our pleasure to give and to go on being able to give. Even the tragedy of the death of our Brothers cannot extinguish our hope and spiritual joy. Thus, like a magnet, the Community continues to welcome all in the name of Christ, children and young people, parents and the elderly, the sick and the needy, the mentally disturbed, the traumatized, the lost and the sinful. For here is a place of acceptance and new life.

This is a blessing of simplicity that is so at odds with the message of our world whose unremitting message is that 'to be is to have'. Rather we proclaim that to be is to be in relationship with God and one another. We believe that obsessive materialism is a sin that keeps us prisoners. God's gifts free us to trust his love and to travel lightly. Like David we set aside the armour which would weigh us down and imprison us. God will be our protection. God will be our guide. The gentle shepherd boy can defeat the giants of fear even when the odds seem to be against him.

And you are blessed with the spirit of sacrifice. Sacrifice may seem more like pain or a curse but it is your sacrifice to God which is at the heart of your calling, for God will not turn away from a heart that is broken and crushed. Sacrifice is essential to love; ask a mother and she will know as she struggles to feed her children. This vocation is about letting go of selfishness because of a greater love for one another. In that place of offering we discover a unity with God, where in fact we have nothing to fear. Our martyred Brothers teach us that. They went to the edge of life, a place where we all fear to go, and there they held to Christ. As St Francis said 'Blessed are those who are found doing God's holy will at the hour of their deaths, for death will do them no harm.' Brother Francis Tofi's last words to me were these: 'I would be frightened to die if I was doing wrong, but I am not frightened to die if I am doing good.'

This then is our blessing: we have been called to be sons and daughters of the New Testament. It is not the old theology of personal gain and selfish power. It is not a religion of cargo cult waiting for material wealth to fall from the sky. It is not self-seeking, it is God-seeking, and yet in finding God we also find ourselves. This is the miracle of our faith, that in seeming vulnerability and powerlessness we too can enter into the mystery of salvation. At the bottom of the fall God takes over. In offering and in service we find the only power great enough to transform the world. Jesus Christ did not change the world with the weapons of political power, with war or atrocity, missile, suicide-bomb or bullet, torture or brutality, he transformed the world with a self-offering love and forgiveness, and we who walk in his footsteps enter into the same paschal mystery. We become one with the heroes of our Church, fishermen, tax collectors and sinners whose lives were transformed, and who in offering those lives transformed the lives of others. We become one with Bishop Patteson whose life was taken by those for whom he would gladly have given it, and in so doing ended the Pacific slave trade. And we become one with a group of humble Brothers who journeyed unknown and defenceless to the Weather Coast in search of their lost Brother, who were tortured and humiliated and who gave up their lives in the darkness, and yet who live on. Their offering has become the seed whose harvest must be the peace of this nation. Their graves are not a place of darkness but of light, not the symbols of death but the celebration of resurrection and hope. The hope is that goodness wins and death shall have no dominion. In offering themselves, it is their goodness that is ultimately victorious, and not the horrific violence of the misguided. Yes, like Jacob, in these deaths we glimpse the doorway to the eternal with the angels of God going up and down through Jesus Christ the Son of Man. Their message is at the heart of our gospel: 'A new commandment I give unto you, that you love one another as I have loved you.'

And the human family will widen.

The graves of the seven Peacemakers of the Melanesian Brotherhood. Tabalia, October 2005.